On Our Own

Patient-Controlled Alternatives to the Mental Health System

by Judi Chamberlin

On Our Own

© Judi Chamberlin 1977

This edition published by MIND 1988

ISBN 0 900 557 83 4

MIND publishes a wide range of books and pamphlets to promote understanding and debate about what is meant by mental health and mental illness. MIND considers it important to publish ideas which would not otherwise be generally available.

The views and opinions expressed in this book are the author's and not necessarily MIND's.

Text:
Designed by David Burton & Associates
Printed by RAP Ltd. England

Cover:
Design by Windhorse Assocs.
Illustration by Ian Whadcock.
Printed by Shadowclean

Acknowledgements

This book would not have been possible without the help and support of many, many people in the mental patients' liberation movement. I would particularly like to thank members of Project Release in New York, the Network Against Psychiatric Assault in San Francisco, and the Mental Patients' Association in Vancouver for answering my numerous questions and allowing themselves to be interviewed. Members of Mental Patients' Liberation Front in Boston, of which I have been a member for the past year and a half, have been helpful in these and many other ways.

To thank by name every person in the movement who has helped with suggestions, ideas, and criticism is impossible. A brief list would have to include Diane Baran, Su and Dennis Budd, Jenny Collins, Leonard Roy Frank, Howie T. Harp, Jordan Hess, Dan Kesselbrenner, Arlene Sen, and Barbara Wallen. But such a list leaves out many more people than it includes, and I thank all of them as well. Over the years, through many conversations, Ted Chabasinski has helped me immeasurably to understand the full dimensions of psychiatric oppression.

People outside the movement have also been helpful. I would especially like to thank people from the Vancouver Emotional Emergency Center, particularly Ellen Frank, Isobel Kiborn, David Myers, and Tom Sandborn, who helped to care for me when I needed help, and who later showed by their actions that they did not consider me in any way a lesser person because I asked for their help. Our discussions about humane alternatives to mental institutions have been conversations among equals. Many thanks also to those people from all the organisations mentioned in this book, who spent hours with me, and provided me with a great deal of useful information.

My agent, Ellen Levine, believed in me and the book — without her it never would have happened. My editor, Elizabeth Backman, provided invaluable suggestions and encouragement.

Howi Cahn has been unbelievably patient and loving through the endless day-to-day crisis that go into the writing of a book. My daughter, Julie, has also been remarkably patient, showing a maturity far beyond her years.

Although my mother is no longer alive, I would like to thank her, along with my father, for helping to instill in me the determination to fight on when I knew I was right.

Preface to the British edition

By Judi Chamberlin

It's hard to believe that ten years have passed since I wrote the original edition of *On Our Own*. At that time, the ex-patients' movement was far smaller than it is today, with only a handful of struggling ex-patient run alternative programmes. Unfortunately, some of the programmes I described ten years ago have disappeared, or changed beyond recognition, but many, many more have come into existence.

This is, then, a particularly good time to be writing a new preface, one directed specifically at a British audience. Ten years ago, contacts between ex-patient activists on an international level were tenuous. I remember hearing vaguely of a militant Mental Patients' Union, but by the time of my first trip to England (1982), the level of activism had subsided, and it was hard to get a sense of the similarities and differences between British and US ideology and practice.

In the US now (late 1987), the ex-patients' movement is in a state of growth and change. On the one hand, the existence of many more ex-patient run projects, often funded by governmental entities, is a positive sign. On the other, many of these projects have soft-pedalled their ideology, sometimes to the point where they are indistinguishable from traditional mental health services. Co-option is everywhere; there is even a 'consumer' organisation, the National Mental Health Consumers Association, that proclaims its desire to 'work with' and 'improve' the mental health system. This is certainly not the movement for which so many of us have picketed, sat-in, organised, and sacrificed over the years.

However, liberation ideology continues to thrive in the US. In late 1985, many long-time activists joined with newer members of the movement to form the National Alliance of Mental Patients, a group dedicated to the abolition of involuntary psychiatric interventions, and to the development of user-run programmes that are true alternatives to the psychiatric system. We explicitly reject the label of 'consumer', with its depoliticising implications of freedom and choice. We know that the system gave us little freedom and fewer choices, and we refuse to obscure that fact for the sake of bogus 'co-operation'.

From my distant vantagepoint, the British survivors' movement appears to have some unique strengths. The ability of psychiatry's critics to come together, whether as system survivors or as radical workers, simply has not happened in the US or in any other country of which I am aware. If British activists can develop an ideology which combines the knowledge gained from both these viewpoints, respecting the different expertise of each, it will mark a major achievement in the struggle against psychiatric power. Both psychiatric survivors and radical mental health workers propose an ideology of empowerment and autonomy; it remains to be seen if these two groups can overcome their historic differences, including class and power differentials, to promote these ideals for all.

We need more interaction between activists from different countries. I have learned a great deal from my opportunities to compare experiences with ex-patients from England, Scotland, Ireland, Denmark, Germany, Holland, Australia, and New Zealand. Unfortunately these contacts are few and far between; even nearby Canadian and US activists have too few opportunities to exchange ideas and work together. Although each nation's particular political and social structure presents unique opportunities and difficulties, our similarities are amazing. Often even language barriers have not prevented ex-patients from developing deep friendships and mutual understanding based on the shared experience of psychiatric control and the struggle against it. This bond can become the basis of a viable international movement against psychiatric power.

I hope that *On Our Own* can be useful to everyone who reads it: mental health professionals, students, family members, and interested outsiders. But it is directed most specifically at current and former psychiatric inmates — 'mental patients' — especially those struggling to define their own identities outside of psychiatric labelling and control. In 1977, as I daily faced the difficult task of crafting the words that would convey the experiences of ex-patient activists, I would often daydream about the people who would read my words, such daydreams being a welcome escape from the work. Perhaps, I would imagine, or hope, the book would bring our dream to others still suffering and alone. Perhaps it would make a difference in a few people's lives, leading them toward working with others for liberation. In the years since, I have had the tremendous reward of hearing from many people, in many places, that the book has played a part in their breaking out of isolation, joining or founding groups that have continued to enrich and enlarge the movement.

Now, I am hopeful that British ex-patients will find our US perspectives helpful as they develop ways to work either in specifically ex-patient groups, or as identified ex-patients affiliated with workers and supporters. Whenever I meet ex-patients from other countries, I am struck by the ways in which our stories of our encounters with the psychiatric system, despite differences largely of customs and terminology, are over and over again the same. So it is to you, the ex-patients, psychiatric inmates, clients, system survivors, most especially, that I offer my wish for *On Our Own* to be a source on which you can draw as you work for the alternative structures we need to heal and grow strong, and for the legal and societal changes that will allow us to control our own lives and determine our own futures.

Introduction

This is a book about psychiatry and alternatives to it, written from a patient's point of view. For too long, mental patients have been faceless, voiceless people. We have been thought of, at worst, as subhuman monsters, or at best, as pathetic cripples, who might be able to hold down menial jobs and eke out meagre existences, given constant professional support. Not only have others thought of us in this stereotyped way, we have believed it of ourselves. It is only in this decade, with the emergence and growth of the mental patients' liberation movement, that we ex-patients have begun to shake off this distorted image and to see ourselves for what we are — a diverse group of people, with strengths and weaknesses, abilities and needs, and ideas of our own. Our ideas about our 'care' and 'treatment' at the hands of psychiatry, about the nature of 'mental illness,' and about new and better ways to deal with (and truly to help) people undergoing an emotional crisis differ drastically from those of mental health professionals.

Many people, including many ex-patients, are doubtful of our ability to help ourselves and one another. Mental health professionals are even more sceptical. There has been vigorous debate in mental health circles about the nature of mental illness and just who should treat it. But few psychiatrists, psychologists, social workers, nurses, or other mental health professionals have questioned the basic assumption that some people are incapable of defining their own best interests and are proper subjects for involuntary 'care.'

The existence and widespread use of involuntary commitment affects all aspects of mental health care. A lonely woman who calls a suicide prevention centre, intending only to converse with a counsellor, may find herself seized by the police and confined against her will if the counsellor decides, without the caller's knowledge, to have the call traced. A jobless man may walk into a storefront clinic operated by a community mental health center, looking for sympathetic advice; but if the staff member he sees thinks that he is odd or bizarre, hospitalisation could be ordered. Most clients never face commitment, but they know that the power is there. Even those people whose involvement in the mental health system is as fee paying clients of psychiatrists in private practice, supposedly the arrangement most protective of clients' rights, are not immune to involuntary commitment or the threat of it. Psychiatrists who decide that their clients are suicidally depressed, for example, will often hospitalize their patients with or without their consent. Many patients sign 'voluntary' admission forms under these circumstances.

The growing move towards community mental health centres, usually seen as progressive, is viewed with alarm by many ex-patients. Where once the state found it more convenient to incarcerate us permanently, it now seeks to control us through a network of facilities, through which we will be moved in accordance with the correctness of our behaviour. Meanwhile, hardly any of us, patients or nonpatients, are able to find help for the very real pain we all experience at times in our lives. There are some things, we all learn, which we should *never* tell mental health professionals, certain things that are signs we have 'gone crazy'. People who hear voices, or see things that are not there, are somehow different from and inferior to people who learn to handle their pain in socially acceptable ways. This process dehumanises us all.

So-called 'radical therapy' has come into existence in opposition to psychiatric excesses. But radical therapists themselves often overlook the wishes of those of their clients whom they define as disturbed. Radical therapist Ted Clark, for example, says that 'severely disturbed' clients should not undergo radical therapy. He leaves it up to the therapist of course, to decide which clients are too disturbed.[1] Most radical therapists, like other mental health professionals, and like the rest of society, believe that certain 'crazy' people are different and inferior.[1]

Antipsychiatry, as exemplified by R.D. Laing, holds other dangers for patients. Laing, who has eloquently criticised the dehumanising case presentations of traditional psychiatrists, has also continued the tradition, especially in his earlier works, which contain many descriptions of patients, usually tragic young women. Althugh they are sympathetically described, and their symbolism defined (by Laing, not by themselves), it is clear that Laing found them, and left them, inside the mental health hospitals where he trained as a psychiatrist. Laing grants that what these 'schizophrenics say has meaning, but only through his translations. The glamorisation by some self-styled radicals of Laing's therapeutic commune — Kingsley Hall — ignores its most glaring contradiction, the unacknowledged separations and distinctions between those who came as healers and those who came to be healed. Mary Barnes, Laing's and Kingsley Hall's most famous 'case,' was clearly not thought of as an equal by the 'well' members of the household, nor did she think of herself as equal. These attitudes can be seen clearly in the book written by and about her.[3]

In the mental patients' liberation movement, we have examined the ways in which we were treated when we 'went crazy.' Occasional instances of kindness and compassion stand out in sharp contrast to the overwhelming isolation and contempt imposed by most forms of 'treatment.' We came together to express our anger and despair at the way we were treated. Out of that process has grown the conviction that we *must* set up our own alternatives, because nothing that currently exists or is proposed, fundamentally alters the unequal power relationships that are at the heart of the present mental health system.

Power, not illness or treatment, is what that system is all about. It is a power that usually is not spoken about. Patients who do are often labelled 'paranoid.' Thomas Szasz's reputation as a rebel psychiatrist rests on his forthright discussions of the role of power in the so-called therapeutic relationship. But even Szasz stops short of a thorough analysis of power, recommending a contractual relationship between client and therapist as one where the client retains his or her own power. But this will work only if the therapist explicitly rejects the power to commit, and how many do?

No one denies that people in emotional pain can use help, the questions arise over what kinds of help, and under what circumstances. The present mental health system focuses much of its attention on people who do not want help, people who have been defined as mentally ill and unable to judge their own best interests. This system necessitates involuntary commitment and forced treatment, and leads to the dehumanisation of the patient and to the more subtle, but no less real, dehumanisation of mental health professionals. Although all is done in the name of care and concern, the underlying coercive nature of the system constantly makes itself felt. Patients are not supposed to speak of it; calling a mental hospital a prison and its staff jailers is a sure way to be considered 'paranoid.' Only when the patient learns the rules of the game, that black is to be called white, and punishment called treatment, does the staff consider him or her to be on the road to recovery. The real lesson is that one must always hide one's true feelings, hardly a prescription for emotional well-being.

Some patients have found help through the mental health system. Needles have been found in haystacks, too, but this does not recommend haystacks as good places to store needles. Patients who find help do so in spite of the structure of the mental health system, not because of it. Meanwhile, that same system neglects others who also have come looking for help, and imprisons others who never wanted 'help' at all.

Many ex-patients are angry, and our anger stems from the neglect, indifference, dehumanisation, and outright brutality we have seen and experienced at the hands of the mental health system. Our distrust of professionals is not irrational hostility, but is the direct result of their treatment of us in the past. We have been belittled, ignored, lied to. We have no reason to trust professionals, and many reasons to fear them.

A word about terminology. I have used the term 'mental patient,' rather than the term 'psychiatric inmate' as used by some groups in the movement, because it is the term used by the organisations with which I have been involved, and is the term that I believe will be most understandable to the general public. To those members of our movement who reject the term 'mental patient,' my apologies for using it. I hope they will consider what I have to say despite their wish that I had used different phrases.

Patient-controlled alternatives are not the answer to 'mental illness.' There is no simple answer, because no one has defined the terms. The whole concept of 'mental illness' as an explanation of distressing human behavior has come into question. Calling something an illness does not make it one, and psychiatrists have yet to demonstrate the existence of the illnesses they have named and defined. While psychiatric historians praise our modern enlightened ability to recognize that the witches and possessed people persecuted by the Inquisition were, in fact, mentally ill, one may well wonder along with Thomas Szasz[4] whether there is really any difference. The Inquisitors made sure that what we know about witches is known only through the words of their persecutors who were, of course, only trying to help them by saving their souls, even at the expense of their bodies. When accused witches disagreed with the Inquisitor, he could label their words 'heresy.' If they agreed with the Inquisitor, often after torture, he might absolve them of heresy and free them.[5]. Similarly, the words of mental patients have usually been filtered through the reports of psychiatrists, who are permitted to label as 'paranoid' or 'delusional' any words of the patient with which the psychiatrist disagrees. When patients express distrust of mental hospitals or psychiatrists, it can be called 'paranoia.' When patients agree with psychiatrists often after painful or debilitating 'treatments', they are said to be 'in contact with reality.' It is the psychiatrists who are blind to the reality that mental institutions are cold, dehumanising places, no matter how hard their patients try to tell them.

We must remember that terms like mental illness or schizophrenia are useful only if they help us to understand what it is that they describe. Medical diagnoses are useful when they help physicians to predict, treat, or control the conditions they describe, otherwise they quickly fall into disuse. This, I believe, is what will happen to 'schizophrenia,' 'paranoia,' and other so-called mental diseases as we learn more about behaviour, our own and one another's. Medical diagnoses and psychiatric diagnoses, despite their similarities, both are mysterious Latin-or Greek-derived terms used by doctors, serve vastly different functions. *Psychiatric* diagnoses are used to justify what is *done* to the 'patient,' with or without consent, while *medical* diagnoses are not, of themselves, justifications for treatment, but are instead ways of providing useful information to patient and physician in coming to conclusions about how to proceed. In fact, administering medical treatment to objecting patients is considered assault and battery except in rare instances, such as that of unconscious patients. Medical patients are always free to select no treatment at all, despite medical predictions of dire consequences. Of course, the physician always has the power to label the objections of the medical patient as evidence of mental illness, allowing nonconsenting psychiatric *and* medical treatment.

Along with many other ex-patients, I don't share the psychiatric faith that the 'cure' to 'mental illness' is soon to be found. We believe that the kinds of behaviour labelled 'mental illness' have far more to do with the day-to-day conditions of people's lives than with disorders in their brain chemistry. We must work to change our own behaviour when it distresses us, and work to help others who seek out help, but we must also work towards a future in which we are not systematically crippled by the imposition of beliefs in the inferiority of some people because of their colour, their gender, or their expression of the pain we all sometimes feel. In short, we must work to eliminate the racism, sexism, and mentalism, which make lesser people of us all.

NOTES FOR INTRODUCTION

1. Ted Clark, *Going Into Therapy* (New York: Perennial Library, 1985), pp.29-32.
2. For contrasting and more truly radical views of radical therapy, see Michael Glenn and Richard Kunnes, *Repression or Revolution? Therapy in the United States Today* (New York: Harper & Row, 1973) and Phil Brown, *Towards a Marxist Psychology* (New York: Harper & Row, 1974).
3. Mary Barnes and Joseph Berke, *Mary Barnes: Two Accounts of a Journey Through Madness* (New York: Ballentine Books, 1973).
4. Thomas Szasz, *The Manufacture of Madness* (New York: Harper & Row, 1970).
5. For a feminist analysis of the witch-hunts, see Barbara Ehrenreich and Deirdre English, *Witches, Midwives, and Nurses* (Old Westbury, N.Y.: The Feminist Press, 1973).

Chapter One

A Patient's View of the Mental Health System

Mental health and *mental illness* are terms that have entered the popular vocabulary. Yet they are terms that few people can define. Lay people and psychiatrists alike tend to call people mentally healthy when they like their behaviour and mentally ill when they dislike their behaviour. Rebellious teenagers, unhappy housewives, dissatisfied workers, or lonely old people, for example, are often diagnosed as mentally ill, which is less a medical, scientific description than it is a judgement that the person so labelled has, in some way, behaved improperly.

We can see this judgemental process at work when we look at the effect that a diagnosis of mental illness has on an individual's life. Unlike physical illnesses, which affect particular parts of a person's body, mental illnesses affect that abstraction known as the mind. Once it has been decided that a person has a sick mind, enormous social consequences ensue. A finding of mental illness, which is often a judicial, as well as a medical, determination, frequently results in loss of liberty. People labelled mentally ill are usually presumed to be incapable of exercising their decision-making power in their own best interest. The compulsory psychiatric treatment of people labelled mentally ill usually involves confinement in a mental hospital, which is widely perceived as an unpleasant and undesirable fate. Mental patients who protest such confinement are seen as being unable to understand their own best interest; and often, once someone has been so diagnosed, even the perception of his or her place of confinement as undesirable or unpleasant is considered a sign of mental illness.

Anything can be called a symptom of mental illness. In ordinary medical usage, the word *symptom* refers to malfunctioning body parts or systems. One dictionary defines *symptom* as the 'the subjective evidence of disease or physical disturbance observed by the patient.'[1] Physical symptoms can't always be seen, but they are almost always apparent (and distressing) to the person they affect. In psychiatric usage, it is an individual's behaviour that is the symptom, and often the distress is felt less by the person being labelled mentally ill than by those around him. Some people find their own actions so distressing that they go voluntarily to psychiatric clinics or emergency rooms, but frequently prospective patients are brought by family, friends or the police. Such people don't perceive themselves as *ill*; their 'symptoms' are bothersome to others. Frequent handwashing, staying out late at night, crying, spending a lot of money, expressing an unusual religious preference, wanting a divorce, having trouble in school or on the job, changing one's life-style — all these and many more have been called symptoms of mental illness.

Nor does one's behaviour have to be particularly bizarre for one to be considered seriously mentally ill and be committed to a mental hospital. Leonard Roy Frank of San Francisco was thirty years old and living in his own apartment. He was fired from his job, and rather than get another job, he decided to live on his savings and take some time to read and study. He became particularly interested in studying the Bible and in the practice of Orthodox Judaism. He grew a beard, in accordance with Orthodox requirements, and began strict observance of the dietary laws. Several months later, his parents came from New York to visit him and were horrified by his way of life.

> I had started going through what I call my changes. I didn't experience fear of the process — I was delighted with this new perspective on who I was and what society was all about. I was reading, studying, and contemplating. When my family visited, they had me institutionalised

involuntarily, since I would not co-operate with them by seeking therapy. The outrageous thing was that I was going through this period of self-exploration and growth, and it was interpreted as my having a serious mental disorder.[2]

In 1974, Leonard Frank obtained the medical records of his involuntary incarceration and published them in *Madness Network News*, a newspaper he helped to start.[3] The records show that the only 'symptoms' the psychiatrists were able to find, 'symptoms' that they used to justify administering to him against his will fifty insulin shock and thirty-five electric shock treatments, were his vegetarianism, his beard, and his denial that he was mentally ill. During the eight months of his hospitalisation, the records show that much medical attention was focused on the question of shaving. After months of refusing to shave voluntarily, Leonard's beard was shaved off while he was unconscious during a shock treatment. Entry after entry in the record is devoted to a solemn recital of the problem of the beard. The record indicates that whenever Leonard was given a mental-status examination, he answered all the factual questions correctly; he was, in psychiatric terminology, 'well oriented.' The doctors' conclusion that he was a paranoid schizophrenic rests on his 'bizarre' eating habits, his long hair and beard, and his refusal to admit he was mentally ill — his 'lack of insight'.

'The Frank Papers' make truly frightening reading. Frank's crime was living his life as he — rather than as his parents and the psychiatrists — chose. After his parents arranged for his commitment and for him to be given shock treatments, they returned to New York. The record contains copies of letters written by the doctors to his parents reporting on his condition. One letter in particular reveals that the psychiatrists had in mind nothing less than the complete changing of his personality. 'He still has all his delusional beliefs regarding his beard, dietary regime and religious observances that he had prior to treatment.

We hope that in continuing the treatments we will be able to modify some of these beliefs so that he can make a reasonable adjustment to life.'[4] It was considered progress that 'he asked for a bowl of clam chowder soup and took some bread and used butter on it'.[5] His 'delusions' — that he should be a vegetarian, wear a beard, and observe his religion — were enough for a court order of commitment, requested by the doctors on the grounds that he was 'dangerous to himself and others under these circumstances'[6] What danger? Whose delusions?

People who are labelled mentally ill become part of a system that deprives them of control over their own life as part of their treatment. Mental hospitals have been called 'total institutions,'[7] in which even such ordinary decisions as when to eat, go to the toilet, and go to bed are made by others. A natural consequence of being subjected to such a regimen is a feeling of depersonalisation. Feelings of depersonalisation are frequently considered primary symptoms of mental illness.[8] To complete the circle, psychiatrists usually attribute their patients' feelings of depersonalisation to their internal state and not to conditions within mental institutions.

The whole experience of mental hospitalisation promotes weakness and dependency. Not only are the lives of patients controlled, but patients are constantly told that such control is for their own good, which they are unable to see because of their mental illness. Patients become unable to trust their own judgement, become indecisive, overly submissive to authority, frightened of the outside world. The antitherapeutic nature of mental hospitalisation has long been recognised.[9]

A tremendous gulf exists between patients and staff in mental institutions. Patients are seen as sick, untrustworthy and needing constant supervision. Staff members are seen as competent, knowledgeable natural leaders. These stereotypes are believed by large numbers of patients and staff members. Communication is difficult across this gulf. Staff members don't believe what patients tell them. Patients don't believe what other patients say. Patients begin to question their own perceptions of situations, including their very accurate perceptions that they are looked down on and spied on by the staff.

Eleven years ago, I spent about five months as a patient in six mental hospitals. The experience totally demoralised me. I had never thought of myself as a particularly strong person, but after hospitalisation, I was convinced of my own worthlessness. I had been told that I could not exist outside an institution. I was terrified that people would find out that I was an ex-patient and look down on me as much as I looked down on myself. For years I feared that any stress, any difficulty would lead to my total collapse. But gradually I had to recognise that I was not the fragile shell I believed myself to be. It was a long process. I had to fight the crippling belief in my inferiority, a belief that I had been given by the people I once trusted as healers. It was years before I allowed myself to feel anger at a system that had locked me up, denied me warm and meaningful contact with other human beings, drugged me, and so thoroughly confused me that I thought of this treatment as helpful. Of enormous help in digging through the layers of mystification has been my involvement, for the past six years, in a number of mental patients' liberation groups, in which ex-patients have come together to validate our own pain and anger.

Out of this anger has come action — working to change commitment laws, to inform patients about their legal rights, to increase Constitutional guarantees to patients, to end the demeaning and harmful psychiatric system and replace it with true asylums, places to which people can retreat to deal with the pain of their existence. We envision a system, in which this pain would not be labelled 'illness' but would be seen as a natural consequence of a system that puts wealth, property, and power above the basic needs of human beings.[10] These asylums would not simply be more humane mental hospitals, they would be true alternatives to the present mental health system — voluntary, small, responsive to their own communities and to their residents. Alternative facilities already exist in a few places, and more are in the planning stage.

Patient-controlled alternatives can provide services to people without the demoralising consequences of the authoritarian, hierarchical structure of traditional mental health services. When the emphasis is on people helping one another, the gulf between 'patient' and 'staff' disappears. Someone can seek help from others without being thought of as sick or helpless. The same person who seeks help can also offer it. People who have been patients know from their own experience that warmth and support (when they were available) were helpful and that being thought of and treated as incompetent were not. Even when a person is experiencing distress, he or she can still be helpful to others. A person who is experiencing extreme pain may temporarily need to be only a 'taker' rather than a giver, but such situations are often relatively short-lived (although being treated badly — as frequently happens in mental institutions — can prolong them). Being able to reach out to another person — even when one is feeling bad oneself — illustrates to the person in distress that he or she is *not* incompetent and worthless. Taking part in making decisions, even such simple ones as what to have for dinner, shows a person that he or she does have some control over his or her life and gives that person the confidence to participate in more substantial group decision making in such areas as financial policy and staff hiring.

There are immense practical problems involved in trying to set up patient-controlled alternative facilities and services. Money is difficult to find. Opposition from professionals, who are accustomed to being in charge and to thinking of patients as incompetent, can be enormous. Ex-patients may be uncertain of their own abilities. In later chapters, I describe some of the alternatives that exist and how their organisers dealt with these difficulties.

The label *mentally ill* implies that a person has a medical problem, one that can be properly treated only by doctors. In mental illness it is the mind that is said to be diseased. The medical model of mental illness — the belief that mental illnesses are directly analogous to physical illnesses — is generally followed by psychiatrists and by the general public, as can be seen in the terms 'mental *illness*,' 'mental *patient*', and 'mental *hospital*'. But there is another way of looking at mental illness. The opinion that mental illness does not exist has been advanced by, among others, psychiatrist Thomas Szasz, sociologists Thomas Scheff and Erving Goffman, and psychologist Theodore Sarbin. Szasz has written that 'although mental illness might have been a useful concept in the nineteenth century, today it is scientifically worthless and socially harmful.'[11] Scheff considers that 'mental illness may be more usefully considered to be a social status than a disease, since the symptoms of mental illness are vaguely defined and widely distributed, and the definition of behaviour as symptomatic of mental illness is usually dependent upon social rather than medical contingencies'.[12] Goffman has pointed out that 'society's official view is that inmates of mental hospitals are there primarily because they are suffering from mental illness. However, in the degree that the 'mentally ill' outside hospitals numerically approach or surpass those inside hospitals, one could say that mental patients distinctly suffer not from mental illness, but from contingencies.'[13] Sarbin believes that 'mental illnesses are not so easily defined as their medical counterparts, physical illness and somatic pathology.... Definition of behaviour pathology is essentially a cultural matter, dependent on local beliefs and practices ... Even within our own culture, widely divergent definitions of mental illness may be found.'[14] Psychiatrists E Fuller Torrey and Ronald Leifer hold similar views. According to Torrey, 'the very term (*mental disease*) itself is nonsensical, a semantic mistake. The two words cannot go together except metaphorically; you can no more have a mental 'disease' than you can have a purple idea or a wise space.'[15] Leifer says that 'the relationship between psychiatry and medicine is historical and social rather than logical or scientific.'[16]

One does not have to be a mental health professional to enter this debate. What is at issue is whether people with certain types of disturbing behaviour are suffering from diseases. Although many psychiatrists claim that their training gives them the expertise to detect symptoms of the various mental illnesses, it is the very existence of mental illness that is in question. Leaving the determination of whether mental illness exists strictly to the psychiatrists is like leaving the determination of the validity of astrology in the hands of professional astrologers. While occasional psychiatrists (or astrologers) may question the very basis of the discipline they practice, such behaviour is understandably rare, since people are unlikely to question the underlying premises of their occupations, in which they often have a large financial and emotional stake.

The equation between mental illness and physical illness is not new. Certain kinds of behaviour, such as hallucinations, have been labelled illnesses in many cultures and periods of history. What is frequently forgotten is that some other cultures have alternative explanations. A 'hallucination' can be an indication that a person has special abilities and should be consulted about major group decisions. Or a 'hallucination' may instead be termed a 'vision', a religious manifestation (if the person doing the labelling shares the religious beliefs of the visionary). Recently, growing numbers of behaviours are being labelled mental illness — far more than have traditionally been called mad.

The question what is mental illness? leads directly to some of the major philosophical questions with which the human race has grappled throughout history: what is the mind, what is the relationship between the mind and the body, what is the relationship between the brain and the mind? These questions are far too important to be left to psychiatrists, whose medical-school training is largely irrelevant to dealing with them. By their training, psychiatrists have already made the assumption that mental illness exists as a counterpart to physical illness.

The law has the power to compel people to receive treatment for mental illness. This almost never occurs in the case of physical illness, except in rare instances when courts overrule parents who have refused medical treatment for their child. The courts in such instances assume the *parens patriae* role, acting in lieu of the parents in what the court defines as the child's best interest. When a person of whatever age is ordered by a court to undergo psychiatric treatment, this same *parens patriae* power comes into effect. This connection between the legal and medical systems puts the mental patient at a disadvantage that is not faced by patients with physical illnesses. Courts usually bow to psychiatric expertise and make the assumption that potential patients *are* sick and in need of treatment — precisely the question the courts are supposed to determine.

In addition to the *parens patriae* doctrine, which assumes that a mentally ill individual is incapable of determining his or her own best interest, an additional doctrine, the police power of the state, is used to justify the involuntary confinement of people labelled mentally ill. This doctrine is based on the assumption that mentally ill people are dangerous and may do harm to themselves or others if they are not locked up. The belief in the dangerousness of the mentally ill is firmly rooted in our culture. It is especially promoted by the mass media, which frequently run stories in which crimes of violence are attributed to a person's mental illness. If the person has been previously hospitalised, that fact is prominently mentioned; if not, frequently a police officer or other authority figure will be quoted to the effect that the accused is 'a mental case' or 'a nut'. In addition, unsolved crimes are often attributed to 'crazies'.

In actuality, people who have been hospitalised because of mental illness are not dangerous.[17] The vast majority of former mental patients do not get in trouble with the law. The occasional ex-patients who commit crimes are noticed; law-abiding former patients are not. The police power of the state to commit people to mental institutions rests not only on the shaky premise that mental illness is equivalent to dangerousness but on the equally shaky belief that psychiatrists can accurately predict future violent acts. Law professor Alan M Dershowitz, who conducted a thorough survey of all the published psychiatric literature concerning the prediction of dangerousness, found that less than a dozen papers involved follow-up studies to see whether those the psychiatrists had labelled dangerous actually went on to commit dangerous acts. The studies indicated that the psychiatrists did a rather poor job, greatly overpredicting violence. They labelled many individuals violence prone who were not in fact violent.[18] However, on the basis of psychiatric predictions of future violence, individuals can be subjected to indefinite detention in mental hospitals.

Both the *parens patriae* power and the police power relate to the stereotyped view of the prospective patient — that he or she is sick, unpredictable, dangerous, unable to care for himself or herself, and unable to judge his or her own best interest. None of these beliefs is scientifically verifiable.

It was in the guise of defining his best interest that the state of Illinois involuntarily committed Robert Friedman to a Chicago mental hospital in February 1975. Friedman's detention made national headlines because he was stopped by the police for panhandling while carrying nearly twenty-five thousand dollars in cash. It was the contention of the state that this showed his poor judgement and inability to care for himself, despite the fact that he had worked for many years (he had been laid off from work a year earlier), lived by himself, and had never been considered in need of care. The psychiatrist who examined him once he was involuntarily confined told the court that Friedman was a 'paranoid schizophrenic'. Friedman had accumulated his money by years of careful living, but the state, which was presumably protecting him, proved far more reckless with his money than he had been. He was charged eight hundred dollars a month for his care, 'care' that so damaged him that seven months later he was unable to live on his own and was placed in a nursing home. In addition, he was required to pay for a lawyer retained by his relatives, who wanted him institutionalised, as well as for his own lawyer, who tried to get him released. On appeal of his case, the state of Illinois filed a confession of error, in which they admitted that there had been no valid reason for his initial commitment. Friedman was by this time suffering from the debilitating effects of confinement and forced medication and was declared legally incompetent. Fourteen months after he was originally found to be mentally ill, Robert Friedman was dead.[19]

Robert Friedman's 'symptoms'were his frugality and his panhandling. For these the state deprived him of his liberty, much of his money, his health, and, ultimately, his life.

Psychiatrist Thomas Szasz takes the position that the only proper role for psychiatry in a free society is to work with individual, consenting clients. Institutional psychiatry, in his view, is inherently coercive, since the institutional psychiatrist is the agent not of his patient, who wishes to be free, but of the people who want the patient locked up — sometimes the state, sometimes the patient's family or friends. The patient has no reason to trust the psychiatrist; often the psychiatrist can see this lack of trust only as a sign of the patient's 'paranoia.' And so the patient gets more of the same treatment he or she has been protesting.

Institutional psychiatric treatment is largely physical in nature. Drugs, the major method of treatment, are known as 'major tranquillisers' or 'antipsychotic agents'. Their main effect is to slow down both thinking and motor activity, and they are responsible for what is widely perceived as a 'revolution' in mental hospitals since the early 1950s, when they came into widespread use. Mental institutions are quieter than they used to be, but the slurred speech and stiffly held bodies of the patients reveal the cost of that quiet. The term *antipsychotic agent* implies that the drug regulates specific malfunctioning parts of the brain, but no proof exists of either the malfunction or the specific corrective power of the drug. The manufacturers of Thorazine, the most widely used major tranquilliser, say that 'the precise mechanism whereby the therapeutic effects ... are produced is not known'.[20]

There is another, far less favourable, way to view the widespread use of these drugs, especially when they are forced on patients in mental institutions. The term *chemical straitjacket* has come into use to describe the effects of tranquillisers. While it may appear far more humane to inject someone with a drug than it is to tie the person up, in actuality they are just two different ways of accomplishing the same thing. And while being tied up can be uncomfortable, it may be preferable to the common side-effects of tranquillisers, which include (for Thorazine) lethargy, drowsiness, pseudo-Parkinsonism, and the possibility of developing an irreversible brain syndrome called tardive dyskinesia (uncontrollable involuntary movements of the mouth, tongue, and jaw, and possibly the extremeties).[21] Other major tranquillisers have similar listed side-effects.

Tranquillisers are used not only in mental hospitals but in many kinds of institutions where large numbers of people are supervised by underpaid, poorly trained staff members: institutions for the retarded, nursing homes, juvenile detention centres, and prisons. The purpose is clearly institutional management. One study of tranquilliser use in a facility for the retarded concluded that the drugs had a beneficial effect because they made 'ward management easier and more pleasant for the attendants, who are now more relaxed.'[22] Of course, it was the inmates, not the staff, who ingested the drugs. At the same time, the side-effects of the drugs may have made it more difficult for the retarded residents to learn basic self-care skills that might have made it possible for them to live outside the institution.

Mental hospitals are similar to prisons, old-age homes, and state 'schools' — all exist to contain various kinds of unwanted people. Mental hospitals add the justification that they are treating illness, but this can be regarded largely as rhetoric.

One of the main functions of the mental hospital, like other 'total institutions,' is control. The lives of patients are minutely supervised. As psychologist D L Rosenhan and his colleagues discovered when they faked the symptoms of mental illness and had themselves admitted to a number of mental hospitals:

> Personal privacy is minimal. Patient quarters and possessions can be entered and examined by any staff member, for whatever reason. His personal history and anguish is available to any staff member ... who chooses to read his folder ... His personal hygiene and waste evacuation are often monitored. The water closets may have no doors ... The pseudopatients had the sense that they were invisible, or at least unworthy of account. Upon being admitted, I and other pseudopatients took the initial physical examination in a semipublic room, where staff members went about their own business as if we were not there.[23]

All the volunteers in the study experienced depersonalisation, not because they were mentally ill but because 'patient contact is not a significant priority in the traditional psychiatric hospital'.[24]

What most psychiatrists call mental illness, Thomas Szasz has called 'problems in living'. People who seek help with their problems in living find that help is frequently unavailable in cold, impersonal mental hospitals. People would find their needs far better served by small, voluntary community facilities where all participated in decision-making and none were seen as less than human. But help must be wanted. Robert Friedman, for example, or Leonard Roy Frank needed simply the right to be left alone. 'My only problem in living,' says Leonard Frank, 'was that other people wouldn't leave me alone'.

When people do have problems in living, they can help one another. Psychiatrists have no monopoly on knowledge about loneliness, alienation, anger, or any other difficulties of living. In fact, psychiatrists (who are often middle or upper class) may never have faced the kinds of problems their poorer patients face daily. The mental hospital, where understanding human contact is at a premium and where psychotherapy (whatever its value may be) is almost unheard of, is hardly the place where people can learn useful new ways of dealing with life. Instead, knowing that there must be a better way, people have banded together to set up all kinds of alternative institutions. Hot lines, crisis centres, and counselling centres of all sorts were set up in many areas during the 1960s. Many have folded, but others are going into their second decade of existence, and new ones are springing up all the time. Psychiatric outpatient facilities such as halfway houses and social clubs are also increasing rapidly.

Alternatives of all sorts exist, but here it becomes important to define what is meant by an alternative. Some are merely mini-institutions in the community, where psychiatrists supervise staffs of nurses and paraprofessionals, where residents' lives are strictly controlled, and where drugs are compulsory. Often a veneer of democracy is provided, in which the residents vote on what to have for dinner or what movie to see, but real decisions, such as who gets to live in the facility or what the rules are, are firmly in professional hands. Other alternatives are more truly democratic, although in almost all, the staff/patient (or staff/resident or staff/client) dichotomy still exists. What I define as a true alternative is one in which all basic decision-making power is in the hands of those the facility exists to serve. Such places are rare, but where they do exist, they show clearly how well people can help one another in environments that have been set up to maximise the strengths and abilities of each participant.

Let me make clear what I do *not* see as models for the future. The typical halfway house is run along the same authoritarian, hierarchical lines as the typical mental hospital, although on a far smaller scale. Dr Richard Budson, a psychiatrist at Harvard Medical School, describes the movement towards halfway houses as 'a truly collaborative programme between professionals, paraprofessionals, the community and its service agencies'[25] — the prospective residents play no part at all. The authoritative survey *The Halfway House Movement* states that 'all facilities defined as halfway houses (in the survey) maintain something of a profession orientation'[26] and notes that 'whether the residents themselves would paint similar pictures (to that provided by the administrators and directors) is, of course, an open question.'[27] Since the residents are still faceless and voiceless, this 'alternative' is still far too close to the old model.

The 'therapeutic community' was introduced by psychiatrist Maxwell Jones as an improvement over the traditional organisation of the mental hospital ward. So-called therapeutic communities have become a fad in progressive mental hospitals — recognisable by the innumerable ward meetings, which take innumerable votes on every minor decision of ward life while the staff continues to make major decisions behind closed doors. Jones has written that 'in a therapeutic community the whole of a patient's time in hospital is thought of as treatment.'[28] The orientation is very much within the medical model — the patient is sick, the staff is well, and the goal of hospitalisation is to cure the patient. The method of the therapeutic community is described as democratic, but only if one accepts the strange definition of democracy of psychiatrist Philip Margolis, who describes it as a situation in which 'one person was responsible but he permitted the group decision to prevail with the understanding that he could overrule it if he wished.'[29] Margolis, describing the therapeutic community he ran at the University of Chicago Hospital, says of it:

> If not a 'true democracy, the ward was truly an egalitarian society, with equality of opportunity. (Almost) all members of the community were subject to the same rules and working conditions and equal rights and privileges, taking into account their particular role in the community. *Staff was staff, and patients were patients*; there was still a staff hierarchy; and some patients were sicker than others. But these conditions and circumstances were understandable and were made explicit and part of the 'game' of which there were definite 'rules'.[30]

The kinds of rules that Margolis speaks of exist in many mental hospital therapeutic communities. Typical is an eight-page list of rules distributed by the Adolescent Unit of Haverford(Pa) State Hospital to its patients.[31] Incoming patients are assigned to Phase I; they are allowed off the unit only when escorted by a staff member and may receive phone calls or visits from their family at the discretion of the staff. In order to 'graduate' to Phase II, patients must satisfy the staff that 'you are actively working on your problems and participating in the therapies provided.'[32] Many adolescents are hospitalised because they do not meet parental expectations; 'actively working on your problems' clearly means modifying one's behaviour in the direction of those expectations. Adolescent rebellion becomes mental illness.

The phase system continues with Phases III to V, which involve the patient in community votes, that is, patients in the higher phases vote on each patient's phase status.

> The community will vote on granting the change you requested. A majority vote decides. However, because the

staff bears final responsibility, it must reserve the right to overrule a community decision when necessary.[33]

In Phases IV and V, patients become 'buddies', assigned to accompany lower-phase patients off the ward. Buddies are responsible for reporting to staff any rule violations by the person they are paired with.

It is very difficult to maintain one's integrity under the therapeutic community system. Patients are required — in plain English — to rat on one another. Resisting the system can result in punishment. For example, 'if areas (of the ward) are found disorderly, the entire community (excluding, obviously, the staff) shall be held accountable and restrictions given.'[34] Patients are required to enforce the standards and expectations of the staff. But is conformity truly a measure of mental health?

People who write therapeutic community rules seem to think so. Restrictions (staying in one's room from dinner to bedtime) are issued for such offences as 'being in cars on the grounds ... excessive use of profanity ... and inappropriate behaviour (a particularly open-ended rule)'.[35] The stated aim is 'to help you learn to get what you want in life by gaining self-control over what you do'.[36] Under this system, a patient has little choice but to decide (or appear to decide) to do what is expected. The mystification inherent in the phrase 'what you wish to do' is obvious within such a coercive system.

Recreational and service facilities for ex-patients are also typically run along authoritarian and undemocratic lines, especially when it comes to major decisions. We will take a closer look at Fountain House and Center Club, two well-known examples, in Chapter 4.

Patient-run and patient-controlled[37] alternatives are quite different. Rather than a hierarchical structure in which some participants are clearly in charge of others, true alternatives feature a co-operative and democratic structure. Although there may be divisions of function, they are fluid, and one who takes the helping role at one point may be the one who receives help at another. Most important, they are places where no one, no matter how poorly functioning, is looked down on as hopeless or as less than human.

Ideally, a network of community facilities for people in acute crisis and for people with long-term difficulties would eliminate mental hospitals entirely. Facilities would differ, depending on the neighbourhood and the kinds of clients they served, but all would be run democractically, with basic decision-making power in the hands of clients. People would not be considered sick or well but would be seen as individuals coping with their lives to the best of their abilities. Unique and special needs would be recognised. Third World people, for example, could run facilities in which all participants understood the experience of being minority group members and useful coping mechanisms would not be dismissed as pathological. Healthy and vigorous elderly people could act as resource people for less able older people. Homosexuals could provide role models for other, troubled gay people. Rather than becoming passive recipients of institutional 'care', troubled people would be helped to see the strong and positive aspects of themselves as they, in turn, help others.

The definition of need would come from the client. People behaving in ways that other people found troublesome but that they themselves found satisfactory could not be forced to partake of any services, no matter how humane, against their will. The social control functions of the current psychiatric system cannot be carried over into the alternative model, or it loses its alternative quality. The alternative system would leave Robert Friedman or Leonard Roy Frank quite properly alone.

It will be objected that this will leave untreated many people who require 'treatment'. But two hundred years of institutional psychiatry have shown that mental hospitals cannot help the unwilling. Incarceration is not treatment.

NOTES FOR CHAPTER 1

1. *Webster's New International Dictionary* ,3rd ed,sv 'symptom.'
2. Personal interview with Leonard Roy Frank, December 7, 1976.
3. Leonard Roy Frank, 'The Frank Papers',*Madness Network News* 2, no 5 (December 1974), pp12-17. 'The Frank Papers' have been reprinted in John Friedberg's *Shock Treatment Is Not Good for Your Brain* (San Francisco:Glide Publications, 1976), pp62-81.
4. 'Frank Papers', *Madness Network News*, p15.
5. Ibid, p16
6. Ibid, p14.
7. See Erving Goffman, *Asylums* (Chicago: Aldine Publishing Company, 1962), particularly the first chapter. 'On the Characteristics of Total Institutions'.
8. See, for example, the definition of 'acute schizophrenic episode' which lists 'dreamlike dissociation' as one of the symptoms associated with the onset of this condition, in The Committee on Nomenclature and Statistics of the American Psychiatric Association, *Diagnostic and Statistical Manual of Mental Disorders*, 2d ed (Washington, DC: American Psychiatric Association, 1974), p34.
9. See Goffman, *Asylums*; WM Mendel, 'On the Abolition of the Psychiatric Hospital', in *Comprehensive Mental Health,* ed CM Roberts, NS Greenfield, and MH Miller (Madison: University of Wisconsin Press, 1968); JK Wing and GW Brown, *Institutionalism and Schizophrenia* (Cambridge: Cambridge University Press, 1970).
10. This phrase is used by the Mental Patients' Liberation Front of Boston.
11. Thomas S Szasz, *The Myth of Mental Illness* (New York: Harper & Row, 1961), p ix. See also Szasz's numerous other books and papers.
12. Thomas J Scheff, *Being Mentally Ill* (Chicago: Aldine Publishing Company, 1966), pp128-129.
13. Goffman, *Asylums*, p135.

14. Theodore R Sarbin, ed, *Studies in Behaviour Pathology* (New York: Holt, Rinehart and Winston, 1961), p7.

15. E Fuller Torrey, *The Death of Psychiatry* (Radnor, Pa: Chilton Book Company, 1974), p36.

16. Ronald Leifer, *In the Name of Mental Health* (New York: Science House, 1969), p28.

17. Among the many studies that come to this conclusion are LH Cohen and H Freeman, 'How Dangerous to the Community Are State Hospital Patients?' *Connecticut State Medical Journal* 9 (September 1945): 697-700; Jonas R Rappeport and Frances Gruenwald, 'Evaluation and Follow-up of State Hospital Patients Who Had Sanity Hearings'. *American Journal of Psychiatry* 118 (June 1962): 1078-1086; Jonas R Rappeport and George Lassen, 'Dangerousness — Arrest Rate Comparison of Discharged Patients and the General Population,' *American Journal of Psychiatry* 121 (February 1965): 776-783; and Jonas R Rappeport, *The Clinical Evaluation of the Dangerousness of the Mentally Ill* (Springfield, Ill.: Charles C Thomas, 1967).

18. Alan M Dershowitz, 'The Psychiatrist's Power in Civil Commitment: A Knife That Cuts Both Ways, *Psychology Today* 2, no 9 (February 1969): 43-47.

19. Material on Robert Friedman from 'The Docket: Test Case Litigation', *Mental Health Law Project Summary of Activities* 2, no 1 (March 1976):4-5; Leonard Roy Frank, 'Robert Friedman Is Dead', *Madness Network News* 3, no 7 (June 1976); 11; and Cercie Miller, 'Robert Friedman Dead', *State and Mind* 5, no 3 (July-September 1976): 17.

20. *Physician's Desk Reference*, 30th ed (Oradell, NJ: Medical Economics Company, 1976): pp1457-1458.

21. Ibid, p1458.

22. Gail Marker, 'Institutional Drug Abuse', *Mental Health Law Project Summary of Activities*, March 1975, p15

23. DL Rosenhan, 'On Being Sane in Insane Places', Science 179 (January 19, 1973): p256.

24. Ibid.

25. Richard D Budson, 'The Psychiatric Halfway House', *Psychiatric Annals* 3, no 6 (June 1973): p83.

26. Harold L Raush with Charlotte L Raush, *The Halfway House Movement* (New York: Appleton-Century-Crofts, 1968), p45

27. Ibid, pp44-45

28. Maxwell Jones, *The Therapeutic Community* (New York: Basic Books, 1953), p53.
29. Alfred H Stanton and Morris S Schwartz, *The Mental Hospital* (New York: Basic Books, 1954), quoted in Philip M Margolis, *Patient Power* (Springfield, Ill: Charles C Thomas, 1973), p150.
30. Margolis, *Patient Power*, p151 (emphasis added).
31. Haverford (Pa) State Hospital, 'Adolescent Unit Phase System and Community Rules', mimeographed, nd, unpaged.
32. Ibid.
33. Ibid.
34. Ibid.
35. Ibid.
36. Ibid.
37. I use the word *patient* to include ex-patients, residents and clients.

Chapter Two

The Making — and Unmaking — of a Mental Patient

The differences between mental institutions and true alternatives are not a subject for dry reporting. The experiences of real people tell the true measure of those differences. This is my story.[1]

I got married at twenty. Of course, that wasn't the origin of my troubles, it just seems that way. Lots of things brought me to that point. Like hating school. Bright New York Jewish girls are supposed to love school, bring home perfect report cards, and make their parents proud. By the time I got to high school, I was counting the days to freedom. Although I had the marks, and the hopeful urging of my parents, I knew I didn't want to go to college.

Which led to a secretarial job, boredom, and marriage. I had freed myself from one trap only by entering another. It's all a familiar story today, but this was 1965. No women's liberation, or even the recognition of the need for it.

We had long talks, my husband and I, about the idyllic future we imagined. We would raise a family, of course — our children would be beautiful, smart, talented, and loving. I would go off each day to work. I don't remember the details of our dream house — maybe it even had a white picket fence. It never occurred to me to question our faith in the American dream. Meanwhile, we lived in an apartment and fought the daily indignities of life in New York City.

When I got pregnant, I felt I was beginning a great adventure. Three months later, after a miscarriage, the adventure was over. Everyone waited for me to 'snap out of it'. I wanted to retreat to someplace inside myself for a while, but everyone — my parents, my husband, my obstetrician — expected me to be up and around, cheerful, getting on with my life. I couldn't explain my need to withdraw — I couldn't find words for it. The more demands people made, the more frightened I became. Couldn't they see that I needed to be alone, to cry, to lie in bed and pull the covers over my head, to figure out what I wanted, what I needed?

For years I was to describe it as an intense depression. But *depression* is a word I was given by psychiatrists, a word that's slipped into everyday language so that we hardly notice it, but a word that nonetheless makes us think of the need for doctors and hospitals. My need was to return to myself, to get in touch with my own feelings. This label, depression, for years thwarted my chances to get my life moving in a positive direction. A depression is something to get rid of and the goal of psychiatry is to 'cure' people of depression. That my depression might be telling me something about my own life was a possibility no one considered, including me.

I went to a psychiatrist unwillingly. I couldn't understand what he was supposed to do for me. I was unhappy — I couldn't see how that could be talked away. But on the first visit it became clear that more than talk was to be used in my cure. The doctor opened a desk drawer and made a selection from the various brightly coloured pills. I was given orange ones and blue ones, and white ones to get me through the long, sleepless, tear-filled nights.

He gave me advice, too. I should go back to work, get out more, be with people. But I had done all that, that's how I had ended up so unhappy. Didn't he see? And take my pills. There was something very important about my taking my pills. If they were supposed to make me happy, they didn't. I felt drugged, lethargic — the very feelings the pills were supposed to cure.

It was the doctor who first planted the idea of the hospital in my mind. If he couldn't help me, perhaps the hospital could. I was confused by everything that was going on around me. I wasn't meeting anyone's expectations — what was wrong with me? The doctor had provided an easy answer — an illness called depression. My desperate unhappiness was an *illness*; all I had to do was find the cure. The doctor didn't seem to have it. Perhaps the hospital would.

I went to Mount Sinai Hospital full of hope. To me, admission to the psychiatric ward meant that at last I would find someone who would know how to bring an end to my suffering. I was almost elated as a nurse showed me around the ward. It was clean and modern, and large windows let in the sun. No snake pit here. Later I learned that the unbarred windows were made of a special glass that would not shatter. I was astonished to see how young some of the patients were — high school students, some of them. There were older people too. I was twenty-one years old.

I hadn't brought a suitcase with me, so the nurse gave me hospital pajamas and a robe and locked my street clothes in a big closet with everyone else's. We were also allowed to wear 'lounging outfits,' which meant that some of the women could look almost normal. I felt sorry for the men, who had no choice but to look rumpled and sick in pajamas, robes, and slippers.

The next surprise was meeting 'my' doctor, a resident who was assigned to my case. My outside doctor, who at least had spent a few months getting to know me, was now an outsider. The new doctor told me we would have two thirty-minute sessions a week. I couldn't believe it. I had been seeing my outside doctor twice a week for forty-five minutes, and he had told me that I was sick enough to need hospitalisation, which surely should mean more, not less, psychotherapy. I argued and argued, but those were the rules.

A nurse came around with medication — and another surprise. Instead of my orange pills and blue pills, I had red ones and yellow ones. I checked, but there wasn't a mistake — new drugs had been ordered. The nurse made the rounds of the 'lounge', and nearly everyone got some kind of pill.

The lounge was a big room furnished with couches and chairs. A TV stood in one corner. There were two telephone booths — we didn't have phones in our rooms. Adjoining the lounge was a small dining room, and beyond that was a kitchen where we could prepare snacks. The rest of the ward consisted of bedrooms, corridors, and a glassed-in nurses' station.

I was assigned to a room with three other women. I was eager to talk, to compare experiences, but no one seemed very friendly. I went to sit in the lounge and found a few people, anyway, who wanted to talk. From the pay phone in the lounge I called my husband to tell him I was in the hospital. We immediately began to fight. He couldn't understand what I was doing there, and I was unable to make him see how deeply unhappy I was and how sure that I would find some answers in the hospital.

Visiting hours came after dinner. My husband arrived, still seething. My parents came too, in anguish and despair. We were so far apart. None of us spoke the same language. But no one was supposed to notice. It was only recently that I'd begun to notice it myself.

At bedtime I asked for my sleeping pill. Rather than my beloved white tablet, my only chance of sleep for months, there was an unfamiliar capsule. I couldn't sleep.

The next day I was introduced to the hospital routine. After breakfast came the nine o'clock ward meeting — all the doctors, nurses, and other staff members, and all the patients. It was hard to talk about yourself in front of such a big group of strangers. After the meeting we went upstairs to either the gym or the occupational therapy department. We went there some afternoons, too. In the evening, we could watch TV, read, or play cards. There were occasional escorted walks (which only some patients were allowed to go on); most of the patients hadn't been outside in weeks. I couldn't quite understand how this routine was supposed to make me well. But I went along with it willingly, convinced that everything had a reason.

I was in the hospital for two and a half weeks. My belief that I was in a caring, therapeutic atmosphere never wavered, despite some puzzling incidents. My husband visited every night, and his visits invariably ended in screaming fights. Rather than working together to find a way out of our difficulties, we turned to blaming each other. Since I had little confidence in myself, I came out worst in these encounters. On one particularly bad evening I asked one of the nurses to please tell him to leave, because I was too upset to deal with him. She refused and told me to do it myself. When I came back into the room, he began to yell at me again. I felt totally friendless.

One rare evening we didn't have a fight. Instead, he was very subdued. Our cat had been sick. He had taken him to the vet, who had diagnosed an illness that is frequently fatal. I started to cry when he told me, and he held my hand. After visiting hours, I felt abandoned and miserable. I went looking for a nurse to talk to and told the story through my tears. She didn't seem to understand. I loved my cat and was afraid he would die. Did that make me mentally ill?

When I was discharged, I expected to feel better. I went home — and discovered that I still couldn't get out of bed or stop crying, and my husband and I were still tearing at each other. I went back to my old doctor, and at least he gave me my white sleeping pills back — eight guaranteed hours of oblivion. I longed for them all day. At the hospital I had been unhappy, but at home I was even more miserable. One day I packed my suitcase and went back to Mount Sinai.

I couldn't believe it when they told me there wasn't a bed. Nor would they allow me to go back home. An ambulance was called and, with a policeman sitting beside me, we were on our way to Bellevue. If you grow up in New York, you know about Bellevue long before you understand what it means. Kids whisper and giggle, and you figure out it's some kind of horrible place, although you're not quite sure what it is. Bellevue is a big general hospital, but it's the psychiatric ward that most people are talking about. Long before you learn those big words, you know *nut house* and *booby hatch*.

The next few hours were a mass of confusion. To begin with they took away my glasses. I could barely see anything that was more than a few feet away, and it was almost impossible to distinguish one unfamiliar face from another. By the time I was brought up to the ward, it was night. Someone led me to a bed in a corridor and told me to lie down and go to sleep. After a while I got up and went looking for a bathroom — groping my way down the hall. A white figure appeared and ordered me back to bed. I waited in terror through the long night. I suddenly realised that neither my husband nor my parents had any idea where I was.

It took me several hours the next morning to find someone who would listen to my story. Finally, a nurse agreed to let me make a phone call. When I heard my father's voice, I started to sob. 'Get me out of here, please,' I begged. The nurse got on the phone and explained that I was in Bellevue Hospital. My parents promised to come later that day. 'And bring me a spare pair of glasses. They took mine.'

After breakfast and lunch (I was afraid to eat the food), my parents arrived with an old pair of glasses, and for an hour I had the luxury of seeing. But when it was time for them to go, the nurse made them take my glasses with them. All they could think of, it seemed, was the damage a piece of glass could do but why couldn't they understand how much more emotionally vulnerable I was when I could hardly see? My parents also found out that they could not take me home. The only way to get me out of Bellevue was to find a private hospital that would take me. 'Try Gracie Square', one of the nurses suggested. 'They'll take anybody'. It was Saturday afternoon, the next day was Easter Sunday. It would be impossible to do anything before Monday, at the very earliest. I would have to stay in Bellevue at least until then.

Easter Sunday. I was urged to come into the dining room, where we would each get a cupcake with a jelly bean on top. I was still afraid to eat the food, but I was also afraid that the nurses would notice that I wasn't eating. I tried to disappear into the corners during mealtimes, and it seemed to work. In three days, I swallowed nothing but water from the fountain. Every Easter I think of those cupcakes with a shiver.

On Monday my parents were able to get me admitted to Gracie Square Hospital. It was mainly a question of money. They weren't wealthy, but they were able to pay the fee. I had to be transported by ambulance again. The doctor who signed my transfer papers told me it was too bad I was leaving, since she was sure Bellevue could help me. 'What would you do if you were my doctor?' I asked her. 'I'd give you shock treatments.' I was thankful that she had already signed the papers.

My suitcase, which had been taken from me when I arrived, reappeared. Patients weren't allowed to keep their possessions because there was no safe place to put things. Anything you wanted to keep had to be carried with you. Some of the other patients, the experienced ones, used large handbags or shopping bags to carry their possessions around. Otherwise, there was no way to keep anything — a change of clothes, a sweater, a comb.

Gracie Square was clean, beautiful, and quiet. I luxuriated in the change from Bellevue. But only for a few minutes. I was led to a barren, deserted area and locked in. No one talked to me or explained that the hospital had required my parents to hire private-duty nurses for me, and until the first 'special' arrived, I was kept in isolation. The fear was overwhelming. I hadn't eaten in three days, and suddenly I had the sensation that I wasn't alone, there was something in there with me. I screamed and cried, but nobody came. Finally, 'it' went away. Later, the door was unlocked and 'my' nurse came and took me to my room.

It took me only a few hours to recognise that Gracie Square was a clean, nicely furnished prison. There was no phone, visitors were allowed only twice a week, and the locked ward door opened with a buzzer. To counteract that, there were carpets on the floor and pictures on the walls, and the food was surprisingly good. 'The Gilded Cage', I came to call it.

There was little to do. Occasionally we were taken through the buzzer-operated door, into an elevator that operated with a key, and onto the first floor for occupational therapy or upstairs to a recreation room. My doctor came to visit me a few times. There were pills to take in addition to my white sleeping pills at night. I didn't tell anyone about the 'thing' I had seen the first day, and it didn't come back. After a few weeks, I was transferred to the third-floor ward where there was a telephone and we could go to activities more often.

I made two friends, and we passed the long days talking and watching TV. Donna was an unhappy teenager who had frequently slashed her arms and had been in Grace Square before. Leslie's story was more dramatic. Even her doctor admitted that there was no reason for her to be in a mental hospital. Leslie, a college student, had been raped, but she hadn't told anyone, because she had been parked in a lover's lane with her boyfriend when it happened. To her horror, she discovered she was pregnant. Abortion was illegal, unless the woman's life was in danger, so she had faked a suicide attempt, and her doctor had put her in the hospital, trying to prove that she 'qualified' for an abortion. The three of us tried to fill the empty hours as best we could.

No one knew what do do with me. My doctor suggested Hillside Hospital, where I would be able to get psychotherapy. Gracie Square was too expensive for my parents, and he told them that Hillside might charge a reduced fee. I knew I didn't want to go home. Maybe this new hospital would be able to cure me. I was still sure that some doctor must have the answer for me. When I was discharged from Gracie Square, I didn't go back to the apartment I shared with my husband, I went home with my parents. Getting into Hillside was a long and complicated process, with admission forms and interviews. Then the wait for a bed. At home, I spent most of my time crying in my room, and the tension level quickly became intolerable.

One night I started to scream in terror and demanded that my parents take me back to Gracie Square. I explained to the doctor on duty that I was terrified and wanted to come back into the hospital. He gave me an admission form to sign. I must have signed others over the preceding months, but this was the first one that made any impression on me. The form I had to sign stated that if I wanted to leave, I had to give three days' written notice. When I protested that I didn't know how long I wanted to stay, I was told that I had to sign the form in order to be admitted. Finally, I grabbed the pen and blocked out the offending paragraphs, not simply drawing lines through the words, but completely covering them. Only then did I sign my name. A nurse came and took me upstairs. I had asked to go to the third floor but was taken to the fifth instead. As soon as the door clicked shut behind me, I realised I had made a mistake.

When my doctor came to see me the next morning, I couldn't explain what had happened. All I knew was that when I was at home, it had seemed that I could get away from the terror I felt by coming back to the hospital. Although neither my doctor nor I recognised it at the time, I was becoming afraid of the world outside the hospital. Psychiatrists call such patients *institutionalised*, and it can happen very quickly. Rather than wanting to be well (which I was beginning to think was impossible), I wanted only the security of Hillside, where I still thought I would find the cure for unhappiness. After a few days my doctor discharged me from Gracie Square, and I went back to my parents' house, to cry and to wait.

By the time the call came from Hillside, I was in pretty bad shape. I wasn't used to being around people, yet I wasn't frightened by meeting so many nurses, aides, and patients in my first few hours. I was sure that I had finally arrived in the place that knew how to give me the long-awaited cure. I was surrounded by people I was sure had the same goal — to make well or be made well. It seemed far removed from the terror I felt about walking down a street among strangers, something I hadn't done by myself in months. In the patients' jargon I was picking up, life in a mental hospital was defined as being *inside*, safe and protected. The word didn't sound ominous to me then.

Hillside didn't have wards, it had 'cottages', small buildings, each with perhaps five bedrooms, a living room, bathroom, and a nursing office. Each one housed both men and women, but there was only one bathroom, with a flip sign for 'Men' and 'Women' hanging on the door. I was instructed to yell out, 'Female', when entering. A nurse explained to me that each group of two cottages was run as a unit. They used to put all the men patients in one cottage and the women in another, but they had decided to 'integrate' a few years back, and that's why they weren't built with two bathrooms. It seemed like an awful nuisance.

An aide explained the rules to me. I was not allowed away from the unit — the two cottages — without a staff escort. Eventually I might advance to 'group privileges' — that is, being permitted to walk to the dining room or to activities with a group of patients — and finally to 'individual privileges'. I would not be allowed phone calls or visitors until the staff decided I was entitled to those 'privileges'. It was Gracie Square with invisible walls. When I had visited Hillside, I had felt reassured by the phone booths that were all around, and I had checked to make sure that there were liberal visiting hours. Now I felt tricked, betrayed. I knew I didn't want to be a prisoner again. If anything went wrong, I was cutt off from the outside world. When the aide told me that he also worked in nearby Creedmore State Hospital, I began to feel very frightened. Everyone knew how bad the state hospitals were. Hillside was supposed to be different.

Then the first interview with 'my' doctor — still another doctor. Again, I was supposed to start from the beginning. Right away, I knew I didn't like him. I couldn't imagine ever feeling trust in him, he was so remote, distant, professional. (Maybe he was just scared. I found out later that it was only his second week as a resident.) It was impossible to get another doctor. The possibility that some people can never develop warmth or sympathy with one another was never even considered. If you couldn't get along with the doctor you were assigned, it was just another sign that there was something wrong with you.

I didn't like my roommate either. Most of the patients were young, but I was supposed to room with a middle-aged woman with grown children. I didn't see how I could ever feel close to her — we were just too different.

The next shock came at medication time. No pills had been ordered for me. I told the nurse what I was accustomed to taking. She checked my chart and told me that I was being evaluated without medication. I was confused. I had been taking various combinations of tranquillisers for about six months, and although they didn't do much to change my mood, I had been assured by all my previous doctors that I'd be far worse off without them. Now I was being told that I could get along without them all, including my sleeping pills. Unlike the tranquillisers, the sleeping pills had a very definite effect on my mood. In the brief period between taking a pill and drifting off to sleep, I felt incredibly good, without a care in the world. Although I woke each morning to the crushing realisation that the good feeling was gone, each night would bring the increasing certainty that one morning I'd wake in the same joyous condition. Now I was afraid to face the night. I listened to my roommate's snoring for hours.

The next day I started trying to get a new roommate and a new doctor. It was impossible, against the rules. I was supposed to adjust. The more I argued, the more I was looked on as sick. It was a sign of health to follow the rules. But the rules seemed designed to drive me crazy. Every minute was scheduled. A nurse took me to my first activity — a woodworking shop. It was a big room with lots of expensive equipment. Patients were busy working on their projects. I didn't like the sound of the machinery. The woodworking teacher handed me a board, which I was to guide past a moving saw. I had always been frightened of machinery, but especially so now. I was sure that the saw would attack me — I could almost see the blood streaming. I had come here to get away from that, and now they were forcing me to put my hands near the rapidly moving saw. I started to push the board against the blade, then dropped it and ran from the room.

Next I was taken to a ceramics workshop. This was better — no ominous machines here. I took a lump of clay and began to pound it against a board. Clay has to be solidly packed down, and I enjoyed slaping it down again and again. My hands were covered in clay. Suddenly, as I held the ball of clay in my hands, it began to change. I had an enormous desire to stuff the slimy mass into my mouth. At the same time, it disgusted me. I told the nurse that I couldn't stay here anymore, and we went back to the cottage. I found that I was sweating and shaking. Maybe the staff were right — I was crazy, and my demands were unreasonable. I was dizzy, disoriented, confused. I went outside to sit under a tree and think about it. I got my first 'therapy' at Hillside under that tree, and it came from another patient. Harry had been admitted at the same time I was. He was the first patient I met. Harry had been at Hillside before and knew the ropes. The printed instructions I had been sent had said to bring only clothes and personal articles, and no radios. I arrived with a single small bag. Harry was stumbling under a huge pile of his belongings, including fencing equipment and a record player. He had offered to let me listen to his records. Now, under the tree, I told him how angry and confused I was. Why did I have such an unfriendly room-mate, such a cold doctor, and why did I feel so awful? I was alternately sweating and shivering in the warm sunshine. My flesh was crawling and my stomach churning. Harry asked me what medication I was on, and I repeated to him that I was being evaluated without medication. When I told him what I had been taking, he understood. 'You're having withdrawal symptoms', he told me. I realised I wasn't going crazy after all. The physical feelings had a cause. My anger and frustration were also real.

No one would respond to my requests for changes. I talked to nurses, to my doctor, to an administrator. I listed the reasons why I thought I should be able to get another roommate and another doctor, but it was clear that no one was taking me seriously. After several days of fruitless rational argument, I tried screaming. I demanded to be discharged — my right as a voluntary patient — but again no one took me seriously. I began to scream and cry. I was a prisoner, no one would listen to me, I was trapped in a situation that made me feel worse instead of better. Everyone around me clearly thought that I was crazy. After all, I was screaming and crying like a crazy person. What else did crazy people do? I picked up a bedside lamp and began to smash the little windows of the door to my room. Swinging the lamp was the only way left to feel powerful. It only lasted a few minutes. Several nurses and aides subdued me, although I fought them with strength I didn't know I had. In my exhausted state following this last outburst, they told me that I would be discharged.

Later they told my mother that I was 'too sick' for them. She puzzled over that one for years. 'It was supposed to be a hospital: they were supposed to know what to do for you', she told me much later. 'We certainly didn't know what to do. There they were, saying they didn't know either. There was nowhere to turn.'

This time I went back to my husband, trying to pick up the pieces of our life together. It wasn't easy. We had so little warmth to give each other. Our cat finally died. We cried together over that. At least then I knew why I was crying. I was afraid to stay alone, and he hired a woman to come each day to watch me. Even though I had asked for her, I hated the whole idea of having her there to guard me, kind and well meaning as she was. It was just further proof that there was something desperately wrong with me. Even my home had become a mental hospital. Not knowing what to do, I demanded that my husband fire her, only to discover that I hated being alone even more. My mother started to come each day, a further reminder that I couldn't take care of myself. My life had become a nightmare that had no end. There were little things that could make me feel better — it was summer, and I could lie in the sun or go swimming — but the relief was never more than momentary and many days I felt too much dread even to face the people around the swimming pool.

Was this what the rest of my life was going to be? I knew I didn't want that, but I had no idea how to change. The doctors didn't know, the hospitals didn't know. I tried going back to my psychiatrist again, but he could offer nothing except pills, and after going through the withdrawal at Hillside, I knew I didn't want them again. Except for the sleeping pills — only they had the power to bring on a few minutes of good feeling at the end of each endless day. Sometimes I thought about swallowing them all and following that good feeling to its end, which I dimly realised was death, but I didn't want to die, I wanted to live.

I needed someone to teach me how to stop crying. For some reason I still thought I could find it in a hospital. One morning, in desperation, I went into the bathroom and cut both my wrists with a razor blade. My mother took me to the emergency room at Montefiore Hospital, and once again I was a mental patient. It wasn't good, but it was something.

Montefiore wasn't a prison. It was a small ward, perhaps twenty patients, and it was easy to learn everyone's name. In the bedrooms, the beds were disguised as couches. Everything was colourful and comfortable. For the first week or so I stayed on the ward, calming down. I realised that I did not have to die. 'My' psychiatrist was another young resident, but he didn't have the glacial remoteness of my Hillside doctor. I told him I felt better without tranquillisers, and he agreed I didn't need them. But he wouldn't give me the white sleeping pills I craved. With the capsules I was allowed, sleep became difficult again.

Two of the aides were nuns, which I thought was strange. One of them asked me why I always slept with stuffed animals in my bed. Because she was a nun, I felt embarrassed to tell her that it was because I liked the feeling of sleeping next to somebody. I felt she wouldn't understand. But when I told one of the nurses, she said I should have answered the nun. No one would acknowledge that it was normal for me to feel strange about talking to a nun, even though I'd never done it in my life.

It must have been even harder for Alan, a fourteen-year-old patient who was an Orthodox Jew. He always ordered kosher food, but one day there was a mix-up, and he was given a regular tray, which of course he wouldn't eat. An attendant tried to talk him into eating, since he was thin and shouldn't miss a meal. Alan tried to explain his religious beliefs — to a nun with a quizzical smile and a cross around her neck.

Twice a week we had 'TC' — therapeutic community meetings. These were ordeals — talking in front of a whole room of people about your problems and feelings. Attendance was compulsory, and if you didn't speak up voluntarily, one of the doctors was sure to put you on the spot with a pointed question. The doctors talked a lot about how we were 'a community'.

During the day some patients went to the day programme. Stuck on the ward, I envied them for having an activity to go to. I couldn't understand why people grumbled about it — until I was assigned to the programme. Arts and crafts, cooking — every minute was scheduled, and the activities were about as challenging as they had been back in day camp. We tried to play hooky, but you had to have a good excuse — not liking it wasn't good enough. The day programme was supposed to be more therapeutic than staying on the ward watching TV.

There was a backyard where we had occasional barbecues — the high chain-link fence wasn't there simply to mark off the space. I hated it, it felt like being in a cage. Sometimes we went on outings to the real world. It was fun to go to the movies, except for the ordeal of going into the theatre itself. The hospital had an arrangement with the manager to let us in for free, and we were always lined up and counted in the lobby. We obviously weren't an ordinary group, even though the aides wore street clothes and took off their name tags. I always wanted to hide.

One Monday morning, it was clear that something had happened. Frank, a patient I didn't know very well, hadn't returned from a weekend pass. All kinds of rumours were flying around. We were all called into the dayroom, where the entire staff was assembled. One of the doctors told us that Frank had committed suicide at home the previous day. He told us that we were all very upset and frightened that the hospital couldn't protect us. Then he announced that there had been 'a community decision' to lock the ward for a while, until everyone felt better. I spoke up and told them that a locked ward certainly wouldn't make me feel better, it would frighten me. I didn't want to feel like a prisoner again. The only response I could get was the bland assurance that we all 'needed the security' of a locked ward.

I tried pounding on the door, but it was solid and wouldn't give. My doctor told me that I was to be put on tranquillisers. My anger at being locked in was a symptom. I didn't want the heavy, drugged feeling of tranquillisers — I was now feeling more alive than I had for a long time. I held the pills in my mouth and spat them into the toilet as soon as I could.

When I told my doctor I wanted to leave the hospital, he said I couldn't. 'But I'm frightened of locked wards', I told him. 'I've been on a locked ward, it was terrifying. Until this happened, I was feeling better, but now the things that frighten me are right here in the hospital'. He told me I was too sick to go home. 'It's not fair', I said. 'All along this has been an open ward, and now you've changed the rules.'

I decided that there was no reason to obey any of the rules, since it was obvious that they could be changed at the will of the staff. I refused to get dressed. 'Why can't I stay in my bathrobe all day', I argued. 'We can't go anyplace.' They told me I couldn't come into the dining room in my robe, so I started taking my trays to my room, until that was outlawed too. Then I started asking my visitors to bring me food from the coffee shop. A nurse came into my room and tried to take away my hamburger. There was a struggle, and I found myself in a locked, barren 'quiet room'.

The two seclusion rooms were located behind the nurses' station. Each had a heavy door with a small safety-glass opening. On the opposite wall was a window covered with thick 'psychiatric screening' — far more aesthetic than bars, but equally impenetrable. Although I had seen patients locked into seclusion from time to time, it was not something I thought could ever happen to me. Patients in seclusion were 'crazy' — they screamed and banged on the door. Now it was me, and suddenly banging and kicking became logical. I had attempted to be reasonable, to explain myself — and this was what they thought of me. My anger mounted. I was not only a prisoner, I was a caged animal. Suddenly nothing was important except freedom. And freedom lay on the other side of a locked door.

When they got tired of listening to me pounding and screaming, they came into the room and gave me an injection. They let me out a few hours later, exhausted and demoralised.

There was no way I could convince the staff that being behind locked doors was harming me. The terror that had been receding for the past few weeks was back, only this time I knew where it was coming from. But I couldn't do a thing about it. They had already decided that the locked door was reassuring. Evening walks had been cancelled, of course. Too unsettling. I prowled the ward, restless. They increased my dosage of tranquillisers. I was still spitting them out as often as I could, but I couldn't always get away with it. I complained constantly that the drugs made me feel worse, remembering all the side-effects I had experienced in the past. I didn't know if they suspected.

I was taken for two days for psychological tests. It was a chance to get off the ward, anyway. The psychologist had me fit blocks together, answer all kinds of questions, interpret ink blots. It went on for hours. When the nurse came to escort me back to the ward after the first day of testing, I could feel myself shrinking back down to a small, caged animal. To the psychologist I might have been an object, but I was at least an interesting object.

It was not only that I thought of myself as shrinking. I felt it. With enormous pain, my face started to collapse. My nose was withdrawing into my face. I couldn't breathe. I screamed and grabbed my face. As the pain subsided, I gasped out an account of what was happening to the nurse and the psychologist, who were holding me. I saw disbelief and contempt in their eyes. I was still crying softly when I was brought back up to the ward.

At the end of the second day of testing, the same thing happened, but the pain was not as severe, and it subsided more quickly. This time, knowing that it was not 'real', I fought it, and pushed away the knowledge that it was my world that was shrinking. The psychologist told me the results of my IQ test — my mind was shrinking, too. The score was fifteen points lower than the one of my school records.

After they tested my mind, they tested my brain. An EEG didn't sound frightening at all. I remembered the electrocardiograms I had to take after the doctor thought I'd had rheumatic fever when I was a kid. The technician told me to sit in a chair and started attaching the wires to my scalp. To my surprise, each wire was inserted into my skin. After the first few I started to protest. He kept saying soothingly that there were just a few more wires, but more and more went in. I demanded to know how many there were all together. There were to be more than twenty. I started to scream and tried to pull the wires out. The nurse and the technician kept trying to hold my hands away from the wires. I protested that I wasn't going to sit still and let them stick wires in my head — and that there must be some other way to hold the electrodes in place. They kept insisting that I had to have the test. I was too tired to fight anymore, and I let the technicians put the rest of the wires in. Some went behind my ears. The skin there itched and burned for days afterwards.

The next day I got off the ward again, for an appointment with my doctor. Before I had a chance to discuss anything with him, he dropped a bombshell. I was being transferred to Rockland State Hospital. Waves of terror moved within me. My ears were ringing, everything suddenly seemed unreal. I started to cry. 'Why can't I stay here?' 'This isn't a long-term hospital. You need long-term care.' 'Let me go home. I'll go back to my psychiatrist. I'll see him every day.' 'You're too sick to go home.' 'But a state hospital — they don't give any care there. Let me go someplace where I can get treatment.' 'You don't need treatment. You need long-term custodial care.' 'What's wrong with me?' 'You're very sick.' 'But what's *wrong* with me? What's the name of it?' 'You have a character disorder. You need to be in a place with a rigid structure. You may never be able to live outside a hospital.' Still in tears, I was returned to the ward.

I realised that I needed a lawyer and called the New York Civil Liberties Union. When I explained the situation, they told me there was nothing they could do. Under New York law, once two doctors stated a person was mentally ill, he or she could be committed for sixty days. No court hearing was required. Sixty days — it sounded like eternity. I wouldn't accept that there was nothing I could do. Next I called the Legal Aid Society. The woman I spoke to was no help at all. 'If that's where they're sending you', she told me, 'you must need to be there'. There was nothing I could do, nothing my husband or my parents could do once the doctors had made up their minds.[2]

I felt that a death sentence had been pronounced on me. The doctor's words, 'long-term custodial care', echoed ominously in my head. Would I ever get out of there? I went into the room I shared with three other patients and began to search methodically. I found the mirror in Carol's bureau drawer. I shattered it and began to cut my arms with one of the fragments. It was a long time before anyone checked to see what I was doing. Then it was back to the seclusion room. This time I quickly realised that I was just giving them more reason to commit me. I told the nurse through the seclusion-room door that I knew I was upset and wanted some Thorazine to help me calm down. I knew Thorazine didn't calm me, but 'acknowledging your illness' was supposed to be a good thing to do. I needed some foolproof way to kill myself, and until I found it, I was determined to play it cool. So I didn't fight the injection. I lay on the mattress on the floor of the seclusion room and wished that I was already dead.

There was no way I could stop the day from coming. One of the nurses took me down to the emergency room, where I was put into an ambulance and taken to Bellevue Hospital. At Bellevue, I waited in a room full of benches and people being processed for the various state hospitals. Everyone going to Rockland was put aboard a bus — an old school bus, now marked 'Ambulance' and 'Rockland State Hospital'. A woman in a white uniform patrolled the aisles. I spent the ride mulling over the absurdity of her job — she was called a 'transfer agent', and we were being delivered. There was a paper bag on the seat behind me, on which someone had written 'For LeRoy Lemons, Age 7'. I tried to imagine him — seven years old. Why was he there? What could he have done? I looked out the window at the cars on the highway. Did they realise we were being taken away. Did they care?

Rockland was huge. Building after building. Hideous, forbidding architecture. I was taken to a building called Female Reception. An aide escorted me to my ward, stopping repeatedly to unlock various heavy doors and then carefully relock them behind us. The elevator operated with a huge key. They didn't bother to disguise the fact that this was truly a prison.

The ward, when we finally got there, looked like every nightmare or horror movie about insane asylums: barred windows; a huge, barren dayroom; long, dark hallways. I sat in a chair and looked around. There were other patients sitting around quietly. Some were watching TV. A woman in a wheelchair came over, and we started to talk. An hour or so passed; then an aide came into the dayroom and called my name. With much locking and unlocking of doors, I was taken to another ward and locked into another dayroom. This one wasn't so quiet. A TV blared in one corner, a radio in the other. The dayroom was crowded with patients. Some sat, but some were dancing to the radio, others were engaged in loud conversation. There were shouts, waving arms, gales of laughter. Then an aide called out some names, mine among them, and we were taken out of the dayroom and into 'the section'. I never found out why they called it that. There were benches, stall showers, a row of sinks with steel mirrors above them, and a row of toilets, lacking both seats and partitions. Two aides told us to undress. When we were naked, they examined our bodies for identification marks. One aide called out hair and eye colour, and the locations of scars, while the other one took notes. We were told to stand over the toilet bowls and bend forward for a quick rectal search. Then we were provided with 'state clothes' — thick cotton panties and enormous, faded cotton dresses. The faded letters RSH were inked across the back. Before we were escorted back into the dayroom, each of us were handed a printed sheet with information about the Mental Health Information Service, a legal aid service for mental patients. It sounded good, but after the humiliations of the past half hour, I recogised that it didn't matter. What had just been done to us showed that there was no justice for mental patients.

Back in the big, noisy dayroom I sank down on one of the wooden benches, drew up my knees, wrapped my arms around them, lowered my head, and began to cry quietly. A woman sat down beside me and leaned toward me. 'Don't do that', she whispered. 'They'll think you're depressed'. The consequences were unknown but ominous. I dried my eyes, straightened up, and looked around for something to do. There was the TV, on a high shelf, with some chairs gathered below it, but the programme looked uninteresting, and besides, the sound was drowned out by the rock 'n' roll on the radio. In a far corner was a bookshelf, and I went to investigate. A few old, battered books, some of them with pages missing, none of them particularly exciting — yet they were to be my salvation. Over the next two weeks, I read each of them two or three times.

The dayroom door was unlocked, and a group of aides entered. Once more my name was called. What now? I walked up to them and one of them handed me a small paper cup. 'What is it?' I asked reasonably. 'It's concentrate. Drink it.' When I hesitated, she repeated the order irritably. I lifted the cup to my lips — liquid fire poured down my throat. Tears streamed from my eyes. I was bent over practically double trying to catch breath. My lips and tongue felt as if they were dissolving. The group of aides watched, no one saying a word, until I was once again standing erect and breathing almost normally. Then they left the dayroom and locked the door behind them. I looked around for water, but the only fountain was out in the hall; I could see it through the small window in the dayroom door. Nor was there a clock, and they had taken my watch 'for safekeeping'. It was midafternoon, but I couldn't pinpoint the time any closer. There was no way of knowing how long we were to be locked in this room or what would happen next.

Hours later, the door was unlocked again, and we were lined up for dinner. An aide pulled me and the other new arrivals out of the line. While the others left the ward, we ate in the dayroom. Dinner was a plate of something soupy and unrecognisable, with a battered tablespoon the only utensil. I didn't want to eat, but I was hungry and nibbled at it. It wasn't long before the others were marched back from the dining room, and we were locked in again.

Still later, an aide came in pushing a medication cart. I watched in dread. Would I be given the ghastly liquid again? I cringed when the aide handed me a paper cup, but there were two pills

in it. I popped them into my mouth, and she filled the little cup
with water. When I had swallowed, she had me open my mouth
and looked inside. I hadn't even considered not swallowing the
pills — the unspoken threat of another dose of 'concentrate'
was quite effective.

I had imagined an enormous dormitory with rows of beds, but
instead I was taken into a tiny room furnished with nothing but
a bed. The heavy door was closed and locked. I climbed into
the high bed and tried to sleep. I dreamed I was back in
Montefiore, telling my roommates about a nightmare that I had
been committed to Rockland. It had all been a nightmare, the
sense of relief was overwhelming. Then I awoke to the crushing
reality.

The days passed in incredible sameness. We were awakened
at six by the lights going on above our heads. No lingering in
bed was permitted. Beds had to be made, then we were handed
bedspreads. The absurdity of it — spreads to be put on in the
morning, taken off at night, and the bedroom doors locked all
day. Whose sensibilities would have been offended if the beds
had been without spreads? Then two hours spent locked in the
dayroom before breakfast. No one ever explained why we
couldn't sleep till seven, or even seven-thirty. After breakfast
we were taken in groups to 'the section', where we washed.
I hated sitting on the toilet in full view. You had to remember
to ask for toilet paper. Three times a week we were allowed
to take showers, and clean dresses were issued. I kept asking
for my clothes, but it was weeks before they came back from
the marking room, ruined by having my name inked on (despite
the fact that all were neatly name-tagged). Was it just accident
that I always seemed to draw a dress in the largest size? Then
back into the dayroom until lunch. Then until dinner. Then until
bedtime and the end of another endless day. After the second
day I was allowed to walk with the others into the dining room
— not out of the building or even off the floor, but still it was
a change of scene. No dawdling over meals — it was important

to get us back into the dayroom as quickly as possible, it seemed.

The food remained as bad as it had been the first day, although in the dining room we were issued forks as well as spoons. We were allowed to help ourselves to bread spread with margarine, and this became the mainstay of my diet. There was never any fruit or fruit juice, and the 'coffee' resembled that beverage only in that it was hot and served in cups. The 'milk' obviously came from a package, not a cow. One day there was ice cream, which was exciting until we tasted it.

The smallest diversion became an enormously exciting event. Sometimes we were taken into the courtyard, where you could play outdoor games or just sit on a bench and breathe fresh air. Once an aide came onto the ward and organised us into teams for relay races. Games I hadn't played since grade school, yet I found myself cheering for my team and jumping up and down with excitement. It happened only once, yet I never saw that aide again without hoping she would bring in the plastic rings and tenpins and organise another round of games. At the same time, I burned with humiliation that I could be diverted so easily. It was only years later that I found out that 'concentrate' was liquid Thorazine and that customarily it is mixed with juice. Nurses have been warned by the manufacturer to wear rubber gloves while handling it to avoid irritating the skin.

I was frightened when an aide called my name and I was taken off the ward. No one ever bothered to tell you where you were going. She took me to a small office. I never found out why the psychologist asked to see me. None of the other patients on my ward were tested, but I went through the same tests I had just taken at Montefiore. The whole time I was in Rockland, only the psychologist treated me as a person who might possibly have a life outside. He sent for me perhaps once a week, and our talks were one tiny oasis of sanity in this mad-house. We talked about nothing of great importance, but being treated like a person was significant enough.

On the ward, I tried to find someone to talk to, but it was hard to find anyone who would answer and still more difficult to sustain a conversation over more than a few sentences. Still, there were five or six women whom I learned to seek out. Eleanor, a tall, striking black woman with a deep voice, was one. She told me about her husband and the children and, as the days passed, of how she would soon be going back to them. Her voice turned warm and soft when she described her children. Elsie and Molly, both middle-aged women, became my friends too. We came from similar New York Jewish backgrounds and talked about our families. And there was Dina, a flamboyant redhead who talked incessantly about the glamorous life she had led. Other patients I learned to know by name. Evelyn and Lily were teenagers. Full of energy, they constantly chattered to one another and danced to the rock 'n' roll music on the radio. Sometimes I danced with them for a few minutes, but even in the summer heat they could keep it up for hours. I always wondered how they ended up there. Dolly preached a never-ending sermon. I avoided her as much as I could, because she would hold my hand and call down endless blessings on my head as I tried politely to get away.

A few patients were universally hated. Becky was brought onto the ward, screaming curses, after I had been there for three or four days. A few patients recognised her, and there were mutters of 'Oh, no' and 'Not again'. It didn't take long to find out what they meant. Becky had something nasty to say to everyone. She broke up conversations, cursed at anyone who came across her path, and increased the noise level tremendously. There was no way to get away from her, except to ignore her and hope she would go away. When she realised no one wanted to be near her, she burst into tears and shrieks. Her face got redder and redder, and her screams got louder. Suddenly the door was unlocked, and two aides came in and grabbed her. Becky was taken into 'the section'. We could hear her screaming through the door and across the hall. A few minutes later the door was openend, and Becky was pushed back into the dayroom. She had been laced into a strait-jacket. I had never seen one before, but I recognised it instantly. I could remember reading in a magazine article, long before, that they hadn't been used in years, but I had already discovered that everything else in the article was lies. I couldn't quite remember the title — 'The Miracle in America's Mental Hospitals' or something like that.

Becky's arrival upset everyone. Even patients who had formerly been so quiet you hardly ever noticed them were suddenly more noisy and excitable. The most dramatic change was in Eleanor. Instead of quietly planning her arrival home, she began to scream messages to her husband and children as she ran through the dayroom. I tried to talk with her, but she hardly heard me. 'I'm coming, I'm coming', she screamed and ran off. Aides rushed into the room and pulled Eleanor out. I could hear them calling for 'a camisole', which I discovered was a straitjacket when Eleanor reappeared. I felt close to tears as I thought about my quiet talks with this once stately woman. I became almost nostalgic for the ward before Becky's arrival. Anything was better than this.

It was hot, and patients put into straitjackets used to sweat and itch. They were usually left on for several hours. I was determined never to give the aides any excuse to put me into one. Whatever they ask me to do, I thought, I'll do it. I volunteered to mop the floors in the hallway. It was a break from the boredom, it was quieter than the dayroom, and the aides liked it. Staying on their good side became enormously important.

One aide clearly hated me. I never found out why. Miss Byrd had more rules than anyone. Other aides let you crowd around the medication chart and call out your name, but with Miss Byrd it was different. Everyone had to be seated, and she would roll the cart into the centre of the room. Then one by one she would call out the names. It took forever, and I would sit there in dread that this time they would give me the liquid again. It was the same when she took us to 'the section' for showers. When other aides gave them, we would get in line ourselves. I was usually near the front because I watched carefully for the signal. But Miss Byrd made us sit on the benches in 'the section' and called out who got to go next. The towels were small and thin, the water was never hot enough, I hated standing naked in the impersonal glances of the aides, and still I longed for those showers — a few minutes of being gorgeously, luxuriously clean.

Visitors could come twice a week. We would all be taken into 'the section'. The door was closed, but we tried to look out and see if we could recognise anyone. There was no way to know if your visitors were coming — there were no telephones. When Miss Byrd was there, we weren't allowed near the door. An aide would call out a name, and that patient would be allowed into the dayroom to meet with her visitors. If no one came, you had to spend two hours in 'the section' — the bathroom. My mother came every Wednesday, and she, my father, and my husband came every Sunday. I felt sorry for the women who didn't have visitors.

I always used to ask my visitors for the same thing — a roast beef sandwich from a New York delicatessen. With a Coke from the machine in the lobby, it was ambrosia. And on Sundays, they brought the *New York Times*. Unimaginable wealth — a whole week's worth of reading if I rationed it out carefully enough. I hid the paper under my mattress and took one section with me to the dayroom each day. The bedroom doors were locked each morning and weren't opened until bedtime — I only forgot the paper once. I didn't ask for books, there was no safe place to keep them. The newspaper, once I had finished it, was picked up by one patient after another. Some read it, others who got hold of it later tore or scattered the pages.

Every morning the doctors came onto the ward for a few

minutes. If you had a question, you had to get the doctor's attention quickly. A few patients got answers, the rest had to wait for tomorrow. I had met 'my' doctor briefly the first day, an Indian woman with adequate, but not fluent, English. I felt sorry for the patients assigned to another Indian doctor, who spoke virtually no English. Even when she answered their questions, what she said showed that she often misunderstood.

One morning the aides unlocked the dayroom door before it was time to go for breakfast. I was told to push one of the chairs across the doorway and sit in it to prevent anyone from going out into the hall. Of course, the hall led only to the locked ward door, there was nowhere for anyone to go. Still, a few patients tried to wander past me. I didn't want to say anything; I wasn't an attendant; I didn't care if patients were wandering in the hall. It made absolutely no difference to me. At the same time, I recognised it as a test. 'Hey, stay inside, Donna. Marie, go sit down and wait for breakfast. Come on, get away from the door.' I hated myself. After breakfast, my doctor told me I was being transferred to another ward across the hall. I had been there thirteen days.

It took me two days to hate the Quiet Disturbed Ward. All these women were so sunken into themselves that I could find no one to talk to. I tried, but they moved away. I missed Eleanor, missed Dina, even though over the last few days both had become increasingly remote. At least they responded to me sometimes. Here, there was no one. I had three roommates, but even we exchanged only an occasional hello.

The first morning a man came through the ward calling 'Group therapy, group therapy'. I asked an aide if I could go. Mr Cole led a group of us outside, where we sat in a circle of chairs on the lawn. It was like no group therapy I had ever seen or imagined, but it was enough just to sit outside for an hour several times a week. Mr Cole did just about all the talking. It was like attending a boring lecture by a not very good speaker. I never found out who Mr Cole was or just what this was supposed to accomplish. Once, as he was taking us back to the ward, I asked Mr Cole what the average length of stay was at Rockland, and he said proudly that it was now down to four months. I wondered how I could survive another three and a half months.

On this ward we weren't locked in the dayroom. The door that led off the ward was locked, of course, but we were free to go to the water fountain or into 'the section'. There were partitions between the toilets — even without doors, it seemed almost private.

It was always frightening when an aide came into the dayroom and began to call out names. One morning about ten of us were called. We were told we were being taken to the gynaecology clinic, and instructed to go into our rooms, remove our panties, and then come back to be escorted to the examination. Our dresses would hide the fact that we wore no underwear. I went to my room, shaking. I had no intention of walking through the hallways that way and yet realised the seriousness of disobeying an order. Was it worth it? Would I be sent back across the hall? I returned with my panties still on. The aide unlocked the door, and we walked forward. It was a long way, through the tunnels that connected the buildings, down corridors full of strangers. At the clinic we were taken into the examining room one by one. When my name was called, I stepped inside the door and hesitated a moment to remove my panties before lying on the doctor's table. The doctor and nurse looked up, annoyed, at this momentary interruption in the smooth flow of patients. The quick, impersonal exam took only a minute or two. I stepped off the table and picked up my panties, while the next patient was already being led to the table. It was the only time I ever deliberately disobeyed an order during my entire stay at Rockland.

My doctor told me about the open ward downstairs, where the

patients weren't locked in and could go to activities. 'Would you like to go there?' Would I! but I didn't want to appear too excited. 'Yes, it sounds very nice', I said quietly. Showing I could handle it was important. The next day I was brought downstairs and turned over to Miss O'Brian. I sat in her office while she read through my file. I was good at reading upside down. Suddenly two little notations jumped out at me — 'sui' and 'homi'. If they thought I was a homicidal maniac, I was never going to get out of there. Where had they ever gotten such an idea? I saw even more clearly how important it was to be on my best behaviour at all times.

The Open Ward was really misnamed. Although the door was unlocked, you weren't allowed through it, except for activities and meals. My roommates were all elderly. The only one I tried to talk to was too deaf to hear very much. But in a few hours I found a friend. We were allowed to visit in the ward across the hall, and Patty and I quickly spotted each other. She was seventeen, four years younger than I, but far closer in age and attitude than anyone else there. We spent most of each day together. Miss Collier, who ran Patty's ward, was much stricter than Miss O'Brian. We gave the ward a quick cleaning under Miss O'Brian's direction each morning, but when I would go across the hall to find Patty, Miss Collier had them washing the windows and polishing the floors. I usually volunteered to help Patty so she could be free sooner. Then we would sit in her room and talk. Her room was a tiny cell similar to the one I had had upstairs, but she had a dresser and a chair, and she could go there whenever she wanted. We never went to my room, because one of my elderly roommates was invariably napping. I was glad to see that it wasn't against the rules.

Patty and I went everywhere together — to meals, OT, movies, and dances. Any excuse to get off the ward. We could go to OT — occupational therapy — every day if we wanted. The occupational therapist was a cheerful woman who chattered on about her home and her husband while we sat around a table with our projects. Her husband was graduating from college, and we were kept informed about all the graduation festivities. 'What college?' I asked politely. It turned out to be a college of mortuary science. One day Patty and I were given permission to try to find the OT department by ourselves, and we promptly got lost. We wandered through the mazes of hallways looking for something familiar, then peered through a small window onto a ward where we thought we could ask directions. I saw old, white-haired women wandering around inside and suddenly realised that the 'old' women on my ward were nothing like this. These women were toothless, ragged, lost. Who had put them here to die? I shivered. Eventually we found our way back to our wards. After that we waited for someone to escort us to OT.

I hated the dances, but I always went. Having something to do was far more important than whether I liked it or not. It was the same with the movies. It didn't matter what they were showing. It was a chance to walk across the grounds (even though we were lined up and counted) to the auditorium, to sit for a few hours in the dark and pretend I was in a real theatre, just an ordinary person who had decided to spend an evening at the movies.

One of the patients on the ward really frightened me. There really wasn't anything frightening about Rose, except that she seemed so comfortable and at home in the hospital. There were all kinds of rumours about Rose. Someone told me she had been there twenty years. I peeked into her room once. She had one of the tiny private rooms, crammed full of odds and ends of furniture, including a sewing machine, where she made pot-holders and other small items. One day she came up to me when I was sitting and reading in the dayroom, to display some of the things she had made. I admired a red oven mitt, and she promptly told me it cost two dollars. Each time I saw her after that, she asked me if I had made up my mind about the oven mitt. The next time it was visiting day, I asked my parents for the money. It seemed the least I could do for Rose.

One day an aide came for a few of us. We were taken into a room, then, one by one, led in front of a screen, where a picture was taken. After the picture came something worse. An aide held my hand and pressed my finger across an inked pad and then a sheet of paper. She complained that my fingers were too stiff for the prints to mark clearly. I couldn't get my hands to relax — every muscle fought the indignity. But she waited and took another set. 'I guess these will have to do.'

On Sundays, my doctor gave me an afternoon pass to go out with my parents. Every moment was magical — sitting in the car, driving out past the forbidding hospital walls without challenge. In the restaurant, I looked at the menu, dazzled. I could pick anything I wanted! The only hard part was going back. I stood beside my parents in the lobby, knowing that in a moment they would go through the door and back to the world, while I would be led through corridors whose doors would be carefully locked behind me. When I got back to the ward, I found Patty, who questioned me eagerly about every detail of the day, and I gave her the chocolate bars and gum I had brought back.

One day Miss O'Brian decided I was ready for a private room. Instead of a dresser, it was furnished with a mirrored vanity table. There wasn't too much room for my stuff, but it became Patty's and my new hangout. Every morning after breakfast and the cleaning of the ward, I would help clean Patty's ward, and then we would come back to my room to sit in front of the mirror, comb our hair, and put on makeup. We always wanted to look clean and well groomed. On the Open Ward we could take showers whenever we wanted; we always had shining clean hair. Both Miss O'Brian and Miss Collier thought highly of looking one's best. In the laundry room, we washed and ironed our clothes. Wearing my own dresses and underwear felt so good.

One morning Miss O'Brian came looking for me. I had been scheduled for an EEG. 'But I had one a month ago at Montefiore', I protested. Apparently it didn't matter. Miss O'Brian turned me over to an aide, who escorted me through the mazes of corridors and tunnels. I was trembling, remembering the other EEG and realising that this time I couldn't protest. But it turned out not to be too bad. Instead of sticking wires into my scalp, this time a claylike substance was spread over my head to hold them. When I came back to the ward, Miss O'Brian said it was fine to take another shower. It took ages to get all the gooey stuff out of my hair.

Another day a group of us were taken to the dental office, where a technician cleaned my teeth and complimented me on my regular brushing. Once again, I was both pleased and humiliated at the same time.

It was getting hard to fit into my clothes. I knew it was from eating so much bread and margarine, but I couldn't stop. I still wasn't eating much of the regular food, and even that wouldn't have been much better. There were no fresh vegetables, no salads, just the same gooey messes that made me gag. One day I discovered a menu pinned to a bulletin board outside the dining room. Each day, the slop had a different name. I wondered if the people who made up the menus ever saw the food.

My Sunday afternoon passes had become a regular event. One Sunday, my husband went to talk to my doctor and ended up screaming at her about the miserable treatment I was getting in this miserable hospital. Even though I agreed with him, I was terrified. Didn't he realise the importance of staying on her good side? When it was time to go out, the pass hadn't been signed, and it took hours to find her and get things straightened out. That afternoon we didn't have time for dinner in a restaurant.

My mother brought me some new clothes. I had never been

fat before. I felt so ugly. My hair was scraggly, my body huge, my skin covered with pimples. When I went out on Sunday afternoons, I was sure everyone was looking at me, that they could tell where I came from. Even though I hated to go back, it was almost a relief to be where no one stared at me, where no one cared what I looked like.

The drugs I had taken for so many months affected every part of my body. My eyes kept going out of focus, especially when I tried to read. My mouth was dry, my tongue swollen, my words slurred. Sometimes I forgot what I was trying to say. My body was puffy. I hadn't menstruated in months and was able to move my bowels only with enormous amounts of laxatives. I had no energy at all. If walking around in a constant haze is supposed to be tranquillity, I was successfully tranquillised.

Actually, I had just about given up. My unhappiness was the crime that brought about my imprisonment. I was learning to hide my misery. I told Miss O'Brian that I was feeling better. I didn't want to tell her I felt like a piece of me had died. Even though I knew I would never be happy again, I was learning to pretend to be like everyone else. I didn't care about finding an end to my unhappiness anymore; there was no end. But I was determined to be free; no one must know my secret.

A group of student nurses came to spend a week of their training. They were a pain in the neck. It was funny to watch them try to carry on conversations with the patients. Clearly they had been told both that we were seriously mentally ill and that they should try to talk normally with us, and they were having trouble trying to reconcile those opposites. Even worse were the volunteer workers who came around occasionally. They always brought treats — cookies or candy. 'Lollypop ladies', I used to call them to myself. I always expected them to try to pat our heads.

My doctor told me she was sending me home for a week's trial visit. It was working, she actually thought I was 'better'. I spent the week with my husband in our apartment. It was all very calm, very dead. This was what my life was going to be. It was awful, but it was bearable. Rockland wasn't. It was as simple as that. The last days were shadowed with the knowledge that I had to go back. I felt like crying as we drove across George Washington Bridge, and a few tears actually rolled down my face when we saw the sign for Orangeburg. But when we went into the lobby of the building, I had dried my eyes. I knew I wasn't allowed to cry.

I was put in a homemaking group in the occupational therapy department. There was a model house, and we played at making beds and setting tables, making sure everything was lined up properly, and won an approving glance from the teacher. I didn't know who to hate more, her or me.

I was sitting in the dayroom when an aide came in with some papers for me. I opened the envelope nervously. My name had been filled in on a form letter informing me that I had been converted from involuntary to voluntary status. By this time, I knew something about the law. Voluntary patients were allowed to sign out on three days' notice. My ears were ringing, my hands trembling with excitement. I went to find Miss O'Brian, to find out to whom to send the letter.

The day before discharge a group of patients met with a social worker. She told us to tell the truth about being hospitalised when we tried to get jobs. I didn't tell her I had already planned to lie. She asked me if I wanted to go to an aftercare clinic, and I told her I would go to a private psychiatrist. I was afraid to tell her I was through with psychiatry. I was becoming a skilled liar. I was given a supply of tranquillisers and a lecture on the importance of taking them.

It was hard saying goodbye to Patty. I didn't want to talk about how happy I was to be leaving, when she was staying behind. And when I said I would miss her, we both knew that it was outweighted by my joy at leaving Rockland. I promised to write, but I never did. Whatever I would say about my freedom, it would only be a further reminder that she was still a prisoner.

I was amazed when my suitcases appeared from some storeroom. I hadn't realised that they could keep track of possessions so efficiently. There wasn't much to pack. I kept expecting someone to realise that I had to make a phone call to let my family know that I was coming home, but finally I went to Miss O'Brian. Making a phone call turned out to be incredibly complicated. When an aide escorted me to a phone, another aide came up and challenged me. Patients weren't allowed to make calls. As soon as someone could get there from the city. I wouldn't be a patient anymore. I was allowed to make the call. Two hours later I was on my way back to New York City.

I went to stay with my parents. My husband had given up our apartment and was living with an old college roommate. We saw each other once in a while, but there was no real feeling left between us. I still hated to come out of my room. I had begun to cry again. One day my father threatened to send me back to the hospital. I don't know which of us was more terrified.

I didn't want to see a doctor. Whatever it was that was wrong with me, I knew I wasn't sick. In the weeks after my discharge, I had weaned myself from tranquillisers. I agreed to see Dr Cohen, my father's doctor, only because I had so many physical complaints: my weight, my lethargy, my inability to menstruate. Even though his waiting room was packed with people, Dr Cohen spent hours with me. Gently, he suggested I see a therapist. He told me that after talking to me, he would select a doctor whom he thought was best suited to me. Still, I was skeptical about Dr Jonas. I told him that I was convinced he couldn't help me, that no one could. Dr Jonas asked why.

'Because I'm hopelessly mentally ill', I told him. 'What makes you think that?' he asked.

I poured out the story of my hospitalisations, of all the drugs I had been given. 'At Montefoire, they told me I would never be able to live outside an institution, that my brain was abnormal.' Now it was Dr Jonas's turn to be skeptical. He told me he didn't believe those things about me. 'It's all in my records', I told him. He asked me to sign releases so he could get copies of my hospital records.

A few weeks later, I sat across the desk from Dr Jonas as he glanced through the records. I was sure he would turn from me in disgust. Instead, he told me he was more convinced than ever that there was nothing wrong with me. 'Everything in here,' he told me, 'was written by young doctors just out of medical school. They like to use these big words but don't know what they mean. Who would you rather believe — them, or me, a doctor who's been in practice for years?' 'What about my diagnoses? I've seen some of them — that I'm schizophrenic, that I have a character disorder.' 'Nonsense', he told me. 'What about my EEG? At Montefiore, they said it showed I was having seizures.' He looked at the EEG report. 'A perfectly normal report', he told me. 'Slight variations like these don't mean a thing.'

He really believed in me! I felt the confidence to tell him something I had never told another doctor. 'The first day I was in Gracie Square, they locked me in an unused storage area. I had a hallucination — I felt like there was something in there with me.' 'Did you see anything?' 'No, but I felt it, I knew it was there.'

'And I had another hallucination, just a few weeks ago. I had just woken up, and I had the terrible feeling something was wrong. I went to the door of my room, and there were all these locks and bolts on it. Then I started to scream and they disappeared.'

Dr Jonas explained that in the stage between sleeping and waking it is not abnormal to see things that are not there. And he explained the first 'hallucination' by my state of intense fear and hunger after the weekend at Bellevue.

There were a lot of important things that my treatment with Dr Jonas never touched on. I was too guarded to discuss my deep doubts about what course my life would take. When my husband suggested that we move to Pennsylvania and start a new life together, Dr Jonas seemed to think it was a good idea, and I decided I thought so too. For a few months I travelled to New York once a week to see him. Then he told me he thought I was well enough to end therapy. Perhaps Dr Jonas thought I was well, but I knew better — I knew that, at last, I had managed to build walls thick and strong enough that no one could see through them, to the frightened and worthless person I was sure I would always be.

My hospitalisations occurred during 1966. I saw Dr Jonas through much of 1967. In 1973 I once again experienced the overwhelming sense of my life crashing down around me. A lot had happened in the intervening years. Women's liberation, for one. I left my husband in 1971; with the support of a women's group I was finally able to recognise that everything between us had been dead for years. Later that same year I became involved with the Mental Patients' Liberation Project, the first of a number of mental patients' liberation groups I have worked with. In 1974 I was going through a long and painful attempt to break off a relationship with a man I had been involved with for two years. Although he and I fought constantly, at the same time we clung to each other. He left New York. So did I. We both ended up in Vancouver — not together, but not exactly apart either. We kept saying that it was over between us, but neither could make the final break. One day he started to scream at me, as we had screamed at each other so many times before, but this time he said that he was leaving for San Francisco. I couldn't believe what was happening. Everything began to feel unreal. There was suddenly only one reality — my lover would leave me, and I would die.

If I had been in New York, I don't know what would have happened. But in Vancouver there was a place where I knew I could go — the Vancouver Emotional Emergency Center. When I arrived, everyone was at a meeting in the dining room. Tom, one of the workers, came out of the meeting and sat with me in the living room for a few minutes. He said I could stay, then went back to the meeting. I lay on the couch, feeling the life slowly draining out of me.

Everything I had heard about VEEC was positive — that it was a place where people weren't punished for feeling bad but were helped to learn and grow from the experience. Still, I was frightened. The people who worked at VEEC were called staff, just like in hospitals. Would anyone be able to understand what I was experiencing?

Over the next few hours I met most of the staff and all the other residents. Only five people were allowed to stay at VEEC at one time. The staff worked on shifts, two at a time, throughout the day and hight. There were also volunteers. There was always someone to talk to.

The first afternoon David and Dave were on shift. I sat in the dining room and watched them make dinner. I didn't feel like doing very much or saying very much, but there was something comforting about watching them. There were eight for dinner — the residents, David, Dave, and a volunteer. We sat around a big dining table. The food was delicious. Later David asked me if I wanted a massage. We went upstairs to one of the bedrooms, and I lay down on the floor. The massage was incredibly relaxing. I went downstairs to the living room and sat with a few other people. After a while I lay down on the couch again. When people started going off to bed, I asked David if I could stay on the couch — I wanted to be near other people, and the upstairs part of the house, where the bedrooms were, felt very isolated. He said that I could and brought me a blanket.

The next morning Ellen sat down with me to work on my contract. The idea was to set some goals for what you wanted to accomplish while staying at VEEC. The emphasis was on change. I knew that if I didn't change, I would either be dead or feel dead. I was racing against time. I wrote in my contract that I wanted to learn how to live without my lover and to find out what I wanted to do. I didn't believe it was possible, but I knew I had to try.

The contracts were kept in a file box in the office. The only other notes that were kept were in the logbook. Anyone, resident or staff member, could write anything they wanted in the log. I always enjoyed reading it. I wrote a note about myself, explaining that I didn't want to talk very much, that I felt the need to withdraw inside myself. The staff members were very gentle people. I was amazed to see how openly they touched and hugged one another and the residents. Over the next few days nearly everyone held me or rubbed my back or gave me massages.

I needed reassurance that VEEC wasn't a hospital. I asked Ellen and Tom to pretend that we were in a hospital and they were the staff. They would whisper about me and write 'charts'. Ellen went into the office and wrote something on a piece of paper. Then she came out and started to whisper to Tom. I wasn't sure whether it was pretend or real by that point. I rushed into the office and grabbed the paper. She had written a confused jumble of psychiatric terms. I ran into the dining room ripping it up and screaming, 'This is not a hospital, this is not a hospital'. Ellen and Tom joined me in chanting, 'This is not a hospital.' We talked a little bit about the differences. I felt safe and protected.

But the next day I began to doubt again. One of the staff members had arranged for a psychologist who worked for one of the community mental health centres to spend the day observing VEEC. Although she asked everyone if they minded, it was already arranged. I wanted to say that I minded, but I couldn't. Instead I became very withdrawn. I didn't want him observing me. After breakfast I felt I needed to lie on the couch, to quietly cry and slowly allow myself to feel my pain, but when the psychologist arrived in the late morning, I knew I had to stop. It was one of the first sunny days of Spring, and everyone was lying on blankets in the backyard. The psychologist tried to strike up a conversation with me, but I murmured something noncommittal and ignored him.

That night I found it impossible to tell anyone how angry I was. I wrote a little about it in the log. Dorrie read what I had written and came to sit with me. She said she could understand my feelings. Once I was able to talk about it, I became angrier and angrier. Dorrie encouraged me to express it. 'I feel like hanging a sign on the door telling shrinks to keep out of here. They don't belong here', I told her. 'Why don't you?' she replied. I wrote in big black letters, 'SHRINKS BEWARE'. Even the shape of the letters was angular and angry looking. I taped the sign in the window of the front door, where it remained for the rest of my stay. The sign provoked a lot of discussion. At one point a few staff members wanted to take it down, but I was able to persuade them how important it was to me.

Again, that night, I wanted to sleep on the living room couch. An agreement was worked out so that I could sleep there as long as it didn't interfere with anyone using the living room. I found it comforting to sleep with the lights on and the sounds of people talking and moving around. It was reassuring to feel life going on around me.

The first time I heard the screams I became frightened. But I was quickly reassured. The sounds came from the 'screaming room' in the basement, where people had a chance to let out their emotions and their pain. The floor was covered with mattresses so no one could get hurt. It wasn't only residents who used the screaming room. Sometimes staff members went down there too if their day had been particularly frustrating or difficult. Emotions were allowed here. Because we had a chance to let loose by going down to the screaming room, there was no need to be disruptive upstairs. There was a strict rule against violence, but violence was never a problem while I was there. I remembered the desperation with which I had pounded on the window at Hillside. It was far more satisfying to scream until I was exhausted and collapsed on the mattresses in the screaming room at VEEC.

I began to feel very close to Chris, one of the staff members. He spent a lot of time just sitting with me quietly. He seemed to believe that I could come out of this state of lethargy and find some direction for myself. Sometimes I almost believed it too. But other times the pain was so great that I knew it would destroy me.

During the weekly staff meeting I asked Chris to bring up the subject of the psychologist's visit and how upset it had made me. Residents could come to staff meetings, but I didn't want to speak in front of so many people. I whispered to Chris, and he spoke up for me. I was glad when the discussion came to the conclusion that residents should have absolute veto power in such situations. Although showing professionals how VEEC worked was important, the needs of residents came first.

After being on shift every afternoon for nearly a week, Chris was scheduled to be off for four days. I was frightened when he left. He had been helping me hold off the terror that had the power to sweep me away. I wrote in the logbook that I was very angry because Chris wasn't there.

I felt even more alone when I saw what Dorrie had written in the log about me. She thought my whispering to Chris at the meeting was manipulative. And Dorrie was on shift that evening. Another staff member sat with us and helped us to talk it out. 'I wanted you to speak out for yourself', Dorrie told me. 'Right now that's very hard for me. I'm feeling so bad.' 'But when you were whispering to Chris, I felt like you were refusing to deal with the rest of us. I felt put down.' I was surprised. 'I didn't mean to put you down. I never thought of it that way.' My angry feelings toward Dorrie were changing. It seemed that hers had changed too. We ended up hugging each other.

Still, the next few days were very difficult. One night I woke up with a particularly terrifying nightmare. I stumbled into the dining room and sat shaking. Someone brought a blanket and put it around me. It was a while before I could explain what had happened. I had continued to sleep in the living room, where I could be near to someone at all times.

A day or two later my lover called. He was planning to leave soon and wanted to give me my money, which he had been holding for safekeeping. I didn't want to deal with it, because it meant recognising that he was really leaving. Dorrie came with us to the bank. I didn't want to take the money, but the two of them insisted. They were urging me to buy travellers' checks with it, but I decided to keep the cash. I gave it to Dorrie to hold, about three hundred dollars, all the money I had. When we got back to VEEC, I thought she would put it in the locked box in the office, but she said she was afraid someone might walk off with the box, so she kept it in her pocket. When the night-shift people came, she asked one of them to hold my money for me. This went on all the next day. Finally everyone decided they didn't want the responsibility any more. They told me either to hold it myself or to go to buy travellers' checks. The money was all mixed up with the idea of my lover leaving. I was sure I was dying and couldn't understand why everyone was bothering me about money. It seemed so unimportant.

I went to the bank with Dorrie. My ears were ringing, and every moment seemed deeply significant. I was sure this was the last day of my life, and I wanted to take everything in. After I bought the travellers' checks, I asked Dorrie to come out for a drink with me. I didn't drink very often, but I was sure that being drunk would make me even more sensitive to every sight and sound. I wanted to drink Black Russians, and we went to several places before we found one that served them. I must have had three or four. When we left the bar, I was amazingly drunk. My feet didn't seem to touch the ground. Colours seemed incredibly brilliant and shimmering. I was almost happy that on the last day of my life I was seeing so much beauty. I tried to tell Dorrie how beautiful everything was.

When we got back to VEEC, I lay down on some cushions that were on the floor of the office. (Another resident had been sleeping in the office.) David was there too, and I tried to tell him about the brilliant colours. I was expecting to die very soon. But first I wanted to explore the strange world I was experiencing.

I asked Jennifer, a staff member I hardly knew, to come down to the screaming room with me. I explained to her how I felt that the situation I was in was destroying me, and we decided to act it out. I lay on the mattress-covered floor, and she sat on my chest. 'I'm sitting on you, I'm crushing you, and I won't let you up.' She chanted the words again and again. I lay there listening, overwhelmed with the feeling that there was nothing I could do. Weakness, powerlessness. But underneath those feelings there was something else. Jennifer continued to chant. The new feeling grew stronger. Suddenly I began to push against Jennifer. At first feebly, but as I pushed, strength flowed into my body. With a surge of energy, I pushed her off. As I slowly stood up, I was thinking that I would push her down and sit on her, but by the time I was fully upright, it seemed unimportant. Instead I stood with my arms raised, my fingertips touching the low basement ceiling. Energy and joy were slowly filling me. I turned to Jennifer. 'I don't care about you,' I said defiantly, knowing that she knew I was talking not to her but to the feelings that had crippled me for so long. I remained with my arms lifted and my eyes closed for several minutes, making wordless, joyous noises. After a while I sat quietly, letting these new feelings find a comfortable place within me. Eventually we went upstairs.

The next few days, my last at VEEC, were a chance to use my new energy to solve some very real problems. I had no place to live and had to make arrangements for a place to stay until I could leave Vancouver. I made plans to move to Bellingham, Washington. A new place was no longer a threat, it was a challenge. I was amazed by my energy. I had followed my pain and fear toward what I thought would be death, and instead I had found a source of life, my own sense of self, which had always been hidden from me. Out of struggle and pain, I had been reborn.

NOTES FOR CHAPTER 2

1. For another personal account of mental institutionalisation by an ex-patient who now questions psychiatric practices, see Janet and Paul Gotkin, *Too Much Anger, Too Many Tears* (New York: Quadrangle Books, 1975).
2. A few years later I might have been able to get legal help. In December 1968 the New York Civil Liberties Union set up a special legal project to aid mental patients. But even a lawyer might not have helped. New York State law permits sixty days' commitment upon the signature of two doctors, a longer time than any other state. No court hearing is necessary.

Chapter Three

Consciousness-raising

The barriers to instituting change in the mental health system are enormous. The 'mental health industry' is an entrenched bureaucracy, resistant to change from within and almost totally unresponsive to outside pressures. Mental health is big business; in fiscal year 1974-1975, fourteen million dollars was spent on mental health services in the United States.[1] Psychiatrists, the most prestigious mental health professionals, like other doctors, are reluctant to allow nonphysicians to have very much input into what they see as purely medical matters. Other mental health specialties, such as psychology, occupational therapy, and social work, have their own power bases within the mental health system, positions they have won after struggling with the psychiatric establishment. The nonpsychiatric mental health disciplines have promoted their own alternative facilities, such as halfway houses and ex-patient social clubs. Although these alternatives are not (usually) run by psychiatrists, they are still firmly under professional control.

The alternative programmes that form the subject of this book are different, because their underlying philosophy is different. Nonprofessional, client-controlled services don't divide people into 'sick' and 'well', 'helper' and 'helped.' They see every person as having a combination of strengths and weaknesses, and the need for help in one area does not negate the ability to help others also. But in order to achieve these ends, people have to recognise their own strengths and abilities. They have to discover that sometimes there are no 'experts' to turn to. People who seek out these alternatives, have experienced the harm that the 'experts' and their methods can cause.

These alternatives have been begun in a spirit of anger and

frustration, by people who have had firsthand experience with unresponsive, unhelpful mental health 'care'. But more than anger and frustration is necessary to enable people to set up functioning alternatives. People also need confidence in their own abilities — confidence that has often been damaged by contact with the mental health system. So, side by side with the work of setting up the alternative has gone another essential activity — building up the confidence and self-esteem of all the people involved in the work. This consciousness-raising process seems to have been independently arrived at by groups in many places as an important part of creating meaningful alternatives for people.

Many of the people involved in these alternatives are ex-mental patients, who face a special set of barriers. The crippling stereotypes about mental illness have often been internalised by ex-patients, many of whom believe (at least some of the time) that they are weak, incapable, untrustworthy, 'sick', 'crazy', or whatever. It is difficult or impossible to go through the experience of mental institutionalisation without beginning, to some extent, to hate oneself. Part of the process of institutional 'treatment' is convincing the patient that his or her former ideas, beliefs, and behaviours were wrong. One stands little chance of discharge without agreeing — or seeming to agree — with the staff's assessment of what constitutes mental health. Even a person who struggles successfully to maintain his or her own way of thinking can be damaged by this form of psychological assault. Also, there are many people who go looking for help with their problems, who are quite willing to acknowledge that they need new and more effective ways of coping, but who have not found that help from psychiatry. These people are now joining to set up alternatives in order to get help with their own problems, as well as to help others. They don't see themselves as inherently better than any other potential users of the service.

Mutual-support networks of some sort seem to be an essential part of getting alternatives started. They are directly analogous to the consciousness-raising groups that have served to get women involved in feminism. These leaderless women's groups had no 'experts'; they developed their theory out of the examination of the lives of their members. Self-defeating behaviour was not viewed as illness but rather as a response to a society that imposed a special set of pressures on women. The work of women's consciousness raising and that of ex-patients has enormous overlap. In both kinds of groups participants have often experienced the liberating realisation that they were not 'crazy' after all.

Consciousness-raising is not 'therapy'. Therapy has as its goal adjusting the individual to the 'reality' of his or her own life. Therapists (particularly in mental institutions) seldom question the assumption that the underlying social system is a benign influence on people's behaviour. In a consciousness-raising group, on the other hand, people begin to see that much of what they had viewed as their own individual problems are responses to real frustrations. In mental patient consciousness-raising groups, people have discovered that their dissatisfactions with their own lives (and with the 'treatment' they got in the hospital) were not 'symptoms of mental illness' but were valid perceptions of what was wrong with their lives.

People do not 'go crazy' for no reason. Often they are afraid to recognise that their 'happy marriage' is making them miserable, that their 'good job' is drudgery, that their 'loving family' is a mass of unspoken, simmering tensions. These are pressures that can, indeed, drive one crazy. Psychiatry — especially in the mental hospital — seldom helps people to make these frightening, but potentially liberating, discoveries. The function of the mental hospital is to cool out the anger and rebellion, conveniently labelled 'symptoms', so that the person can return to 'normal' life.

Consciousness-raising, on the other hand, helps people to see that their so called symptoms are indications of real problems.

The anger, which has been destructively turned inward, is freed by this recognition. Instead of believing that they have a defect in their psychic makeup (or their neurochemical system), participants learn to recognise the oppressive conditions in their daily lives.

The realisation that a person has suffered at the hands of a system that is supposed to have helped him or her is an important first step. Often it takes a long time for an ex-patient to realise fully the extent of the damage that has been done. The belief that one has been harmed may coexist with the belief that one is 'sick', that such treatment was somehow deserved or justified. In consciousness-raising, ex-patients find that mistreatment was not an individual error, but is built into the system. The depersonalisation experienced by the investigators in the Rosenhan study (in which 'normal' volunteers had themselves admitted to mental institutions) is an experience common to all mental patients. People struggling to define themselves and their lives face a hostile environment in the mental hospital, where staff is apt to define only the most conventional attitudes as healthy.

Consciousness raising is an ongoing process. Negative stereotypes of the 'mentally ill' are everywhere and are difficult not to internalise, no matter how sensitive one becomes. This stereotyping has been termed 'sane chauvinism' or 'mentalism' by mental patients' liberation groups. Like sexism, mentalism is built into the language — *sick* and *crazy* are widely used to refer to behaviour of which the speaker disapproves. The struggle against mentalism is one of the long-range activities of mental patients' liberation.

I can perhaps best describe the effects of the consciousness-raising process by relating what it did for me. For several years before getting involved in mental patients' liberation, I had become increasingly angry about my hospitalisation. There was no one to share these perceptions with. I knew no other ex-patients, and nonpatients seldom wanted to hear very much about it, even in those cases where they were sympathetic. In any case, I didn't dare confide in most people that I was an ex-patient. My anger existed side by side with my acceptance of my own 'mental illness'. I thought that my story was an isolated example of poor treatment, rather than a representative case of the damaging effects of mental institutionalisation.

My feelings began to change when I discovered the existence of the Mental Patients' Liberation Project in New York, one of the earliest mental patients' liberation groups. We talked about our experiences and discovered how similar they were. Whether we had been in grim state hospitals or expensive private ones, whether we were there voluntarily or involuntarily, whether we had been called schizophrenic, manic-depressive, or whatever, our histories had been extraordinarily similar. We had experienced depersonalisation, the stupefying effects of drugs, the contempt of those who supposedly 'cared' for us. Out of this growing awareness came a deeper understanding of the true purpose of the mental health system. It is primarily a method of social control.

We also began to talk about the kinds of help troubled people need. Having experienced the dehumanising effects of mental institutions, we saw that large facilities with rigid hierarchies could never be the kind of places we had in mind. It quickly became clear that there was no way to fix up the current mental hospital system. What was needed was an entirely new model. People who had been in places with carpets on the floors told the same stories of indifference and cruelty as those who had been in dingy, barren state hospitals. Institutions with lots of staff members (expensive hospitals with good reputations) were particularly oppressive, because they were able to control virtually every move patients made.

David was a patient in one of these highly regarded hospitals.[2] He had been taken there at the request of his parents (he was a teenager at the time) because they considered his interest in religion sick. David was also a vegetarian, and the hospital considered it therapeutic that he become a meat eater, which he resisted. David began to eat a lot of peanut butter at every meal, because he was concerned about getting enough protein in his diet. It was decree that he be limited to one ounce of peanut butter per meal, a ruling that was enforced by a staff member assigned to be there to watch him eat.

It is clear that many of the things that are done to mental patients 'for their own good', in the view of the staff, are experienced as harmful by patients themselves. Mental patients' liberation groups believe that it is the patient's own assessment that is the most valid measure of whether a particular treatment is helpful or harmful. Once again, the semantic confusion caused by the medical model makes this simple fact difficult to see. In medicine, it *is* sometimes necessary to undergo a painful procedure in order to restore health. But psychiatric treatments are *not* analogous to medical ones. It was not in order to restore healthy physical functioning that David was being forced to starve. He was being starved into submission. It should be an individual's decision — not a psychiatrist's — whether or not to be a vegetarian. Defining meat eating as mentally healthy does not make forced meat eating a medical treatment.

In the past six years of activity in the mental patients' liberation movement, I have gotten to know literally hundreds of ex-patients. As we have told our stories to one another, it has been truly amazing how the same themes, often the same words, occur again and again. In answer to the question, How did you get out of a mental institution? I have heard many ex-patients use the identical phrases I once used. 'You tell them what they want to hear. You learn to play the game.'

One common route into the mental hospital occurs when a person experiences a number of life crises at the same time. It can be truly frightening to find oneself suddenly without friends, money, or a place to live, which is what happened to eighteen-year old Nancy[3].

> I was involved in a painful and mutually destructive relationship with a woman whose life-style was very different from mine. Finally, I managed to break it off. We were oppressing each other — it was awful. Just as I was leaving her, leaving New York, she got sick. She couldn't go to a doctor because she didn't have any money. I felt so guilty, but at the same time I knew I had to leave. I came back to Boston, but I had no place to live except with two men that I hated. I thought I had a job, but I lost it. I didn't have any money. I began to hear my lover's voice; she was asking me for help. I thought I was going crazy. I went out for a walk and ended up at Cambridge City Hospital — I guess I was heading there without realising it. I told them I was afraid — there were so many thoughts going around in my head that it was almost impossible to talk.

> What they did — all they really did — was to give me a lot of Stellazine. I was afraid of the other patients, and I hardly came out of my room. The hospital was an awful place to be. After a month, I escaped.

One way to look at Nancy's voices, the psychiatric way, is to see them as symptoms of illness, requiring hospitalisation and drug treatment. But is it really that abnormal, unusual, or 'sick' to react to such overwhelming stress so dramatically? Nancy's 'treatment', which continued with three other hospitalisations within a short period, resulted in her thinking of herself as a chronic patient.

> By the time of the third hospitalisation, I felt comfortable in hospitals. When I wasn't inside, I was scared. Everything was frightening. During the periods when I was home, my parents were very tense. They were

watching me differently — no one believed I could make
it on the outside. I thought I would spend the rest of my
life in hospitals. I would look at people on the street and
wonder what they had that I didn't. It was such a mystery
to me.

Mystification is one of the characteristics of institutional
psychiatric treatment. Nancy believed she was 'different'
because the treatment she received brought that message along
with it. Being a mental patient meant that her problems were
somehow different from other people's, since she seemed to
require drugs and institutionalisation. Instead of helping her to
deal with the reality of her feelings, the hospital mystified them
into symptoms of illness. It is realistic to feel guilt at the breakup
of a difficult love relationship — guilt that Nancy experienced
as 'hearing' her lover's voice calling her. It is realistic to be
frightened at finding oneself penniless and alone. Nancy's
hospitalisations only added to her real-life problems. She began
to believe that she was incapable of finding any solutions, and
her family and friends turned away from her.

For a long time after I got out, I stayed home all the time,
except when I was at school. I stopped going to feminist
meetings, although I had been very active before. Women
in the women's movement, in the lesbian movement,
women I had known for a long time and worked with,
started treating me differently after I had been in the
hospital. They were oppressing me. They wouldn't tell
me things, wouldn't ask me to do any work, because they
thought I couldn't handle stuff. They had been my friends,
but now they would look at me as if I was crazy. When
I tried to talk about it, I was afraid I was being paranoid.

Nancy's experience is a common one among ex-patients. People
have so many stereotypes of mental illness that they find it almost
impossible to react normally to the ex-patient. When they see
an ex-patient get angry or annoyed or express virtually any

emotion, they become afraid that the patient is becoming 'sick' again. The ex-patient, who is usually demoralised by the whole hospitalisation experience, finds this distancing by old friends discouraging, just one more obstacle to resuming a 'normal' life. What changed things for Nancy was her discovery of the mental patients' movement.

I came to the conference not knowing what to expect. What I found were people I could talk to, relate to, people who thought it was all right to be different. There was no one standard of behaviour, except that we all hated hospitals. I would listen to people speak and then find myself thinking. 'That's what I think too'. I kept getting happier and happier. I stayed up all night talking, which is unusual for me. I was elated, but it wasn't like a manic high. I felt calm at the same time. What was happening was that I was finding a direction I could take and people I could take it with. People have to start fighting oppression by fighting their own oppression, and I saw that I was oppressed as a mental patient even more than I was as a woman or a lesbian.

I used to feel that it was important to fight oppression, but since I was one of the weak ones, I had to let others fight for me. I would always be one of the helpees, not a participant. Now I'm fighting — for myself and others. I found a place I could plug in, where I could address myself to my most immediate oppression. It made me so happy.

After the conference, I had the strength to confront my father about his attitudes towards me, his belief that I was sick. And he's been trying to change. It felt really good when he said to me, 'It's been a privilege to watch you grow and change'. I feel strong now. I feel good about myself.

The intensive consciousness raising experience of participating in an ex-patients' conference caused Nancy to change her attitudes about herself. She was able to change from feeling weak to feeling strong because she suddenly discovered support for ideas that she had thought were hers alone, ideas that had made her feel 'paranoid' when she tried to discuss them with her old friends. Suddenly her feelings about herself — and about hospitals — underwent drastic revision.

> A few days after the conference I went back to Human Resource Institute (the place of her second psychiatric hospitalisation). I guess it was my old way of thinking showing itself for the last time. But suddenly I realised that what I got there — the medication, the constant put-downs — it was no good. I left calmly, knowing I would not be back. The hospital had ceased to be an alternative for me.

Frequently ex-patients are afraid to face their real feelings about the experience of mental institutionalisation. Family and friends tend to react negatively to expressions of anger and hatred toward the hospital and staff, seeing these as indications of illness. Patients often feel the same way and may try desperately to believe that the hospital was a basically helpful and positive place. That was my experience, and Nancy's — it is a common one. Ex-patients need support in order to express the outrage they may never have admitted even to themselves. Being with other people who have gone through the same experience can be exhilarating, as it was for Nancy.

This change — from viewing the hospital experience as a positive one to seeing it as basically unhelpful — is crucial. During their institutionalisation patients must believe (or appear to believe) that the hospital is a helpful place in order to be considered 'well' by the staff. To be discharged, a patient must confirm the psychiatric version of reality, including an acknowledgement that hospitalisation has been necessary and beneficial. Patients who maintain that the hospital is a prison and express this opinion to staff do not get discharged, as sociologist Robert Perrucci found when he studied discharge procedures. In one of the discharge interviews he observed, the patient gave a series of 'appropriate' answers to staff questions, until the doctor asked her if she thought she had been helped.

PATIENT: No, I don't.
DOCTOR: What kind of treatment have you had here?
PATIENT: Lobotomy and shock.
DOCTOR: Do you think it's helped you or tortured you?
PATIENT: I think it's tortured me.[4]

The interview continued, with the patient presenting a reasonable explanation of why she preferred to leave the hospital and get a laboratory job rather than take a work-release placement while remaining a patient.

PATIENT: I'd do much better if the hospital would free me.
DOCTOR: What do you mean, 'free you'?
PATIENT: Well, it would be just like the other work placements I've had. You're never really free.
DOCTOR: But if you stayed here on a work placement, you'd be free to come and go on your own time. It would be just like a job.
PATIENT: No. You would still be controlling me if I stayed here.
DOCTOR: Do you mean we control your mind here?
PATIENT: You may not control my mind, but I really don't have a mind of my own.
DOCTOR: How about if we gave you a work placement in −−−−−−; would you be free then? That's far away from here.
PATIENT: Anyplace I went it would be the same setup as it is here. You're never really free; you're still a patient, and everyone you work with knows it. It's tough to get away from the hospital's control.
DOCTOR: *That's the most paranoid statement I ever heard.*[5]

Obviously, the patient did not get her discharge. When Perrucci interviewed her afterward on the ward, she remarked, 'I did learn something from that staff (interview), though. If I ever get a chance to go again, I'll keep my big mouth shut, and I'll lie like hell. This time I said what I really felt, and look what happened'.[6] Unfortunately, Perrucci does not tell us what ultimately happened to this patient.

The recognition that the hospital has not been a helpful place can lead to many new realisations, as it did for Nancy, who suddenly began to think of herself as strong, as capable of taking action, because she had freed herself from accepting the hospital's image of her.

> While I was at Human Resource Institute in a sense I could see that it was a lot of game playing — having to talk about yourself at the meetings every day — but in a sense I went along with it too. I hated all the talking — but I didn't trust my own perceptions that it was all nonsense. It was much easier just to go along and do what they wanted me to do, say what they wanted me to say. But a part of me, even then, recognised that the talks the patients had in the kitchen in the evening, without staff, were much more helpful.

This kind of attitude change can lead to a person making real changes in his or her life. It is not that an illness has suddenly been cured, but that a crippling belief has suddenly been proven false. The belief in one's own inferiority makes taking action impossible; the discovery that the inferiority doesn't exist is liberating.

> In the hospital, a lot of things seemed designed to make you feel lousy about yourself. Once a group of patients were taken on an outing to the circus. It was fun, except during the intermission, when the nurse handed out pills to everyone.

Another activity that would have been fun, except for the staff's attitude, was cooking. When the staff member praised me for doing something well, she said, 'Oh, you did it all by yourself', the way one would praise a small child.

At Newton-Wellesley Hospital, the doctor who ran group therapy would be really sarcastic to the patients. When I would speak up in the group, he would say, 'Do you want to be the star?' At the same time, we would be criticised if we didn't participate.

Not every ex-patient becomes demoralised by the experience of institutionalisation. Leonard Roy Frank (whose story was told in Chapter 1) is one person who never doubted the wrongness of what was done to him.

I never doubted my own sanity. Soon after awakening from the last shock treatment, I almost immediately perceived the situation as one in which I was being imprisoned. I knew something dreadful had been done to me, even though I had no recollection of the immediate past (an effect of ECT). As soon as I had sufficiently recovered from the confusion caused by the shocks and the drugs, as soon as I had recuperated from the aftereffects of the tortures, I decided I would play along with the doctors in order to get out of there. I lied to them. When you lie to psychiatrists in this way, they accept it as the truth. But when you tell the truth — that the treatments are harmful, that you're not sick — that's regarded as 'hostility', and as further evidence of the fact that the disease has persisted, or that you have 'lack of insight'.[7]

But few people have the strength to stand up for what they believe in the face of almost unanimous opposition, especially when their opponents control their lives and their freedom. Most people need a supportive atmosphere in order to recognise and express their negative feelings about hospitalisation.

Not all ex-patients are angry about what was done to them. Some feel it was a valuable experience, even that it has saved their life. There are patients who feel better when they take Thorazine (or other psychiatric drugs). But it is impossible to know how common feelings of anger are, since ex-patients seldom are given the opportunity to express that anger without negative consequences. The positive values attached to psychiatric treatment by the general public often lead to the assumption that ex-patients who speak badly of their experiences are still 'sick' — and the feelings, thoughts, and beliefs of many people believed to be 'mentally ill' are simply not taken seriously. Books written by ex-patients in praise of their psychiatric treatment, on the other hand, find ready acceptance.[8]

The movement to set up true alternatives to the mental hospitals that many ex-patients have found so debilitating provides not only an opportunity for ex-patients to recognise their anger but also the chance to use what they have learned from their own experiences to shape alternatives that will meet real needs. From such experiences I and many others have learned the importance of emotional support from caring people, support that is difficult to find in rigidly structured mental institutions. Yet, it is in search of such support that many people have gone voluntarily into mental hospitals, only to discover that hospitals make true human contact between patient and staff nearly impossible.

Psychologist D L Rosenhan and his colleagues mimicked the symptoms of mental illness (they claimed to be hearing voices) and were admitted as patients to various mental institutions, where they experienced how rare support from staff members is. Rosenhan gives two reasons to explain this lack of contact:

First are attitudes held by all of us toward the mentally ill — including those who treat them — attitudes character-ised by fear, distrust, and horrible expectations on the one hand, and benevolent intentions on the other. Our ambival-ence leads, in this instance as in others, to avoidance.

Second, and not entirely separate, the hierarchical structure
of the psychiatric hospital facilitates depersonalisation.
Those who are at the top have least to do with patients,
and their behaviour inspires the rest of the staff.[9]

The pseudopatients kept records of how much time they spent
with professional members of the staff (psychiatrists,
psychologists, and clinical residents) — it averaged 6.8 minutes
per day.[10] 'Clearly', Rosenhan concludes, 'patients do not
spent much time in interpersonal contact with doctoral staff.
And doctoral staff serve as models for nurses and
attendants'.[11]

The hierarchical organisation of the psychiatric hospital
(leads to) those with the most power hav(ing) least to do
with patients, and those with the least power (being) most
involved with them. Recall, however, that the acquisition
of role-appropriate behaviours occurs mainly through the
observation of others, with the most powerful having the
most influence. Consequently, it is understandable that
attendants not only spend more time with patients than do
any other members of the staff — that is required by their
station in the hierarchy — but also, insofar as they learn
from their superiors' behaviour, spend as little time with
patients as they can.[12]

The mental health establishment frequently claims that increased
funding will lead to increased staffing and better patient care.
Rosenhan doubts this:

I have the impression that the psychological forces that
result in depersonalisation are much stronger than the fiscal
ones and that the addition of more staff would not
correspondingly improve patient care in this regard. The
incidence of staff meetings and the enormous amount of
record-keeping on patients, for example, have not been
as substantially reduced (by fiscal pressures) as has patient

contact. Priorities exist, even during hard times. *Patient contact is not a significant priority in the traditional psychiatric hospital.*[13]

I have given this lengthy account of Rosenhan's opinions to illustrate that it is not only angry ex-patients who have come to these conclusions. Rosenhan's study was published in early 1973, and his opinions were widely publicised. When a psychologist said what ex-patients had known for years, the ideas suddenly became credible. Rosenhan, however, qualified his conclusions by stating that he did 'not pretend to describe the subjective experiences of true patients', whose experiences might have been different, 'particularly with the passage of time and the necessary process of adaptation to one's environment'.[14] It is unfortunate that the Rosenhan experimenters, living side by side with 'real' patients, did not discuss their findings with them and find out whether or not the 'real' patients perceived things differently.

It is important for ex-patients to practice consciousness raising with other ex-patients in order to develop their real feelings about themselves and their experiences. Often patients have accurate assessments of the problems that led them into the hospital, which are far different than the official, psychiatric opinion of what is wrong with them, an opinion that they must accept in order to be seen by the staff as well. This leads to incredible confusion and anger. Arlene Sen of the Mental Patients' Liberation Front in Boston recalls an incident:

> One thing I used to hate was when we had to answer questions about ourselves in front of a lot of doctors and other patients. Once they asked me what I thought my major problem was, and I said, 'I think I'm too dependent on men'. They really ridiculed that — here I was, this sick person, who did all these crazy things, that's the way they saw me, the way they wanted me to see myself. Of course, now, years later, after being in the women's movement

and the mental patients' movement, I can see that I was right. But the institution was working against that realisation, which was something I really needed in order to change my life in a good direction. [15]

By experiencing consciousness-raising together, ex-patients can learn a new trust in their own strengths and abilities. The consciousness-raising process can lead a group in many different directions. One possibility that can arise is a joint effort to work toward alternative facilities. Along with the recognition of the antitherapeutic nature of much psychiatric treatment comes the formulation of what does make a good place for a person to come to in times of emotional distress.

In early 1971 a group of ex-patients in Vancouver, British Columbia, called a public meeting to discuss dissatisfaction with the psychiatric system. The organisers had been patients together in a psychiatric day hospital, a supposedly progressive arrangement that treats patients during the day and permits them to go home evenings and weekends. This group of patients, however, did not find the setup supportive, since they discovered that crises frequently arose precisely during the times when staff was unavailable (evenings and weekends), and it was against the rules for patients to see one another to talk on the phone outside the institution. One Monday morning the patients arrived on the ward and learned that over the weekend one of their number had committed suicide. Many strong emotions were expressed, and one immediate result was the clandestine circulation of a patients' phone list.

As time went on, some of the patients discovered that they were relying on these 'illegal' phone calls far more than on the therapy they were receiving during day hospital hours, and they began to talk among themselves about the kinds of 'help' that were truly useful. By the time all of them had been discharged from the hospital they felt that their informal network was the one form of real support they had. They decided to try to find more people who had similar feelings about psychiatric treatment and to discuss with this larger group what could be done.

A sympathetic newspaper columnist wrote a story about the group, publicising the open meeting they were planning. More than seventy-five people came to the meeting, most of them ex-patients who had equally negative feelings about their treatment. Some had suffered truly horrifying mistreatment — one woman had received more than a hundred shock treatments and had spent years on the 'back wards' of the province's public mental hospital. Out of the enthusiasm of finding one another and discovering that they shared similar feelings, the participants decided immediately to provide the services they had been unable to find through mental health agencies. One man offered the use of his house, and the group soon found itself operating a drop-in centre. The question of what to call themselves arose, and after considering several ambiguous names, the group decided on the straightforward Mental Patients' Association.

Today the Mental Patients' Association operates a seven-day-a-week drop-in centre and five co-operative residences — all on the principles of participatory democracy. Paid staff members are members of the association, no professionals, and are elected by the membership for six-month terms. All decision-making power is in the hands of the membership, expressed by votes taken at weekly business meetings and at general membership meetings held every three weeks. The Mental Patients' Association (which will be discussed in detail in Chapter 6) is living proof that ex-patients can formulate and run services in which the needs of the clients shape the direction and structure of the organisation.

The origins of the Mental Patients' Association clearly show the process of consciousness-raising at work. Originally, the day hospital patients went along with the rules, ignoring their own perceptions that their crises did not fit into the nine-to-five, Monday-to-Friday availability of the staff. They accepted the rule that they may not have outside communications with one another, a rule that implied that only 'experts' (and certainly not mental patients) could help people with their problems. The suicide led to a realisation that they needed one another. Many of the patients wished they had reached out to the dead man and wanted to make sure that if they felt desperate themselves, they would be able to get support from one another. Gradually, as they saw how much they used the phone list and how helpful it was, they saw that the official psychiatric view was wrong and that patients could help one another as well as or better than the staff. From feeling weak and powerless, they had moved toward feeling strong.

At about the same time the Mental Patients' Association was being organised in Vancouver, a group of ex-patients in New York City began meeting together to discuss their dissatisfaction with psychiatric treatment. The two groups were unknown to each other, but their overall outlook was remarkably similar. The New York group called itself the Mental Patients' Liberation Project. Over the first few weeks of their existence, their discussions led to the writing of a mental patients' bill of rights. The production of this document is another example of the consciousness-raising process at work. The membership of MPLP recognised that the abuses each of them had experienced were not isolated examples of mistreatment but were built into the system. The rights they listed were fundamental human rights, yet they were routinely denied to mental patients. 'Because these rights are not now legally ours, we are now going to fight to make them a reality', they stated in the preamble.[16] The rights listed were:

1. You are a human being and are entitled to be treated as such with as much decency and respect as is accorded to any other human being.
2. You are an American citizen and are entitled to every right established by the Declaration of Independence and guaranteed by the Constitution of the United States of America.

3. You have the right to the integrity of your own mind and the integrity of your own body.

4. Treatment and medication can be administered only with your consent and, in the event you give your consent, you have the right to know all relevant information regarding said treatment and/or medication.

5. You have the right to access to your own legal and medical counsel.

6. You have the right to refuse to work in a mental hospital and/or to choose what work you will do; and you have the right to receive the usual wage for such work as is set by the state labour laws.

7. You have the right to decent medical attention when you feel you need it, just as any other human being has that right.

8. You have the right to uncensored communication by phone, letter, and in person with whomever you wish and at any time you wish.

9. You have the right not to be treated like a criminal; not to be locked up against your will; not to be committed involuntarily; not to be fingerprinted or 'mugged' (photographed).

10. You have the right to decent living conditions. You're paying for it, and the taxpayers are paying fot it.

11. You have the right to retain your own personal property. No one has the right to confiscate what is legally yours, no matter what reason is given. That is commonly known as theft.

12. You have the right to bring grievance against those who have mistreated you and the right to counsel and a court hearing. You are entitled to protection by the law against retaliation.

13. You have the right to refuse to be a guinea pig for experimental drugs and treatments and to refuse to be used as learning material for students. You have the right to reimbursement if you are so used.

14. You have the right to request an alternative to legal commitment or incarceration in a mental hospital.

The 'Mental Patients' Bill of Rights' was drawn up in response to specific abuses that had been experienced by members of the group. The popular myth that holds that mental hospitals have improved dramatically since tranquillisers were introduced in the mid-1950s is belied by the existence of these abuses. The members of MPLP found strength in their united outlook and their sense of outrage. Providing an alternative to mental hospitals was a goal of MPLP, but money was not available, and the group turned to distribution of the bill of rights as a means of publicising conditions inside mental hospitals. Later MPLP (which is no longer in existence) was able to obtain a storefront headquarters and ran a crisis centre staffed by members.

Consciousness-raising was one of the main activities of the Mental Patients' Liberation Front in Boston, which was also founded in 1971. MPLF began with two ex-patients, each of whom had the dream of starting an organisation of mental patients who wanted to fight back. Meeting first at the offices of *The Radical Therapist* (an antipsychiatry journal now called *State and Mind*) and then in the apartment of one of the members, the group focused on consciousness-raising because, as Bette Maher, one of the founders, recalls:

> We needed it. Many patients were still into the head-trip of feeling that they deserved what happened to them — they were 'psychologised' into believing it. At consciousness-raising meetings, we would talk about how people ended up in hospitals — it was because their lives had become intolerable. But hospitals made people worse off than they were to begin with.

> We had strategy meetings, too, but we alternated them with consciousness-raising. And if someone came to a strategy meeting and was really upset, the way we dealt with it was that one of us would volunteer to go into another room and talk to that person. We didn't want to

turn the person off, but we needed to have strategy meetings, too.

A lot of people stopped coming to strategy meetings because they didn't want to be involved in anything political. But they kept coming to the consciousness-raising meetings because they said that the meetings helped them to feel self-respect which they never had before.[17]

At MPLF, consciousness-raising led the group toward the writing of a patients' rights handbook. 'Because patients had so few rights, we didn't think the handbook would give patients that much actual help, but we saw it as a tool for consciousness-raising among patients', Bette Maher says now. The handbook took months to write. A small group of ex-patients, although untrained in the law, thoroughly researched the mental health laws in Massachusetts. They had the help of a lawyer as a consultant, but they did all the research and writing themselves. When it was finished, they made the round of activist groups in Boston and got a number of small donations that enabled them to have the handbook printed at the New England Free Press, a nonprofit printing collective.

Your Rights as a Mental Patient in Massachusetts is a remarkable fifty-six-page document that covers the laws concerning commitment, voluntary and involuntary hospitalisation, the special situation of minors, patients' civil rights and treatment, as well as providing an overall strategy for fighting back. The handbook also contains a bill of rights, which, while it contains many parallels with the one written by the Mental Patients' Liberation Project in New York, also contains many differences of emphasis. The final right listed in the handbook is especially significant:

You have the right to patient-run facilities where the decisions that are made and work that is done are your responsibility and under your control.[18]

The handbook also contains a chapter on the special difficulties of ex-patients, such as problems of child custody, government access to psychiatric records, job discrimination, difficulty in getting driver's licenses, discrimination in admission to colleges and graduate schools, and the fear and distrust people feel toward ex-patients. And, the section concludes, 'you probably won't be Vice President of the United States'.[19]

This survey of some of the early mental patients' liberation groups has shown several of the directions in which consciousness-raising can lead. There is no one single direction for ex-patient groups to take. The needs of members are what has shaped these and other groups, not adherence to any formula. Local conditions may differ, as may the energies and specific interests of members. Consciousness-raising (which may not be specifically called that) helps groups to clarify what they want and what they need, as well as what is possible. Consciousness-raising is a process that ensures that the needs of members are met, because everyone participates by contributing his or her own thoughts, feelings, and opinions, and because there is no one right way of doing things.

Mental patient consciousness-raising may lead to many different kinds of action. As we have seen from these brief looks at groups in Vancouver, New York, and Boston, it can lead to the setting up of drop-in centres and communal residences, to action projects that publicise conditions inside mental hospitals, or to focusing on patients' rights. Other possible directions include the setting up of crisis centres (sometimes called 'freak-out centres'), the establishment of new kinds of member-controlled social service centres (such as job-finding services), or the operating of nonprofit businesses to provide nonalienating work for members.

Whatever a group may decide to do as an outgrowth of consciousness-raising will be enhanced by members' growing awareness that they can be strong and competent people. As the group proceeds with its chosen work, ongoing consciousness-raising will help to ensure that members never lose sight of their ability to help one another and will be a constant reminder that there are no real 'experts'.

NOTES FOR CHAPTER 3

1. Frank M Ochberg, 'Community Mental Health Center Legislation: Flight of the Phoenix', *American Journal of Psychiatry* 133, no1 (January 1976): 56-61. This figure is broken down into $8 billion in the public sphere ($4-5 billion for state and county hospitals, $1 billion for community mental health centres, and $2 billion spent by the military) and $5 billion in the private sphere ($1 billion for private hospitals and health maintenance organisations, and $4 billion for private practitioners).
2. David and I were in the same consciousness-raising group in 1972.
3. All quotes from Nancy from personal interview. October 26, 1976.
4. Robert Perrucci, *Circle of Madness* (Englewood Cliffs, N J : Prentice-Hall, 1974), p157.
5. Ibid, pp157-158 (emphasis added).
6. Ibid, p159.
7. Personal interview with Leonard Roy Frank, December 7, 1976.
8. See, for example, Clifford W Beers, *A Mind That Found Itself* (Garden City, NY: Doubleday, 1953); Barbara Field Benziger, *The Prison of My Mind* (New York: Walker & Company, 1969); Hannah Green, *I Never Promised You a Rose Garden* (New York: Holt, Rinehart and Winston, 1964); Nancy Covert Smith, *Journey Out of Nowhere* (Waco, Texas: Word Books, 1973); Ellen Wolfe, *Aftershock* (New York: G P Putnam's Sons, 1969). All were written by people who have been psychiatrically hospitalised. I exclude the large number of books written by grateful ex-patients who received office psychotherapy.
9. DL Rosenhan, 'On Being Sane in Insane Places,' Science 179 (January 19, 1973): p256.
10. Ibid

11. Ibid.
12. Ibid, pp254-255.
13. Ibid, p256 (emphasis added).
14. Ibid, p257.
15. Personal interview with Arlene Sen, January 11, 1977.
16. Mental Patients' Liberation Project, 'Bill of Rights,' nd.
17. All quotes from Bette Maher, from personal interview, March 17, 1977.
18. *Your Rights as a Mental Patient in Massachusetts* (West Somerville, Mass: Legal Project/Mental Patients' Liberation Front, 1974), p41.
19. Ibid p39.

Chapter Four

Alternatives and False Alternatives

Once the decision to start an alternative service is made (whether it is to be a crisis centre, residence, drop-in centre, or whatever), the founding group must make a number of decisions. What will the alternative be like? Whom will it serve? Who will participate in planning? How will decisions be made? The ways in which a group solves these problems will have significant effects on the shape of the service or organisation that develops. Since, presumably, the group is reacting to deficiencies and flaws in existing services, it will want to ensure that the alternative provides fundamental (and not merely cosmetic) differences.

The question of participation is perhaps the most basic. If the founding group consists entirely of ex-mental patients, it must decide what its relations will be with nonpatients and with mental health professionals. If the founding group, on the other hand, consists of a mix of patients, nonpatients, and professionals, it must face the inevitable strains and tensions and evolve ways of dealing with them. Groups that consist solely of ex-mental patients will set up very different kinds of alternatives from groups dominated by liberal mental health professionals. I have identified three distinct models within what are usually recognised as alternative services.

In the *partnership model,* professionals and nonprofessionals work together to provide services. The recipients of services are told that they, too, are partners in the service. However, the distinction between those who give help and those who receive it remains clearly defined. I consider services based on this model to be alternatives in name only. The overwhelming majority of alternative services (most halfway houses, for example) fit into the partnership model.

In the *supportive model,* membership is open to all people who want to use the service for mutual support. Nonpatients and ex-patients are seen as equals, since everyone has problems at some time or another, and all are capable of helping one another. Professionals are excluded from this model (except in external roles, such as writing letters of support) because they use a different model of helping, which separates those who give from those who receive help.

In the *separatist model,* ex-patients provide support for one another and run the service. All nonpatients and professionals are excluded because they interfere with consciousness raising and because they usually have mentalist attitudes.

Alternative services based on the supportive or separatist models are few in number, but they present a real alternative to the dehumanising effects of mental health 'care' in the United States today. 'Alternatives' based on the partnership model continue many of the same abuses.

Mental health professionals are used to taking a controlling role, and they continue to do so even within 'alternatives' based on the partnership model. An excellent example of the workings of the partnership model is provided by Fountain House, a well-known psychiatric rehabilitation service in New York City. The history of Fountain House clearly shows the limitations of this model.

What is now Fountain House began as WANA — We Are Not Alone — a self-help group formed by several patients in Rockland State Hospital in the late 1940s. The group continued to meet in New York City after the patients were discharged, and attracted the attention of some volunteer workers, who found them a place to meet but who also transformed the group from a self-help project to a new kind of psychiatric facility. A professional staff was hired and, in the early 1950s, most of the original founding group of ex-patients quit in disgust. Some idea of the contempt these volunteers felt for the ex-patients may be seen in the words of Auguste Richard, one of the original board members, who quotes an Episcopal hymn to describe the volunteers as 'Angels of Mercy, Angels of Light, working to rescue the afflicted from their plight'.[1] The 'afflicted,' obviously, can play no part in the service except as recipients.

Jordan Hess, who was a member of WANA, remembers how things changed when the group became professionally controlled:

> There was a feeling of solidarity and companionship in WANA that deteriorated when the professionals got involved. For a while, the ex-patients continued to run the club. We raised our own money (by holding bazaars, for example), and we voted in new members. But eventually the administrators decided to take that power away from us. Instead of the members deciding who could join, when new people came in they were interviewed by the staff, who decided if they were 'suitable cases'. WANA was unique because patients ran it — that was abolished when it became Fountain House.[2]

Today, Fountain House occupies a five-storey building, which was built for it at a cost of two million dollars in 1965, on West 47th Street in a poor residential neighbourhood. A staff of more than sixty (including psychologists, social workers, and consulting psychiatrists) provide services to nearly two thousand 'members'. The main emphasis at Fountain House is on work, and although some members use the clubhouse as simply a place to sit and socialise, most are involved in some sort of work programme, either at Fountain House (where members work in the kitchen, on maintenance crews, as clerical workers and switchboard operators, producing the daily 'Fountain House News' on the club's closed circuit TV, or in one of the other work areas), at the Fountain House Thrift Shop around the corner, or on a work placement in private industry. Fountain House also has an apartment programme, in which several members share the rent on an apartment that is leased to Fountain House. Fountain House is a large agency — there are about 120 work-placement positions and more than fifty apartments.

Fountain House doesn't look like a hospital, but it does look like the large and successful institution it is. Although the hierarchy is not rigidly structured, it exists, and the role performed by the director is quite different from that performed by members. Administration and direction of the programme are clearly and unequivocally in the hands of the staff. The staff and members involved in each unit (the kitchen or the clerical office, for example) meet daily to review progress and difficulties, but there is no provision for overall membership meetings. (As we have seen, this makes consciousness-raising impossible).

During my visit to Fountain House, staff member Sheila Sherman told me that Fountain House is run by its members.[3] This is the official ideology of Fountain House, but what it appears to mean in practice is that members do most of the work while professionals make most of the decisions. By this standard, most mental hospitals could be said to be 'run' by patients.

Director John Beard told me that one of Fountain House's main strengths is its flexibility.[4] Members aren't expected to move through the programme at a predetermined speed but can take as long as they like. They can drop out of the programme and come back at any time. But the flexibility goes only so far. It does not allow members to question their need to be 'rehabilitated' or to determine the suitability and qualifications of the staff.

The Fountain House work programme is better than that offered by sheltered workshops, where the pay is often below the minimum wage, but it is still stigmatising. The Fountain House member is known to be an ex-mental patient, both by the employer and by co-workers, and the tendency in such situations is to blame any deficiencies in the work on the 'fact' of the member's 'illness'. The advantage to Fountain House jobs is that members don't have to go through job interviews (which often automatically eliminate ex-patients, anyway) but can make arrangements through Fountain House. Salaries are paid directly and in full by the employer to the Fountain House member. The jobs are entry-level — messengers, clerks, food service workers.

Fountain House (and similar programmes) separate out those ex-patients who are more needy and less competent and make the assumption that they are representative of all ex-patients and their needs. A paper co-authored by its executive director states that 'typically, the members of Fountain House are those ex-patients who find it difficult to make the transition from hospital back into the community'.[5] Members don't get to see competent ex-patients; their role models are staff members — only they have responsible, interesting, well-paid jobs. This reinforces the assumption (held by both members and staff) that ex-patients should not aspire very high. A 'successful' Fountain House member is one who satisfactorily performs a simple, low-paying job, even if he or she is capable of more. Or, occasionally, a member may become part of the staff, but only if he or she is willing to think of himself or herself as someone who has been 'ill' and is now 'rehabilitated'.

Another example of the partnership model is provided by Center Club, a social club for ex-patients in Boston. The club is located in a rather drab suite of rooms in the YMC Union Building in downtown Boston. Several large rooms are simply furnished with tables and chairs; there are shelves of books and a bulletin board. Several more rooms are set aside as offices.

Center Club, like Fountain House, clearly defines some people as staff, others as members. Staff people are mostly professionally trained, primarily in the field of social work. The club was started by Dr Samuel Grob, a clinical psychologist. Membership is open to ex-patients from certain hospitals and geographical areas, since funding for the club is channelled through contracts from several mental health service providers. Ex-patients not covered by these contracts can join at a monthly fee of fifty dollars, which is prohibitive since the club is geared primarily toward people unable to hold jobs.

Activities at the club are primarily social, both informal (card playing, conversation) and structured (trips, activity groups). All groups are led by either staff members or volunteers. Bernard Alderman, the director of Center Club, told me that groups led by members invariably fall apart quickly.[6]

A reliance on staff and volunteers (and an unspoken lack of trust in members) is clear from Center Club literature. Members are seen as 'seriously handicapped', and although the club is described as 'self-governing', this is qualified by the requirement of 'professional guidance and consultation'.[7]

Self-government is exercised through weekly council meetings, open to all members. The functions of the staff and of the board of directors (consisting of charitable minded citizens) limit the degree of control exercised by the membership. A club member is an *ex officio* member of the board. ('This avoids any ideas of self-reference or paranoia', Bernard Alderman told me.) Since day-to-day administration is in the hands of the staff and long-range planning is done by the board of directors, there is little left over for the members' council to decide.

While Center Club states that members and staff are equal, a number of practices make clear that staff is in charge. The initial decision about membership is made by staff, who can decide that a prospective member is 'too sick', or 'unable to benefit from the programme'. Files are kept on each member, and while members are allowed to see their folders on request, the mere keeping of such records reinforces the staff/member dichotomy. Although Center Club is said to be valued by members because it is not a hospital, this record-keeping subtly reminds members that they are looked upon as mental patients. Center Club staff also take responsibility for notifying a member's therapist (usually with, but sometimes without, the member's knowledge and consent) that the member appears to be in difficulty. No rhetoric about members being responsible people can disguise this infantilising practice. Staff can suspend the membership of anyone they deem to be 'too sick'.[8]

Center Club strongly upholds mental health ideology and terminology. Ex-patients are viewed as handicapped people needing services with a mental health orientation. When I asked Bernard Alderman how he saw the club fitting into the mental health system, he replied that the club was part of a member's overall treatment, filling a member's need for social rehabilitation while the member's therapist takes care of the member's emotional problems. The image of the member as a sick, needy person who depends on other people to provide services indicates the distance staff feel from members. Members, of course, experienced this same distrust from hospital staff when they were patients. Obviously, self-government under such conditions is extremely limited.

This is not to deny that alternatives based on the partnership model have a number of satisfied members. Situations that encourage passivity acquire satisfied, passive participants. But by (subtly) encouraging passivity, professionally run 'alternatives' can never evolve toward true membership control.

Consciousness-raising is impossible in professionally run ex-patient services. Because the orientation is totally within the mental health framework, members are seen as people with individual, personal problems or defects. Expressions of dissatisfaction with psychiatric treatment, even if they occurred in alternatives based on the partnership model, would be seen as part of a member's illness. Without consciousness-raising, as we have seen, ex-patients are as likely as professionals to view such anger as 'paranoia', and to view themselves and one another as 'sick'.

From this description of 'alternative' services based on the partnership model, it is clear that true partnership is impossible because the partners are not equal. The staffs of these 'alternatives' keep records on members, consult with others about members, and make decisions members have to abide by. 'Members, on the other hand, can participate in only the most limited kinds of decision making. They can vote to schedule a bowling night instead of a swimming night, but they cannot vote to fire the director or to point out to a staff member that his or her behaviour is 'abnormal'. A member dissatisfied with the basic structure of these 'alternatives' has little recourse. The kinds of changes that are within membership control cannot achieve fundamental changes in the way the service is run. Calling such 'alternatives' membership controlled is just one more form of psychiatric mystification.

'Alternative' services based on the partnership model are typically set up with no (or limited) input from potential users of the service. We have seen that Fountain House, for example, quickly replaced membership control with volunteer control, and ultimately with professional control. A guidebook for starting ex-patient social clubs, published by the National Association for Mental Health, suggests that in order to assess the need in the community for a social club a study committee be set up, with members drawn from 'lay and professional groups directly involved with the care of psychiatric patients'.[9] Clearly, client input is not an essential element in the model.

When the mental health professionals are involved in setting up 'alternative' services, those services will clearly mirror psychiatric ideology. Even when ex-patients are involved in the creation of the service, the involvement of professionals prevents the ex-patients from developing behind this ideology. So long as patients are willing to view themselves as the professionals view them, they can continue their involvement, but any attempt to make the alternative truly membership run is impossible, since psychiatric ideology defines the patient as weak, helpless, and in need of outside support. The members of WANA, who initially remained when the group became Fountain House, finally walked out, not in a fit of pique, but because they had seen their dream of helping one another transformed into a nightmare. They had become 'members', instead of 'patients', but they were still under the direction and control of professionals who viewed them as sick.

Most so-called alternative services for former mental patients follow the 'partnership' model. *They are alternatives in name only.*

Alternatives that follow the supportive model and the separatist model are fundamentally different. Although some professionals may be involved in setting up services under the supportive model, their participation is deliberately limited by the membership. In Vancouver, for example, the Mental Patients' Association has received help from a number of professionals, particularly in the area of support letters for funding purposes, but the professionals do not come to meetings or take part in day-to-day operations.

The supportive model relies on the abilities of the membership. The role of professionals is simply to ensure the organisation's credibility with funding agencies and other bureaucracies that are impressed by professional credentials. Most mental health professionals, conditioned by their belief that patients are incapable of self-directed activity, cannot go along with the limited role allotted to them under the supportive model. Sometimes, professionals in this situation attempt more direction of the group than is needed or desired by the membership. For this reason, it is essential that when a group attempts to get some help from professionals without being dominated, the members hold frequent and regular meetings without the professionals.

Many professionals deeply resent being excluded from meetings and activities of the group. In fact, this is one of the organisational problems with which any group attempting to set up an alternative service will probably have to deal early in its existence. Public meetings called to discuss deficiencies in mental health programmes and the setting up of alternatives will frequently attract a number of well-meaning professionals, as well as a larger number of ex-patients and an intermediate number of relatives and friends of patients. As we have seen, ex-patient consciousness-raising cannot take place in such mixed groups, and without consciousness-raising, the group will probably incorporate psychiatric ideology, which stigmatises and discredits ex-patients as it claims to help them. It must be up to the ex-patient members of the group to determine the degree that nonpatients may participate. This requires that some meetings (consciousness-raising meetings) exclude nonpatients. Those professionals and other nonpatients who fight attempts by ex-patients to exclude them from some meetings are precisely the same people who will probably attempt to control and direct the group. Those nonpatients who recognise the need for consciousness-raising meetings and don't object to being excluded from them are the only nonpatients who can participate successfully in what is basically a patient-run service.

The Mental Patients' Association, while it limits the role of psychiatric professionals to serving as outside supporters, has a number of members who have never been mental patients. Since MPA has never developed an ongoing consciousness-raising process, and many members (both nonpatients and ex-patients) continue to accept psychiatric ideology, this has resulted in some members viewing nonpatients as superior and ex-patients as inferior.

Dissatisfaction with even limited amounts of nonpatient involvement has led to the establishment of alternatives that exclude nonpatients entirely. I have termed this the separatist model. In New York City, Project Release operates a seven-day-a-week community centre that is entirely patient run. They see themselves not as a service but as a supportive community. It is an important distinction, because the concept of a service implies the existence of two roles, the server and the served. No matter how much a group may attempt to break down such roles, some residue of them always remains when a group is delivering 'services'. The concept of community, on the other hand, implies interaction. (I am deliberately ignoring here such tortured constructions as *community psychiatry.*) The separatist model is by far the most radical model of alternative services, but it is also the model that promotes the greatest degree of ex-patient confidence and competence.

Project Release was formed around the issue of SRO (single-room occupancy) hotels on Manhattan's Upper West Side, which house many welfare recipients (including large numbers of recently released mental patients) in totally inadequate and unsafe conditions. Project Release secured office space from a tenants' organising committee and, as it grew and needed an office of its own, was given the use of a room in a neighbourhood Universalist church. From a concern with housing, the group moved into other areas, including publishing an informational handbook on psychiatric medication[10], and working on a patients' rights manual. But providing an alternative had always been a major long-range goal, and in late 1976 Project Release obtained a ten-thousand dollar foundation grant, with which they rented an apartment and opened their community centre.

The Project Release community centre consists of a two-bedroom apartment in a large, older apartment building on the Upper West Side, comfortably furnished with donations and creative scavenging. The community centre is a gathering place for members and prospective members and is busy from late in the morning until late in the evening, seven days a week. A highlight of each day is a community meal in the evening. No one is designated 'staff'. Members are there not because they are running the centre but because it is clearly a place where they enjoy spending their time. In order to discourage anyone from becoming a passive recipient, all members are required to serve on one or more of the committees (fund raising, community centre, newsletter, and so on) that oversee the various areas of responsibility. As the group states:

> Professional supervision creates a dependency pattern which is a cause of recidivism. In the informal programmes of Project Release, members seek to extend acceptance and co-operation, letting each individual set her/his own pace in tasks and responsibilities. Project Release feels that this form of self-help is a strong antidote to the anxiety of isolation and helplessness induced by society and psychiatry.'[11]

In a moving tribute to the impact of Project Release on her life, a member has compared the effects of being in a conventional aftercare facility to those of becoming a member of Project Release:

> Everything at the aftercare facility perpetuates your feelings of helplessness, dependency, and role-playing. You move from phase to phase of a programme: from working at the work area to working at a volunteer job; from a beginning to an advanced group.

> Criteria are purposely kept nebulous; one moves in a track virtually set up and operated totally without any personal exercise of will; you are never asked, nor, under the circumstances, could you ever say, what changes should be made.... You are, in actuality, willy-nilly, learning that the one person who is not able to help you in your relationship to other people is *yourself....*

Project Release exists in opposition to the whole self-perpetuating bureaucracy of 'Mental Health' care in this society.... Here, you can learn a whole different way of *being*; you begin to trust *yourself* and your reactions. Instead of feeling coldness at your core, you feel *warmth* and *strength*.... Here, we are *with* each other to an extent never possible at an aftercare facility. We experience the entire range of emotions as being positive, as all being us; no feelings are ever invalidated.... Most of us feel that a true alternative has to be different *ENTIRELY* from what it is objecting to.[12]

Project Release has also maintained its original interest in housing for ex-patients. The housing programme helps members to get their own apartments, either by themselves or communally with other group members. The apartments are not part of Project Release — they are rented and run by their residents — but they form part of the wider Project Release community. They compare their apartment programme to other kinds of housing programmes for ex-patients:

SRO's and adult homes, halfway houses and residences are horrible and self-perpetuating institutions. We are always being shunted from one form of institution to another or just put back into the same living situation that caused many problems in the first place. Why can't we just live in our own apartments, like other people? Contrary to most 'experts' opinions we can and we are.[13]

Project Release has completely broken down the concepts of staff and clients. They have avoided setting up any more structure than is absolutely necessary, preferring occasional confusion to impersonal efficiency. They are adamant that no one receive a salary for working at Project Release, since they believe that members could not be equal if some were paid for being there. (They are currently trying to get a grant to start a nonprofit printing business, which would provide employment for interested members. And they have recently opened a thrift shop in which members work.) The concept of community, of people helping one another because they care about one another, is dramatically different from conventional conceptions of therapy. The example of Project Release shows clearly how a group of former mental patients working together follow a completely different model from that used by mental health professionals. The separatist model doesn't divide people into fixed categories of sick and well, since everyone experiences stress and reacts in different ways. Rather than setting up one group of people as 'experts', people are seen as equals who can help one another.

This look at three different models for alternative services shows that the role played by ex-patients is the crucial variable. When they are excluded from any meaningful role in planning the service, it becomes an alternative in name only. The same attitudes of condescension and distancing that are found in mental hospitals are also found in many of the halfway houses, rehabilitation services, and social clubs that are the supposed alternative.

On the other hand, the alternatives built on the supportive and separatist models — the true alternatives — have been designed by ex-patients who are not merely passive recipients of a service but who are actively involved in running it. Role distinctions between service providers and service recipients blur and disappear. Mental health professionals tend to be skeptical of true alternatives because they cannot see patients as competent people. In the professional versions of alternatives, based on the partnership model, the professional is always the senior partner. True alternatives are threatening because they do away with the need for professionals.

Mental health professionals and the facilities they control frequently display contempt for the recipients of their services. And the people they think of as incompetent and untrustworthy feel and react to these unspoken attitudes, which exist in supposedly modern, progressive community mental health centres as well as in old-style state hospitals. A few examples:

A small group of staff members come into a room that is sometimes used by patients and sometimes by staff. They tell several patients that they are planning to use the room now, and the patients leave. The staff members then take out a cake and have a small party for one of the staff. When a patient comes into the room for a glass of water, they offer her a piece of cake, but although there are several other patients sitting in the next room, and more than half the cake is left over, they do not invite the patients to join them. (I observed this in the Chelsea Mental Health Center in Massachusetts).

I try to explain to a therapist why I am feeling so depressed. 'For one thing, I miss my daughter, who lives 3,000 miles away with my ex-husband. Sometimes I just can't help thinking about it, and I feel so lonely.' 'You shouldn't let that bother you', the therapist says glibly. 'I hardly ever see my kids, and it doesn't bother me.' I looked at him in horror, wondering if he wanted me to be as cold and unfeeling a person as he seemed to be. (This happened to me at the Whatcom Counseling and Psychiatric Clinic, in Washington State.)

Several attendants enter the dayroom, where a group of patients are gathered in front of the TV, watching a programme. Without a word to the patients, one of the attendants changes the channel, and then the group of attendants pull up their own chairs in front of the patients so that they can watch their chosen programme. (This happened to me at Rockland State Hospital in New York.)

These attitudes occur in many so-called alternatives, as well as in traditional psychiatric facilities. 'Clients', 'residents', and 'members' are still looked on by staff members as patients, as essentially different from themselves. In halfway houses, residents seldom get to decide whom to room with, let alone who the director should be. Ex-patient social clubs have rules against staff members and club members socialising — yet the rhetoric claims they are equal. At Fountain House, which presents itself as a model rehabilitation service, all job placements are deliberately in entry-level jobs, ignoring the differing educational and aspirational levels of members. Once you've been a mental patient, the staff thinks you're suitable only for a job as a waitress or a file clerk, and you're expected to go along meekly with their judgement.

Journalist Anthony Brandt, who feigned hearing voices and was admitted to a state hospital, was amazed how easily he and the other patients submitted to becoming 'creatures of no significance to be herded through the day, to be managed and controlled'.[14] Drugs were used extensively to numb patients and slow them down.

> But drugs were not the whole story. What subdued us even more effectively was this mindless routine and our mindless participation in it. By treating us routinely as if we lacked the ability to make any choices for ourselves at all, little by little they persuaded us it was true. Subjected to a routinised disrespect and indifference, we began to believe something must indeed be wrong with us, something fundamental must be missing. We began to behave like the empty beings we were supposed to be.[15]

After only two days as a mental patient, Brandt had already become dehumanised in the eyes of the psychiatrist assigned to him. Without making any inquiries as to his interests, education, or abilities, she mapped out her life plan for him. As he recalls:

> I was to stay in the hospital three months or so to stabilise

my life, she said. When I seemed up to it I would go to work in the hospital's 'sheltered workshop' where I would make boxes for IBM and be paid on a piecework basis. When I had made enough boxes I would then be moved to the halfway house in Kingston, across the Hudson, where they would arrange a job for me in a special place called Gateway Industries established for the rehabilitation of mental patients. There I would presumably make more boxes. Eventually I might move out of the halfway house into my own apartment.[16]

Brandt, of course, was horrified by this limited vision of his future. When he told the doctor that, instead, he might try to go back to his wife (from whom he had claimed to be separated in his admission interview), she ridiculed him, asking him if perhaps his wife wouldn't rather have a 'real man'.[17] Mental hospital, halfway house, rehabilitation service, psychiatrist — some are considered alternatives, yet all have the same limited view of the mental patient and demand that the patient believe in it as well.

Staff are so conditioned to viewing anyone who comes before them in the role of a patient as sick that they have a hard time picking out impostors. Both journalists and scientific investigators have posed as mental patients and are seldom if ever, found out by staff, although several of the Rosenhan investigators, for example, were challenged by patients.[18] People who have been hospitalised for mental illness are simply presumed by staff to be mentally ill.

Even people who are not mental patients and who are behaving quite 'normally' (whatever that may be) may be perceived by psychiatrists as mentally ill. Maurice K Temerlin reports a study in which an actor was coached so as to portray 'a mentally healthy man'. Many psychiatrists who viewed the tape, in which the actor provided 'normal' answers to mental-status questions, diagnosed various mental illnesses. One psychiatrist who found the man on the tape to be 'psychotic', is quoted as saying, 'Of course he looked healthy, but hell, most people are a little neurotic, and who can accept appearances at face value anyway'?[19] On the basis of such casually made decisions, people can be, and are, committed to mental hospitals to be made into mental patients.

The casual disregard for individuals that is commonly displayed by mental health professionals, in all kinds of mental health facilities, communicates an unspoken message. 'Good patients' are patients who know their place, who go along with these subtle put-downs. And since the penalty for failure to co-operate is so great, since any protests can be dismissed as merely pathological symptoms, since the power professionals hold over patients is so enormous, is it any surprise that most of the patients go along?

Even outpatients at community mental health centres can be subjected to enormous penalties. (Community mental health centres, introduced with great fanfare in the early 1960s as a replacement for state hospitals, have become simply another layer of the psychiatric bureaucracy.) During 1976, along with other members of the Mental Patients' Liberation Front, I participated in a weekly patients' rights meeting held with patients at a community mental health centre near Boston. Despite the fact that these patients were officially voluntary day patients, we witnessed a great deal of coercion. One patient 'voluntarily' entered a mental hospital after the head of the centre threatened her with commitment. Another patient was unable to get his medication changed or to get any information about side-effects.

We also saw patients demeaned and degraded. One woman had to wait in the hall if she arrived late for the day activities programme, which caused her to feel like a small child. The one room in the entire centre where people could smoke and drink coffee had to be vacated by patients whenever staff wanted to use it. A poster designed by a patient to publicise the patients' rights group was torn down under circumstances indicating that it had been done by a staff member.

Becoming a client of *any* mental health service may result in being subtly degraded. Whether the service is a 'traditional' mental hospital or an 'alternative,' such as a halfway house, it is likely to view its clients as incompetent people who constantly need looking after. These attitudes prevent professionals from helping their patients to move toward independence and self-sufficiency, even when that is precisely what they claim to be doing.

Alternative services must be designed so that this psychiatric elitism is eliminated. People who are having difficulties in living and who seek help with their problems are *not* served by a system that maximises their inadequacies and ignores their strengths, nor by one that implies that only incompetent people have problems. 'Professionalism' demands that mental health practitioners project a neutral, impersonal manner. Sometimes this may be concealed by a bland friendliness, such as an insistence on first names, but it is, more likely than not, only a pretence of friendliness. Real friendliness would break down the role structures of 'professional' and 'patient' and lead to the acknowledgement that everyone may experience difficulties. Some therapists may genuinely want to be friendly with their clients; but the structure of therapy interferes. Friends don't stop talking when the hour is up, nor does their relationship involve payment. One therapist I had insisted on first names, wore jeans and boots, and sat on the floor during sessions. This did not negate the fact that he had power over my life; his game that we were friends did not change this fact.

In alternative services, the entire question of role structure is confronted openly. Distinctions between staff and clients are kept fluid, if not eliminated, not only in the area of service delivery but also in terms of administration. When ex-mental patients run an alternative, they have opportunities to prove their competence as well as to get help with their problems. If someone makes a mistake (and not only ex-patients make mistakes), people work together to straighten things out. Alternative organisations tend to work in some form of collective structure, which encourages the sharing of responsibility. Rather than delegating authority to a director or administrator, which implies that only a few special people are capable of exercising authority, collective structures allow people of varying abilities to work together. Many people's lives have been transformed by their participation in alternative services. Group support, for many, has been far more helpful than various psychiatric services they may have used in the past.

Although some participants have had to return to mental hospitals, this has usually been for short periods and can usually be attributed, at least in part, to limitations imposed on the group by the lack of money to provide some of the services the group has defined as necessary. Project Release, for example, is currently trying to get funding to open 'sanctuaries,' where members can receive short periods of intensive support from other members.

All this is not to deny that some people occasionally become dramatically disturbed. They may hear voices, for example, or see things that other people do not, or take actions that appear irrational and impulsive. But most people who do become disturbed in these ways are reacting to extremely difficult circumstances that have been a part of their lives for long periods of time. If people could find nonjudgemental, supportive services that can provide help with their ongoing life problems, it is likely that there would be fewer incidences of dramatic 'breakdowns'.

Most people maintain stereotypes of the 'mentally ill' that are far different from the reality that leads to some people being labelled mental patients. Most mental patients (excluding those who have suffered damage from having been kept institutionalised for long periods of time) are not strikingly different in their problems and their concerns from so-called normal people. Although the public stereotype of the mentally ill would indicate that most mental patients have hallucinations and delusions or that they speak in incomprehensible gibberish, such behaviour is comparatively uncommon.

Many studies have shown that the incidence of 'mental illness' among people who have never been hospitalised or received psychiatric treatment is quite high. In other words, according to psychiatrists, there are a lot of 'mentally ill' people walking the streets. Perhaps the best known of these studies, the Midtown Manhattan Study, found that less than a fifth of the residents they interviewed could be rated psychiatrically well and that between a fifth and a quarter of the population they studied were psychiatrically impaired.[20] The authors of the study interpreted these figures to mean that there is a great unmet need for more psychiatric services. There is, however, another way to look at the results of the Midtown Manhattan Study. The huge numbers of people that the authors of the study felt needed mental health services but weren't receiving them *were managing and functioning in the community.* They weren't screaming in the streets or disrupting their neighbourhood. They were making do, as best they could, like most people, and they did not define their problems and difficulties as psychiatric in nature. What makes mental patients different is not the nature and severity of their problems but that their difficulties have been redefined as psychiatric 'symptoms', requiring professional help. Since more and more kinds of behaviour are being redefined as psychiatric in nature, psychiatry is creating an ever greater 'need' for its services.

The creation of patient-controlled alternatives stands in sharp contrast to the psychiatric system. Instead of creating clear and stigmatising distinctions between those who are competent to give help and those who are weak enough to need it, these alternatives are creating new communities of equals, counteracting the alienation and powerlessness most people rightly sense to be a prime cause of their unhappiness.

NOTES FOR CHAPTER 4

1. Auguste Richard, *The Early Days of Fountain House* (New York: Fountain House, nd), p4.
2. Personal interview with Jordan Hess, July 14, 1977.
3. Personal interview with Sheila Sherman, December 28, 1976.
4. Personal interview with John Beard, December 28, 1976.
5. Bonnie R Bean and John H Beard, 'Placement for Persons with Psychiatric Disability', *Rehabilitation Counselling Bulletin* 18, no4 (June 1975): p253.
6. Personal interview with Bernard Alderman, October 27, 1976.
7. Samuel Grob, 'Psychiatric Social Clubs Come of Age', *Mental Hygiene* 54, no1 (January 1970): pp133, 135, 136.
8. Information and quotations in this paragraph are taken from an untitled, undated, unsigned ten-page mimeographed paper describing Center Club and given to me during my visit.
9. Mabel Palmer, *The Social Club* (New York: National Association for Mental Health, 1966), p8.
10. David H Briggs, *Consumer's Guide to Psychiatric Medication* (New York: Project Release, 1975).
11. 'Project Release: A Statement of Purpose', nd
12. Joyce Kasinsky 'Why Am I in Project Release?' *Silent No Longer! The Newsletter of Project Release* 1, no4 (n d): p6-7.
13. 'What's Happening', *Silent No Longer! The Newsletter of Project Release* 1, no5 (nd): p1.
14. Anthony Brandt, *Reality Police* (New York: William Morrow & Company, 1975), p168.
15. Ibid
16. Ibid, p170
17. Ibid, p171.
18. D L Rosenhan, 'On Being Sane in Insane Places', *Science* 179 (January 19,1973): p252.

19. Maurice K Temerlin, 'Suggestion Effects in Psychiatric Diagnosis', in *The Making of a Mental Patient,* ed. Richard H Price and Bruce Denner (New York: Holt, Rinehart and Winston, 1973), p235.
20. Leo Srole et al, *Mental Health in the Metropolis: The Midtown Manhattan Study* (New York: McGraw-Hill Book Company, 1962), pp143-144.

Chapter Five

When People go Crazy

There are no commonly accepted definitions, among either phsysicians or the general public, of *mental health* and *mental illness.* The kinds of behaviour that get labelled mental illness are deviant acts that don't fit into neat categories, such as 'crime' or 'immorality'. Sociologist David Mechanic has concluded that 'mental illness is regarded usually as a residual category for deviant behaviour having no clearly specified label'.[1] Calling certain kinds of deviance 'illness' is a widely accepted convention in this society, but rather than conceding that it is just a theoretical construct, most people accept it as a scientifically verifiable fact. Most of the scientific literature about mental illness is biased in just this way; the possibility that the behaviour being described might be explained in other ways than by calling it mental illness is not even considered.

Psychiatrists can have expertise in 'diagnosing' and 'treating' mental illness only if it truly is an illness; otherwise psychiatrists are merely making moral pronouncements about behaviour disguised as objective medical opinions. By calling some kinds of behaviour mental illness, psychiatrists invalidate any meaning that behaviour might have, since the behaviour is merely a 'symptom'. It is, of course, possible that by calling some behaviour mental illness, psychiatrists are obscuring the causes even as they attempt to explain them. As psychiatrist Thomas Szasz has observed:

> The term 'schizophrenia' is supposed to explain so-called insane behaviour just as the term 'protoplasm' was supposed to explain the nature of life, and 'ether' the transmission of energy through space. Not only have these

words failed to explain the phenomena in question, but
... they hindered our understanding. We realise today that
words like 'ether' and 'protoplasm' obscured important
problems in physics and biology; but we fail to realise that
words like 'schizophrenia' and 'psychosis' might obscure
important problems in psychiatry.[2]

Szasz calls these terms panchrestons — words that seem to
explain all, yet explain nothing. Only history, Szasz of course
concedes, will judge whether *schizophrenia* is a term that
obscures more than it explains, but he offers forceful arguments
for the essential meaninglessness of the term.

Szasz has also offered persuasive arguments for the essential
similarity between the treatment of witches in the past and the
present treatment of mental patients:

> In actuality, Institutional Psychiatry is a continuation of
> the Inquisition. All that has really changed is the
> vocabulary and the social style. The vocabulary conforms
> to the intellectual expectations of our age. It is a
> pseudomedical jargon that parodies the concepts of
> science.[3]

What Szasz does by questioning the concepts that many people
in contemporary society accept without questioning is to attempt
to shake us out of conventional ways of thinking and encourage
us to examine these questions for ourselves. It is impossible
to summarise adequately Szasz's voluminous and exciting body
of work. Readers are encouraged to familiarise themselves with
it and assess it.

Defenders of the medical model of psychiatry tend to be quite
dogmatic. The history of psychiatry is frequently presented as
a record of steady progress out of a previously benighted period
in which the insane were persecuted, followed by the dawning
of an enlightenment in which the insane became recognised as

ill and as proper subjects for beneficial psychiatric treatment. [4] That the 'insane' might have objections to their 'treatment' is either ignored or presented as evidence of illness, which is a form of circular reasoning.

A spirited defence of the medical model of mental illness is sociologist Miriam Siegler's and psychiatrist Humphry Osmond's *Models of Madness, Models of Medicine.* In a nearly three-hundred-page work, Siegler and Osmond never discuss the problem of involuntary treatment. In their fairy-tale world, so-called schizophrenics 'present themselves for help, either to a private physician or psychiatrist in his office, or in a hospital admitting office' [5] — hardly the way most mental patients come to the attention of psychiatrists. It is interesting to note that Szasz, whom Siegler and Osmond denounce, treats only those patients who come to him voluntarily. Siegler and Osmond argue that the medical model, better than any other model of explaining deviant behaviour, fulfills 'the first rule of medicine — to do the sick no harm', [6] ignoring the long history of agonising (and discredited) 'medical' treatments for mental illness (and also ignoring their own circular reasoning). Mental illness is an illness because it is diagnosed and treated by psychiatrists, they argue, totally ignoring the historic social control functions of psychiatry and mental institutions.

In the medical model of mental illness, human emotions are transformed into symptoms. Behaviour has meaning in the context of people's lives; psychiatric labeling separates out certain behaviours and calls them part of a disease process. It is impossible to understand what is going on in the life of a person in crisis if his or her behaviour is discredited in this way. People behaving in unusual ways are not helped to understand what is going on by the psychiatric labeling process. And despite the arguments of Siegler and Osmond and other defenders of the medical model, psychiatric labeling is an inherently stigmatising process. People fear the 'mentally ill'; and the distress felt by a person in crisis is magnified by the drawing away of those around him or her at a time when he or she most needs closeness and emotional support.

Nor is 'mental illness' a morally neutral term. As Szasz has pointed out:

'Schizophrenia' is a strategic label, like 'Jew' was in Nazi Germany. If you want to exclude people from the social order, you must justify this to others, but especially to yourself. So you invent a justificatory rhetoric. That's what the really nasty psychiatric words are all about: they are justificatory rhetoric, labelling a package 'garbage'; it means 'take it away!' 'get it out of my sight!' etc. That's what the word 'Jew' meant in Nazi Germany; it did not mean a person with a certain kind of religious belief. It meant 'vermin', 'gas him!' I am afraid that 'schizophrenia' and 'sociopathic personality' and many other psychiatric diagnostic terms mean exactly the same thing; they mean 'human garbage', 'take him away!' 'get him out of my sight!'[7]

Or, as an ex-mental patient puts it, 'If mental illness is an illness like any other, which I don't believe it is, the illness it most resembles is VD'.[8]

A person is suspected of being mentally ill most often because his or her behaviour disturbs other people. Because of the stigma, being labelled mentally ill is an eventuality people attempt to avoid, and those who end up with the label are those with the least power to resist. Terming someone mentally ill is a judgement by others that one is not behaving up to expectations.

Of course, people do experience difficulties in their lives, and may often respond by behaving in strange or frightening ways. Contemporary American society, with its emphasis on competition and individual accomplishment, makes extremely high performance demands. People who aren't 'successful' (whether financially, in their careers, or in their personal relationships) are made to feel that their failure is their own fault, attributable to some flaw or deficiency. Even people who appear to others to be financially or emotionally secure may be plagued with doubts and insecurities. But explaining human unhappiness in medical terms is still nothing but a hypothesis, one which minimises the possibility that people can change, grow, and develop.

My own experiences with 'mental illness' illustrate the nonutility of the medical model, as do those of many other former patients. As I have more fully described in Chapter 2, on two occasions, about eight years apart, I experienced the intense distress, depersonalisation, and sense of unreality that is often described as the onset of acute psychosis. During the first experience, believing that I needed medical help, I voluntarily admitted myself to a mental hospital. For six months I was in and out of hospitals (several times involuntarily), was given large doses of 'tranquillising' drugs, and was generally made into a mental patient. I was told, and I believed, that my feelings of unhappiness were indications of mental illness. At one point, a hospital psychiatrist told me that I would never be able to live outside a mental institution. By the time of my final discharge I was convinced of my own inferiority, a feeling that lasted for years.

The second experience was different. Although I was gripped with terror, I was able to recognise that I was not 'mentally ill' and that what I needed was not psychiatric treatment but warm human contact. Fortunately, an alternative in the form of a residential crisis centre was available, the Vancouver Emotional Emergency Center, and over a two-and-a-half week period, I lived through an intense emotional experience culminating in a spiritual rebirth that has had lasting effects on my life. When I was defined as 'ill', I felt 'ill', and I remained 'ill' for years, convinced of my own helplessness. In an atmosphere that emphasised nurturance I was able to grow.

Mental hospitals as they currently exist cannot provide this atmosphere of nurturance and growth. If the whole rhetoric of illness and pathology means anything, it means that parts of people's personalities are defective and diseased, fit only for medical tinkering. The reliance on medical expertise leads to passive patients submitting to 'treatments' such as the heavy use of psychiatric drugs, which is often perceived by the patients as torture. But patients cannot object to treatment without bringing on more treatment. Only agreeing that one is indeed ill and in need of help brings the possibility of ending the treatment. Mental patients are caught in a vicious circle, where their own feelings are discredited (unless they are in agreement with the psychiatric viewpoint).

Situations that often end in mental hospitalisations involve emotional conflict, and it is the weakest participant who risks ending up as a mental patient. The process of psychiatric diagnosis and hospitalisation is about power far more than it is about medicine. Even people who enter hospitals voluntarily, believing themselves ill, have already gone through a process of defining their problems as psychiatric in nature. Again, it is often the least powerful of the people involved in a situation who come to the conclusion that the cause of the problem is their own mental illness. People who end up as mental patients are people in trouble — with their family, their job, or the community at large. A diagnosis of mental illness lets everybody else off the hook — the mental illness of one participant is responsible for whatever difficulties or conflicts have been occurring. Business can go on as usual. That a particular family or relationship or job might be truly intolerable is not even considered as a possibility. The illness model means that once the sick individual has undergone psychiatric repair, he or she should return and fit smoothly into his or her old life. Further signs of disruption or dissatisfaction can easily be redefined as relapses requiring further medical treatment.

Institutional psychiatry works to preserve the status quo.

Psychiatric 'reality' is defined in the most conventional terms. Making drastic and unconventional life choices is frequently cited as evidence of mental illness. A wife who leaves her husband and children, a homosexual deciding to 'come out', an adolescent moving away from home — all these are undoubtedly crises, but are they medical ones? When psychiatry gets involved in situations such as these, it is clearly dealing with morals far more than with medicine. Defining the rebellious person as sick invalidates his or her perception of the situation — his or her personal reality. Only the testimony of the 'sane' parties to the situation is accepted as reality. In these kinds of situations, where the emotions of all parties run high, it is quite natural to expect that each person will have a different view of what is happening. Invalidating the personal perception of the weakest participant by psychiatric labeling is a demand for conformity masked by medical terminology.

A dramatic example of this kind of invalidation is found in a personal account by Dianne Jennings Walker:

> My life story differs in only very particular details from the stories of so many other women who have been labelled schizophrenic. I could escape the label today; I could 'pass'. When I chose in 1975 not to pass, it was the most nurturing thing I have ever done for myself. For once I feel that my mind, soul and body are *mine*. I was lied to for so many years that I still fear the feeling of being split apart from my body. This so-called symptom of schizophrenia is what happens to us when the perceptions we have of our environment are attacked and ignored and denied over and over again. Ironically, our perceptions are accurate. Even after we are terrorised, drugged or socialized out of expressing ourselves directly we do it symbolically and the feelings are right. I believed as a child that my soul had been stolen from its rightful body, that my real parents lived on a satellite of Betelgeuse. That was not an insane delusion. It was a poetic and actually

logical way to handle the unliveable environment that I had the ill fate to be born into.

In my late teens I discovered psychology and psychiatry, which I believed for many years were my salvation. I read case histories in college textbooks and thought, 'Oh wonderful: I'm not from another planet ... I'm simply crazy!'

Meanwhile my parents' marriage was publicly dissolved. The private dissolution came much earlier. Other long-standing family problems were also kept secret. Oh yes, we had good taste. From time to time I would point out things were not well with us, that, for example, my father and older sister had not spoken to each other in about two years. This was met with any of the following; grunts, silence, hysteria, abrupt change of subject, an assertion that our family was normal, a suggestion that I not worry, an accusation of ingratitude. Every so often my mother would say, 'Where did I get this strange child. She must have come from another planet'. Whenever she said that it naturally reawakened my desire to return to my real home in the constellation Orion. Of course I didn't tell anybody. I mean you just can't tell anybody that. Except your friendly shrink.

I went voluntarily to several psychotherapists. I even, God help me, went voluntarily into the insanery. I was suicidal and sought refuge in a private Catholic asylum. I imitated Lisa of the movie *David and Lisa*. I had planned on resting for three weeks. I was discharged one year, ten months and eleven days later, my doctor's pride and joy because evidently I had been cured of schizophrenia....

For a long time I was so grateful to have my story listened to, so grateful that I was kept in the insanery that I did not notice the crimes being committed against me. My hospital psychiatrist met with my parents, older sister, and brother-in-law in various combinations. He failed to meet with them when I was present. Had he done so, perhaps he could have given me moral support to challenge the way I was treated. He remarked that my history was much like that of other people who had had childhood schizophrenia. Three years after I began seeing him he said, 'Everything you told me about your family is true'. I was happy to be validated and did not think to demand my money back or to demand an apology for being called crazy.

Years passed. My relatives never admitted their complicity. I was alternately regarded as sick and as uncharitable for bringing up the past. The terrifying feelings returned. I sought help from a psychologist, then turned to another psychiatrist. I said, 'I feel like I'm falling off the earth and I think my mother hates me'. He asked, 'Does that really bother you?'...

Psychotherapy oppresses us by teaching us that we are sick, crazy, maladjusted. We should forget grandiose and paranoid ideas (such as that) some societies just aren't worth adjusting to. My last psychiatrist couldn't understand why I wanted to work and be friends only with people who knew I was an ex-patient. He said, 'I don't understand your obsession with honesty'. He and another psychiatrist, who was allegedly radical, told me I was not going to change the world by being militantly ex-crazy. Maybe not. Then again I hear there are more than twenty million of us in this country alone.[9]

When people are caught in such emotional tangles, everyone reacts in characteristic ways. These reactions can be defined as either normal or sick; the making of this decision is moral judgement disguised as medical diagnosis. 'Sick' is only another way of saying 'wrong'. What makes it worse is that everyone (except possibly the 'crazy' person) denies what is going on.

A poignant instance of this process is shown in the documentary film *Hurry Tomorrow*[10], which was shot in California state mental hospital in 1975. One of the patients whose story is portrayed is a middle-aged fireman who, because of a heart condition, has been forced to retire. He cannot adjust to this enforced idleness, and his wife cannot adjust to having him at home all day. One day the wife, believing that her husband is planning to commit suicide, calls the police, and the man is taken against his will to the state hospital. He is unable to make anyone believe that he is not suicidal. The ward psychiatrist tells him that he will not be discharged until he admits his suicidal feelings. He tries to refuse medication, claiming he is not sick, and is forcibly injected. During a visit, he begs his wife and daughter to allow him to come home. 'You can come home', his wife tells him, 'when you are well'. The man's continual protests that he is not sick are seen by both the doctor and the family as confirmation of just how mentally ill he really is. Only by accepting his wife's version of the emotionally charged events between them will he be defined as well.

Hurry Tomorrow is filmed evidence that supposedly modern and progressive mental hospitals are different only in their outward appearance from the snake pits that (nearly everyone will concede) mental hospitals used to be. The ward we are shown is clean and airy; the dayroom has a TV set and a pool table; there seems to be plenty of staff. The horrors are subtle. Most of the patients wander about in a daze; a veteran patient explains to a newcomer that the stupor is caused by the psychiatric drugs they are receiving. The staff members lock patients into tiny rooms or tie them by wrists and ankles to beds. A slight, Mexican-American youth begs in broken English not to be locked in, then the door closes in his face. Patients being held against their will insist that they are being held prisoner, only to be told by the ward psychiatrist that they must abandon such ideas in order to be considered well. The psychiatrist has the power to determine the authorised version of reality.

'Brainwashing' is the emotionally laden term used to describe certain kinds of psychological manipulation. Only indoctrination in unauthorised versions of reality is labelled brainwashing; indoctrination in the ways and mores of the prevailing culture is called education or moral training. Psychiatric treatment is a method of socially acceptable indoctrination; calling it brainwashing is likely to be taken as a sign of paranoia.

Psychiatric medication can be viewed similarly. Brainwashing a person by means of drugs is looked on as reprehensible. Drugs, euphemistically called psychiatric medication, are given to patients (often against their will) with the avowed purpose of changing their 'sick' thoughts, and the process is called treatment.

Modern mental hospitals, where every method of control has been euphemistically renamed, can be frightening places. The actions of every staff member — the aide who holds a patient down, the nurse who injects the medication, the doctor who prescribed it — all have been defined as benevolent. Patients who dare to utter the unauthorised reality — that they are prisoners and that their 'helpers' are jailers — only provide further evidence that they are indeed ill. Succumbing to brainwashing, accepting reality as defined by one's captors, differs from a psychiatric 'cure' only because in the latter case the accepted reality is the prevailing one. Holding a minority position makes a person a potential subject for psychiatric brainwashing.

When is it brainwashing and when not? The Patty Hearst case provides an interesting example. When she was being held prisoner by the Symbionese Liberation Army, Hearst made a series of tape recordings. At first, she begged her parents to help her, but in later tapes she denounced them as fascists and capitalist pigs. Public reaction was that she had been brainwashed by her SLA captors. When Hearst was captured by the FBI and jailed, she initially retained her SLA beliefs;

listing her occupation as 'urban guerrilla' and telling an old school friend that she was committed to feminism and revolution.

Patricia Hearst's family and defence lawyers claimed that her actions after she decided to join the SLA were the result of brainwashing, and a number of psychiatrists were engaged by the defence to examine her. From newspaper reports, it appears that Hearst at first refused the psychiatric examinations, claiming that they were in violation of her rights. It also appears that she was given psychiatric medication while in jail. By the time of her trial for bank robbery, Patty Hearst had changed her views. She now claimed that the SLA had indeed brainwashed her, charges she had previously angrily denied.

One of the psychiatrists in the Hearst case, Louis Jolyon West, had been involved in an unsuccessful attempt to start the Center for the Study of the Reduction of Violence at the University of California at Los Angeles, which would have used experimental techniques, such as psychosurgery and aversion therapy, on prisoners labelled violent. West was well known for his views that participants in ghetto rebellions were exhibiting symptoms of mental illness, as were people who chose a hippie life-style. Of course, with these preconceptions, it would have been difficult for West even to consider the possibility that Hearst had chosen voluntarily to stay with the SLA.

When Patty Hearst mouthed the rhetoric of the SLA, it was called brainwashing. When she instead mouthed psychiatric slogans, the charge of brainwashing did not come up. This is not to say that Hearst may not have been psychologically coerced by the SLA; it is only to point out that she may have also been coerced by her family, her lawyers, and her psychiatrists. Only the SLA's 'treatment' was called brainwashing, because only the SLA espoused radical and unpopular causes. Psychiatric 'treatment,' on the other hand, which Hearst possibly tried to reject, was seen as a neutral force, rather than one that implicitly espouses a particular version of reality.

A number of people, including many psychiatrists, also claim as victims of brainwashing people who have converted to the Unification Church, the Hare Krishnas, and other religious sects. There have been a number of cases in recent years of parents kidnapping their adult sons and daughters from the sects with which they were living, imprisoning them in hotel rooms, and 'deprogramming' them of their alleged brainwashing. Clearly, a form of semantic mystification is in use here, since one kind of coercion is being called by the sinister name of brainwashing, while another form of coercion, of which the speaker approves, is given the far more neutral name of deprogramming. Advocates of deprogramming claim that their method is successful, but many of their successfully treated 'cases' continue to espouse their unpopular ideas once they are free of psychiatric control. The American Civil Liberties Union has called deprogramming a serious threat to freedom of religion in the United States. Only the extreme cults are threatened now, but deprogramming sets a dangerous precedent for dealing with religious dissent, and ultimately other kinds of dissent.

When psychiatrists label as brainwashed people who express minority political or religious opinions, they are taking a moral position and disguising it as objective medical diagnosis. People *may* be coerced into joining cults; but they may also be coerced into joining established religious or political groups without risking the possibility of being kidnapped and 'deprogrammed'. Only when they join small and unpopular groups are they considered brainwashed.

Many former mental patients refer to their institutionalisation as 'brainwashing' and 'torture', even though, as patients, they went along with what was done to them. Patients who complain to their doctors that they are being brainwashed are frequently called paranoid; only those who go along with the psychiatric reality (that they are ill and need psychiatric treatment) are considered on the road to recovery. Like religious and political dissidents, mental patients are thought to need incarceration and curative 'treatment' because they see reality in unauthorised ways.

Psychiatric mystification makes it extremely difficult to see that the protests of its victims might have any validity. Modern mental institutions cosmetically disguise every facet of coercion. Isolation cells are called seclusion rooms or quiet rooms (in at least one institution, 'the blue room'). Drugs (bad) are called medication (good). Psychiatric medication has been referred to as the chemical straitjacket, but real straitjackets are far from outmoded, although they are euphemistically called 'restraints' or 'camisoles'. When doors have been unlocked, patients are punished (although it is not, of course, called punishment) for walking through them without permission. And the locked door, often said to be a thing of the past, is very much present. On one psychiatric ward where I was a patient, there were no locked doors, but we were required to wear pyjamas at all times, and our clothes were kept in locked closets. Although not locked in, we were neatly prevented from leaving.

The availability of 'therapy' varies from hospital to hospital, but all therapies have in common that the ideas and actions of the patient must be changed. The moral questions raised by the involuntary status of most patients are seldom considered. The patient's ideas of what is wrong are often given less credence than the psychiatrist's assessment.

Psychiatrists often attempt to enforce rigid adherence to traditional sex roles, calling any deviation 'sick'. Bette Maher recalls going to a staff presentation conference (for which patients had another name):

> I had to wait in a small crowded corridor with about twenty other new patients. I waited for more than two hours for my turn. I watched each patient come out from the Inquisition — each one looking as if he'd been demolished. I knew I had to play it cool when my turn came. When

> I walked in, I was as composed as possible. I saw the clinical director of the hospital, Dr. Benjamin Simon, sitting by himself at the end of a long table. Surrounding him, crushed together, were about fifty staff members. I sat down at the table without being invited to do so. Dr. Simon's first question was, 'Why isn't an attractive girl like you married yet?'[11]

Cynthia Cekala consulted a psychiatrist after she decided to drop out of graduate school. The psychiatrist was alarmed by her sexual relationships and recreational drug use and urged her admittance to a mental hospital. 'Only now after I have seen my records do I know why I was sent up ... My admitting diagnosis was 'Sexual acting-out — if not hospitalised might get pregnant or get VD'.[12]

> Throughout my stay there I wore what I had worn at school — boots and jeans and sweaters. The shrink told me that if I didn't give up being a hippie and wear skirts I could not be considered to be cured. In my records I was 'masculine'.... I nagged my parents to get me out. I wore skirts with a wrathful submission. Finally I was sent to my doctor. He asked me what I was going to do when I got out. I said I was going to get a job at Bell Telephone and go back to graduate school in the fall. I felt that peculiar tightening of the throat one feels when lying outright, and though I kept my eyes unblinking, fastened on his face throughout, I felt he knew I was lying. He didn't. 'Patient is better motivated toward life.' I got released a week later.[13]

Bette Maher didn't see herself as needing marriage, and Cynthia Cekala didn't think she needed a job with the telephone company to prove that they were healthy women, but their psychiatrists had the power to label them sick because they did not conform to conventional female stereotypes.

Similarly, homosexual patients are called sick as long as they express their unconventional sexual preferences; and whatever problems they may have are commonly attributed to their homosexuality. Although the American Psychiatric Association eliminated 'homosexuality' as an official diagnosis in 1973 a new diagnosis of 'sexual orientation disturbance' was created, which referred to homosexuals 'who are either disturbed by, in conflict with, or wish to change their sexual orientation'.[15]

Mental hospitals tend to call therapy everything that goes on inside them — making the beds and sweeping the floor can be called 'industrial therapy', going to a dance or movie 'recreational therapy', stupefying patients with drugs 'chemotherapy', and so forth. Custodial mental hospitals, which offer little treatment, frequently make reference to 'millieu therapy', as if the very hospital air were somehow curative. But the availability of more treatment would not improve things much. A horrifying example of the 'treatment' provided at one of the country's most highly reputed mental hospitals — the Menninger Foundation in Topeka, Kansas — can be found in the story of Sarah, which appears in Anthony Brandt's *Reality Police*.

Sarah was committed by her parents at the age of nineteen and spent three and a half years in the institution. For the first year she refused to co-operate with any part of the treatment, which she accurately perceived as being designed solely to break her will. When she finally agreed to talk to the doctor, she found he was unwilling to listen to her own ideas about her problems, and she quickly gave up trying to talk to him, except to try to get 'privileges'. (In mental hospitalese, 'privileges' are such basic human rights as wearing one's own clothes, being able to walk around outside, going to the dining room, and so forth.) After she became twenty-one, Sarah attempted to sign herself out of the hospital, which legally she had the right to do. However, they refused to release her until she got her parents' consent. Shortly after her discharge Sarah's parents, still displeased with her way of life (she was living with a black man and planning to marry him), had her committed to Topeka State Hospital, a truly grim institution, where she was kept in a seclusion room for nine months. Eventually, she managed to escape, and is living successfully on her own. Sarah's assessment of the two 'hospitals' where she was imprisoned is illuminating:

> As compared to my experiences at Topeka State, Menninger's was more destructive and painful through its more subtle yet undermining techniques. In the state hospital faced with a harsh reality you had to work hard physically and otherwise to keep up with it. Menninger's on the other hand led to a total disintegration of personality and personal autonomy. [16]

Treatment aimed at restructuring the personality of unwilling subjects is rightfully viewed by them as torture.

The important thing about Sarah's story is that her experience is not unique. Mistreatment takes many forms — anything from insensitivity by staff members to outright physical brutality — and it is far too common. Even isolated instances of mistreatment should be intolerable in a system devoted to healing the sick. But a great deal of evidence seems to show that mental hospitals exist to control their inmates. What happens to mental patients, just as what happens to prisoners, arouses little concern. And because mental patients are supposed to be mentally ill, out of touch with reality, their testimony carries little weight. Ex-patient Kenneth Donaldson ironically defines various 'substrains of schizophrenia, such as 'being unco-operative' (refusing to buy an attendant a pack of cigarettes), 'being emotionally volatile' (telling an attendant to go to hell when he accused you of having sexual relations with your mother), and 'having hallucinations' (saying an attendant broke your arm when the report says you fell)'. [17] In his book, Donaldson describes his fifteen years of horror in Florida State Hospital, culminating in a landmark Supreme Court decision that nondangerous mental patients have a Constitutional right to liberty.

Brutality is not incidental to institutional psychiatric treatment. The history of mental hospitals is the history of the various tortures that have been perpetrated on the insane. Benjamin Rush, a signer of the Declaration of Independence, is sometimes called the Father of American Psychiatry. He ran one of the earliest mental hospitals in the United States, the Pennsylvania Hospital, from 1783 to 1813. His picture appears on the seal of the American Psychiatric Association. Among the treatments recommended by Rush were venesection — bleeding (at that time one of the leading medical treatments for many illnesses), purges and emetics (also popular as general medical treatment), hot and cold showers, and the application of two of Rush's inventions, the 'tranquilliser' and the 'gyrator'.[18] Deutsch describes the 'tranquilliser' as 'a chair to which the patient was strapped hand and foot, together with a device for holding the head in a fixed position'.[19] The 'gyrator' was a board to which the patient was strapped; it was then rotated rapidly, causing blood to rush to the head.[20] Deutsch describes a number of 'treatments' popular in Rush's time, noting frankly that they were 'ingenious mechanisms for terrorisation'.[21] In one 'treatment', the 'patient' was immobilized while a powerful pump directed a stream of water onto the spine for four minutes. Or a patient might be placed on a trap door that concealed a pool of water. At the proper therapeutic moment the trap door would be released and the patient plunged into the 'bath of surprise'.[22] Another 'treatment' consisted of placing the patient in a box pierced with many holes, which was then immersed in water. Understandably, the patient had to be revived after the box was fished out again.[23] Deutsch is not horrified by these practices: 'Strangely enough, tortures and terrors that had been applied as outright punishments in previous ages received in this particular age the blessing of respectable medical theory as praiseworthy therapeutic measures'.[24] In Thomas Szasz's view, however, it is not strange at all. It becomes completely comprehensible once we recognise mental illness as 'a successor notion to heresy; psychiatrists as ... successor-enforcers to the inquisitors; and psychiatric interventions as ... successor-punishments to inquisitorial tortures'.[25]

In standard psychiatric histories, Phillippe Pinel's striking the chains from inmates of the French mental institution he ran after the French Revolution is presented as 'liberating' the patients. Historian Michel Foucault presents another view. 'It is within the walls of confinement that Pinel and nineteenth-century psychiatry would come upon madmen; it is there — let us remember — that they would leave them, not without boasting of having 'delivered' them'.[26] According to Foucault, Pinel favoured psychiatric confinement for three broad categories of people: religious fanatics, people who refused to work, and thieves.[27] Although no longer physically chained to the walls, inmates of Pinel's institution were subject to coercion and forced 'treatment'.

Modern methods of treatment can also be viewed both as treatments (by those who administer them) and as tortures (by those who receive them). Because psychiatric treatments are so often administered against the will of their subject, it is very difficult to accept unquestioningly the often stated views of psychiatrists that these treatments are both painless and beneficial. Nowadays, the most common method of psychiatric treatment, both in and out of hospitals, is the administration of psychiatric drugs. While psychiatrists have speculated that they are correcting disordered brain chemistry by means of these drugs, there is no proof that this is so, and there are as many different theories as to how psychiatric drugs work as there are research psychiatrists.

Psychopharmacologists frequently compare their drugs to insulin, which controls diabetes although it does not cure it. This analogy, although widely accepted, is flawed. Insulin is naturally produced in the body; some people (diabetics) are deficient in it. When diabetics take insulin, their body chemistry is restored to a more nearly normal state. No one, however, naturally produces Thorazine or lithium; these drugs are given to people based on a pharmacological theory that their body chemistry is, in some unknown way, abnormal. Megavitamins, another 'treatment' for 'mental illness', have the virtue of being less dangerous than tranquillisers and related drugs, but there is no proof that 'schizophrenics' suffer from vitamin deficiencies, either. All drug treatments for mental illness are based on unproven theory.

Out of the laboratory and onto the wards, and things begin to appear a bit different. Anthony Brandt, who tells Sarah's story in *Reality Police,* signed himself into a mental hospital as part of the research for his book. After a brief interview with a psychiatrist, in which he claimed to be hearing voices, he was turned over to two aides and a nurse. Without explanation, he was given an injection.

> It was the drug, however, which really took me over. Serintil is a powerful, fast-acting tranquilliser used for the immediate treatment of hallucinatory symptoms. It also has powerful side-effects. I could not sleep after the aide put me to bed.... After about an hour I got up for a drink of water and staggered out to the hall. But why am I staggering? I thought. What is happening to me? I couldn't control my legs. I was weaving back and forth like a drunk reaching for walls. Sweating and scared, I barely made it to the water fountain. I had no strength in my body at all. On the way back to bed I fell down twice.... The drug was not designed specifically to transform people into jellyfish. Nevertheless, there was no question of my giving the staff trouble while under its influence.[28]

It is not just in the area of drug administration that what actually goes on in mental hospitals differs so drastically from the theoretical formulations of psychiatrists, whose writings frequently indicate an ivory-tower view of psychiatric treatment. Psychiatrists often state that straitjackets are historical relics;

meanwhile, patients on the wards are frequently placed in them. Psychiatric historian Gregory Zilboorg, writing in 1941, stated that 'the number of people without special training who take care of mental patients is now almost negligible'.[29] As Zilboorg was writing, conscientious objectors in the United States were assigned to staff mental hospital wards, not because of any special interest or inclination, but because the work was considered sufficiently unpleasant to be a suitable punishment for those who refused to fight. Innumerable examples of the discrepancies between the psychiatric view of the mental hospital and the experiences of mental hospital workers and patients could be supplied.

For many years psychiatrists thought that the deterioration seen in their 'chronic schizophrenic' patients (that is, patients who had been labelled schizophrenic and who remained in the hospital for many years) was an inevitable effect of the disease process. It now appears, however, that long-term residence in a mental institution is what causes the loss of social skills, the lack of interest in the outside world, and the stuporousness that were previously attributed to schizophrenia. J K Wing and G W Brown, who studied the patients in three British mental hospitals over an eight-year period, concluded that, 'The various stages of this study point towards a conclusion which is very difficult to resist — that a substantial proportion, though by no means all, of the morbidity shown by long-stay schizophrenic patients in mental hospitals is a product of their environment'.[30] Patients who spend long periods of time in mental hospitals become 'institutionalised' — they adapt, as best they can, to the limited world within the institution.

As psychiatrists themselves came to recognise how harmful mental institutionalisation can be, some of them began devising 'alternatives'. The therapeutic community was introduced by Maxwell Jones in England in the late 1940s and early 1950s and was widely hailed by the psychiatric profession as providing a real change in treatment, one that would involve the patient in his or her own recovery rather than making the person a passive resident of a hospital. As described by Jones:

> In a therapeutic community the whole of a patient's time spent in hospital is thought of as treatment. Treatment to be effective will not only involve the handling of the individual's neurotic problems, but also an awareness of the fresh problems which the fact of being in a neurosis hospital will create for the patient, and what aspects of the social situation can be used to aid treatment. The patient, the social milieu in which he lives and works, and the hospital community of which he becomes temporarily a member, are all important and interact on each other.[31]

But in Jones's own glowing account of his new methods, we find that things have not changed very much at all from the patients' point of view:

> Modified insulin treatment is used extensively, and there are always a few patients on electrical convulsive therapy. Abreactive techniques with ether or sodium amytal are used very occasionally, as is the operation of leucotomy (a form of psychosurgery). Insulin coma treatment is used fairly frequently....[32]

> A placement conference is held weekly, and attended by all members of the staff of the unit.... The patient himself is interviewed by the conference when this is considered necessary.[33]

Patients in this 'alternative' were subjected to physically intrusive treatments and were discussed at staff conferences from which they were excluded, the same kinds of procedures that patients find objectionable in more traditional facilities. Jones does not even discuss whether patient consent was obtained for hospitalisation or for treatment.[34]

Therapeutic communities are usually described in the psychiatric literature as places where strict roles (doctor, nurse, patient) are broken down and all members of the community are equally involved in decision making. But psychiatrist Joe Berke, who worked in one, saw things somewhat differently:

> At best, (the therapeutic community allowed) the staff and patients a large measure of self determination. They then got on with their daily lives as best they could, and with the knowledge that all the rules of interpersonal behaviour were open to question and that definite channels of communications existed among all concerned. A community had been created.

> At worst, the programme degenerated into organised brain-washing. Patients were supposed to talk honestly about their feelings, and were often punished for what they said, but the staff was under no pressure to do so. Power remained in the hands of the administrator, although everyone would be told that the group was free and open. Minor trappings of therapeutic community life, like men and women patients meetings together, and being allowed to wear their own clothes, substituted for the basic issues of personal autonomy and sexual identity.

> Unfortunately, $99 \cdot 44/100\%$ of the programmes that laboured under the aegis of 'therapeutic community' were of this latter variety.[35]

My own experience in a 'therapeutic community' was far closer to Joe Berke's view than to Maxwell Jones's. As a patient in a hospital following the therapeutic community model, I found that the doctors frequently made authoritative statements but misleadingly phrased these as coming from 'the group', even though they were clearly coming directly from the psychiatrists.[36] The most notable example occurred when a patient on the ward committed suicide while on a weekend leave (mentioned earlier, in Chapter 2). The ward meeting on Monday morning began with the doctors entering together after the other staff members and patients had already assembled. One of the doctors then made a peculiar series of statements. 'The group is quite upset by Bill's death.' None of us had yet had a chance to express our feelings. 'Everyone is feeling insecure, since the hospital is supposed to be a safe place where people are protected from their suicidal feelings.' There was no chance to find out whether or not that was true, since he quickly went on, 'In order to help everyone to feel more secure, the group has decided to lock the ward for the next few weeks'. The group, of course, had decided nothing. The psychiatrists had decided, but by attributing their actions to 'the group', they were mystifying the source of power within the group, causing the patients to doubt their own perceptions of what had gone on.

The next innovations in mental hospitals also came from England. Psychiatrists David Cooper and R D Laing experimented with changes in hospital wards that they ran. Cooper ran 'Villa 21', a nineteen-bed ward in a British mental hospital, from 1962 to 1966, and tried to break down the usual staff hierarchy, as well as staff responsibility for every aspect of patients' lives. Patients and staff ate meals together, and patients were permitted to call staff members by their first names (both starting innovations at that time in traditional staff/patient relations). Cooper realised, however, that the role distinctions were expressions of real differences: 'Staff are paid to be there, patients are not'.[37] Cooper's suggestion that ex-patients be employed as staff on the ward met with official disapproval. After four years, Cooper recognised the limitations of innovation within the mental hospital framework:

> The 'experiment' of the unit has had one quite certain 'result' and one certain 'conclusion'. The result is the establishment of the limits of institutional change, and these limits are found to be very closely drawn indeed — even in a progressive mental hospital. The conclusion is that

if such a unit is to develop further, the development must take place outside the confines of the larger institution.[38]

Early in his career, R D Laing also introduced innovations within a mental hospital setting. He selected twelve long-term out-of-contact patients who had been diagnosed as schizophrenic and brought them together in a large room, where they were treated with dignity and respect and were able to do as they liked. The first day the patients were led to the room and were led back to their wards in the evening. The second day there was a dramatic change. All twelve of the patients gathered before the door of the room where they were treated so differently, talking and laughing with each other. Although many of them had been hospitalised for years, within eighteen months all were able to be discharged. But within a year all had returned to the hospital, leading Laing to formulate his theory that 'schizophrenia' is something that is done to the patient by his or her family.[39] Laing soon stopped working in hospital settings.

Laing believes that schizophrenia is not an illness, but a 'metatanoic voyage' — literally, a 'mind-changing' experience.[40] Traditional mental hospitals — indeed, traditional psychiatric practices generally — are set up to thwart this voyage rather than aid it.

Mental hospitals define this voyage as *ipso facto* madness *per se,* and treat it accordingly. The *setting* of a psychiatric clinic and mental hospital promotes in staff and patients the *set* best designed to turn the metanoiac from a voyage of discovery into self of a potentially revolutionary nature and with a potentially liberating outcome, into a catastrophe: into a pathological process from which the person requires to be cured. We asked: what would happen if we began by changing our set and setting, to regard what was happening as a potential healing process through which the person ideally may be guided and during which he is guarded? Essentially it is as simple as that.[41]

Laing and his colleagues, realising that there were limitations to the kinds of meaningful changes that could be made within the hospital, set up a house where patients and staff could live and work together, the famous Kingsley Hall. Mary Barnes, who lived at Kingsley Hall for several years, and experienced the regression and rebirth that Laing believes are the natural outcome of the 'schizophrenic' experience, has written an astonishing book about her experiences. Long before she had ever heard of R D Laing, Mary Barnes realised that she wanted to 'go down' into herself, 'to be reborn, to come up again, straight, and clear of all the mess'.[42] This was impossible in a mental hospital. When she met Laing, Kingsley Hall had not yet been set up, and for more than a year, as she felt herself beginning to 'go down', she held on until the community could be set up. Within days after moving into Kingsley Hall, Mary began to regress, taking to her bed, refusing to eat, drinking milk from a bottle, lying in the dark without talking. She returned to infancy and then began to grow up into a truly different person. Mary discovered a previously unknown artistic talent, and when she left Kingsley Hall, it was to a far more satisfying life as a painter.

Kingsley Hall was not a hospital, it was a large old house in a poor section of London, where people could come to live, to work, to experience a stimulating intellectual atmosphere, and to experience their own madness. In theory, no distinction was to be made between staff and patients. Joe Berke, a psychiatrist who worked with Laing at Kingsley Hall, found that 'many a person came to Kingsley Hall with the idea of helping others in the community and wound up having to be looked after by the community'.[43]

Kingsley Hall was one of a network of houses set up in London by the Philadelphia Association and the Arbours Association, which were run by Laing and people closely associated with him. David Parker, who lived in several Arbours Association residences, tells a somewhat different story of what these 'alternatives' were like:

I was in a house run by the Arbours Association in London. The Arbours Association is a research and training group and a residential centre for persons experiencing distress — often ex-mental patients or people who would have to go into a hospital. Arbours Association was a shrink-run colony. In any decision of any importance the shrinks made the decisions, and you could just forget about the others. The shrinks had their meetings and made all the decisions.

There were some positive things. They were against psychiatric drugs in general, although they did keep one fellow I knew on drugs. The shrinks also had meetings about the patients with the patients not there. I have a tape of a meeting (I got permission from everyone there to tape it) in which they talk about the 'psychopathology' of one particular resident.

There were people who worked in the houses — I always thought of them as stooges for the psychiatrists. One time one of the residents in the house was being criticised for throwing garbage out of the window. The stooge told him he would be kicked out of the house. It was really terrifying — it was done in such a brutal manner. So this resident ran away that night. All the psychiatrists came down to the house and decided to call the police to try to get him back. And this was supposed to be a completely free place where no one was forced to stay.

Another resident — the shrinks who ran Arbours had a meeting about her and decided to put her into a hospital for electroshock. I visited her after the shock treatments, and she didn't even remember me, even though we had lived in the same house for months and had been quite friendly. She didn't even remember me.

The one benefit I got out of staying at Arbours was talking with the other patients.[44]

David Parker's criticisms raise an important and disturbing question. To what degree are psychiatrists willing (or able) to give up their tremendous power over patents? As we have seen, 'therapeutic communities' commonly mislead patients about the distribution of power within the 'community'. The Laingian houses, although they were far more real communities than any hospital ward could ever be, housed people who had taken on roles as different as 'psychiatrist' and 'chronic schizoprenic'. Without conscientious efforts to break down these roles, those used to assuming power will do so, as will those used to yielding it.

Perhaps the whole idea of having psychiatrists living in the house makes true equality impossible. In San Jose, California, Soteria House (based in part on Kingsley Hall) was a place where six 'patients' and four 'guides' lived together. Although set up under psychiatric auspices and employing a social worker as house director and a consulting psychiatrist, the emphasis at Soteria was on nonprofessional staff who could 'be with' the patients, rather than do things *to* them.

Soteria House specifically rejected the medical model, seeing 'schizophrenia' not as a disease but as a 'developmental crisis' with positive learning potential.

> It is believed that by allowing and helping the resident to gradually work with and through this crisis in living, or schizophrenia, he will be better able to understand himself and his fears. So rather than ignoring or quelling this altered state, he will explore it, understand it, and finally learn from it. Our House believes that this growth process may leave him with an even stronger sense of identity than before his episode.[43]

Alma Menn, a social worker who was the live-in director at Soteria House (the name is taken from the Greek word for 'deliverance'), has described life in the house:

We buy food, bake bread, sew, tie-dye, plant our garden,
play ping-pong. Anyone who wants to (can) take a turn
preparing a meal and cleaning up afterwards. We write
diaries, play guitars, sit on the front stoop, collect data,
go to the beach, do yoga and massage, in short, do things
that are necessary and interesting to the people living there.
We have house meetings from time to time to discuss house
problems, such as people using up all the towels,
annoyance at another person's freakiness, people running
away and getting picked up by the cops or getting taken
to the hospital. We have no nursing station, no ground
privileges, no group grounds, no weekend passes, no
medication room.[46]

Soteria House was set up as a research project to compare the
efficacy of a nonprofessional, nonmedical approach with
conventional hospitalisation. Residents formed the 'experimental
group'; a matched 'control group' consisted of patients
hospitalised at a community mental health centre and treated
by drugs and other conventional psychiatric methods.[47] This
procedure raises disturbing (and unanswered) questions about
voluntariness and consent. It appears that the Soteria House
residents were there not because they fit the project criteria
(unmarried, between fifteen and thirty years of age, and not
previously psychiatrically hospitalised) and were randomly
assigned to the experimental group. I have not found any
discussion of this important factor in the published articles by
Soteria's founders. Soteria House, although started by a research
psychiatrist and funded by the National Institute of Mental
Health, is, nevertheless, an alternative because it rejects the usual
psychiatric dehumanisation and invalidation of the 'mad' person,
but its definition of itself as an 'experiment in the treatment
of schizophrenia', shows that it basically accepts the illness
model.

Totally nonprofessional alternatives for people in crisis are truly
separated from the mental health system. In Boston, for example,

the Elizabeth Stone House provides an alternative both to mental hospitals and traditional half-way houses. The first two floors of the house, located in a working class Boston neighbourhood, are the Refuge Center, where women in crisis situations who might otherwise have to enter mental hospitals can stay for up to two weeks. Staffing is provided by women who volunteer their time for one or more eight-hour shifts per week. The volunteers are drawn mainly from Boston's feminist community and include students and some former mental patients. The upper two floors house the Therapeutic Community, a long-term residence that provides 'a supportive living environment without the restrictions of a half-way house programme'.[49]

The Stone House was started in 1974 through a conference called 'Women and Madness', which led to the formation of a group determined to bring into existence an alternative centre for women. They found a house and raised the rent money through a series of fund-raising appeals to the Boston women's community. Once the house was operating, they were able to get several small foundation grants, as well as a grant from the National Institute of Mental Health (from a fund for starting innovative programmes). The Elizabeth Stone House operates on the incredibly tiny budget of twelve thousand dollars a year, of which the bulk goes for rent on the house. None of the staff members receive a salary. At the present time there are about forty volunteers, most working a single eight-hour shift each week. Decisions are made in a weekly co-ordinating council meeting, which delegates specific responsibilities to those women who have more time and energy to devote to the house.

Women come into the refuge centre as residents through referrals from a number of social service agencies or through self-referral. The Stone House does not take women who are actively homicidal or suicidal or those whose primary problem is drug or alcohol addiction (although it does accept women with drug or alcohol problems in addition to other difficulties). A prospective resident is given an intake interview by the volunteer on duty and by any interested residents, and the decision on whether the woman becomes a resident is made together. Some women decide not to stay at the Stone House because they are looking for a more structured environment than the house provides. While the house provides informal counselling and makes referrals to sources that can help women with their emotional, medical, and legal difficulties, the main emphasis is on providing a positive and nurturing atmosphere:

> Women often experience emotional crises as a survival reaction to an oppressive environment. Often, not only is it necessary for an individual to change, but also for her environment to be changed. With the Women's Refuge Center Program we have attempted to provide a place for women to make needed personal changes and changes in their environment. We believe that emotional crises are not permanent, disabling 'sickness' but a temporary experience often necessary for coping with life. Most residential programmes that now exist for women in crises are mental hospitals or quasi-institutional halfway houses which lock people into the role of 'sick', strip their decision-making power, and do not allow them to effect change in and have control over their lives and perpetuate the environment which has led to emotional crises in the first place. The Women's Refuge Center is attempting to create an environment which will provide women with space to recreate their lives with support from other women, but without a rigid structure. In order to do this, there is little division between clients and staff. Because of the short-term nature of the programme a staff is necessary to provide continuity. However, both clients and staff have equal decision-making power in all decisions affecting the refuge centre. In this way, the traditional professional roles which place the authority outside the woman and in the hands of the 'experts' are de-mystified and the authority to make needed changes is returned to the individuals.[50]

The Elizabeth Stone House is a true alternative because it is consciously trying to break down the roles of 'staff' and 'patient'. Women who live in the house are *not* patients. Although they are temporarily experiencing extreme distress, they are not seen as incompetent. Co-operation is stressed, but each woman (resident and volunteer alike) is seen as ultimately responsible for her own life.

Drawbacks to the Stone House model include the constantly precarious financial state, the need for maintaining the enthusiasm and dedication of an all-volunteer staff, and the development of some real divisions between staff members and residents. Fund raising is an ongoing problem, and the Stone House has never been able to count on any long-term financing source. This results in much valuable staff time being absorbed by constant fund-raising efforts. Keeping an adequate number of staff members is another ongoing problem. Even those volunteers with the most enthusiasm and commitment have to fit their activities into the free time left over after work or school. Having a paid staff creates its own set of problems, but it at least frees staff members to devote most of their time to the exhausting (but satisfying) work of being with people undergoing crisis.

Even without a paid staff, however, the Stone House has developed some clear-cut distinctions between staff and residents. Volunteers are drawn mainly from Boston's feminist community and tend to be middle class and well educated, while residents tend to come from poorer backgrounds, are less educated, and do not identify themselves as feminists. Poor women, of course, have less time or energy to do volunteer work. Few former residents have returned to the Stone House as volunteers.

In running a crisis facility, it is of course necessary to make some distinctions between staff and residents, since residents are there because they are experiencing distress. What is important is that the distinctions do not become arbitrary — being in an emotional crisis does not mean that the person is incapable of making decisions, only that she may need a supportive atmosphere so that she will be helped quickly to resume management of her own life. The Stone House's requirement of a short stay (which can be extended briefly, depending on individual circumstances) is a forceful reminder that residents are expected to work on resolving their personal situation and not become passive and dependent.

It is hard to know how successful the Stone House is, since there is no formal follow-up procedure. Some residents keep in touch with the programme, but many others do not (and it is those residents who had positive experiences who are, of course, most likely to stay in touch). It is the impression of the women who staff the refuge centre that about half the residents have been helped to make positive changes in their lives.

An important aspect of the Elizabeth Stone House is its recognition that mental hospitals are harmful places. Originally, the house worked closely with the Mental Patients' Liberation Front, in two-pronged opposition to the mental health system. (The two groups are no longer connected.) Even the choice of the name for the house had political significance — Elizabeth Stone was a nineteenth-century crusader against psychiatric oppression, having been committed by her family, who attributed her conversion from Methodist to Baptist to 'insanity'. Elizabeth Stone was a strong woman who dared to fight back, and the Stone House, fittingly, is dedicated to helping other women to find strength within themselves.

In the summer of 1977, the Elizabeth Stone House collective decided to close the refuge centre and the therapeutic community. The collective is re-evaluating their programmes and procedures and planning a funding search, which will enable them to reopen the refuge centre with a paid staff. The therapeutic community was scheduled to reopen shortly.

In 1974 and 1975 a unique crisis facility existed in Vancouver, British Columbia. It is hard for me to be objective about the Vancouver Emotional Emergency Center (VEEC) because as I related earlier, I was a resident of the house for a few weeks in 1974, and my stay at VEEC had a profound effect on my life. My account of VEEC is based on my own experiences and on many hours of discussion with VEEC staff and residents.

VEEC and the Elizabeth Stone House are the only alternatives discussed in this chapter that were set up completely outside psychiatric auspices. VEEC was started by a group of nonprofessionals who had become concerned about the unavailability of supportive services for people undergoing intense emotional crises. As they saw it, people in crisis had no choice but to apply for admission to psychiatric wards or to the provincial mental hospital, where, rather than getting personal care, they often faced institutional indifference, acquired the stigma of having been psychiatrically institutionalised, and often were started on a round of repeated hospital admissions. VEEC got an initial six-month grant from the Local Initiatives Project (LIP), a Canadian federal agency that funds innovative local service programmes; they rented a house in a mixed residential and light-industrial neighbourhood in central Vancouver and hired ten staff members. The house had a capacity of five residents, allowing for a great deal of one-to-one personal contact, which was seen as the primary therapeutic tool. A two-week maximum stay was established since VEEC aimed its services to people in intense crisis situations, and its method was helping people to use this emotion-laden period as an opportunity to make drastic changes in their lives. They did not want to create a dependency relationship, which a longer stay might have encouraged.

Some of VEEC's founders were involved with the Mental Patients' Association (MPA), an organisation of ex-patients that provided supportive services for its members but was not set up to provide intensive support to individuals in crisis. (MPA will be discussed in detail in the following chapter.) Some MPA members who wanted to help returned to hospitals and clinics, but most were dissatisfied with the services they received there. VEEC provided a nonhospital setting where the emphasis was on intensive emotional support rather than confinement and drugs.

VEEC was organised as a collective, with all ten (later twelve) staff members taking equal responsibility for the various jobs involved in running the house: staffing the shifts; cleaning, maintenance, and cooking; fund raising; and community relations. At various times one or another staff member was given a title for purposes of signing applications and fulfilling the bureaucratic requirements of other agencies, but throughout its existence VEEC operated in a completely nonhierarchical manner. All decisions were made at weekly staff meetings, and there was an attempt to make decisions by consensus rather than by majority vote.

One of the basic VEEC principles was that as little distinction as possible was made between staff and residents. Although residents entered the programme in a state of crisis, in which they had little energy to give to helping others, frequently by the time a resident was ready to leave the programme, he or she had become quite actively involved in helping. Former residents were encouraged to become volunteers (who staffed the house along with paid staff members), and some later became staff members. It worked in the opposite direction as well: several staff members and volunteers became residents when their own life situations became difficult. In addition, staff members were open with residents about their own lives and the difficulties they might be having; exactly the opposite of traditional psychiatric neutrality.

VEEC was dramatically different from a mental institution. Rather than offering distance and 'objectivity', VEEC staff members made direct personal contact with residents. There were only four rules at VEEC:

1. No drugs
2. No alcohol
3. No verbal or physical violence
4. No sex between staff and residents

The no drugs rule originally applied only to illegal drugs. But after several months of operation, the rule was modified to include prescribed psychiatric drugs as well.

At VEEC, we try to provide an environment of human support for people undergoing life crisis; the experience of the past four months persuades us that the use and abuse of psychiatric drugs seriously interferes with the possibility of this happening.

We recognise that this decision closes VEEC to a large population of people who would otherwise be appropriate residents. We are saddened by this, but we are convinced that a life pattern involving drugging fear and pain into dullness at best, and serious overdose attempts at worst, cannot co-exist with the growth/communication/autonomy promoting work we try to do with folks who use VEEC.

An important point must be made; people do not become drug dependent in a social vacuum. Institutional psychiatry, psychiatrists, general practitioners, and drug companies share responsibility for their promotion of drug dependence. We believe these drugs are flagrantly over-prescribed, in the coercive context of involuntary committal, or the unequal and mystified power relationship between doctor and patient. These drugs, in far too many cases, serve as internal strait-jackets or invitations to dulled-out apathy....

What we attempt at VEEC (is to) invite residents to explore ways of meeting the needs that psychiatric drugs dull and mystify. We hope VEEC can serve as a pilot and demonstration of this approach.[51]

There were also practical problems connected with drugs. After several residents tried to overdose, drugs were kept in a locked box. Staff members objected to being placed in the nurselike role of doling out pills. The no drugs rule was worked out in a number of staff meetings.

The no-drugs policy caused a strain in the relations between VEEC and MPA, since many MPA members were regular users of psychiatric drugs. Although MPA remained supportive of VEEC (and VEEC of MPA), fewer MPA members became VEEC residents after the establishment of the policy.

The rule about sex was also worked out through practice and discussion. Sex between staff and residents was prohibited because of the recognition that residents were vulnerable to exploitation. Sex between residents was felt to be a private matter, but the staff would intervene in instances of manipulation, and sexual harassment was not tolerated. Sex between staff members was prohibited when they were on shift in the house; on their own time, it was considered a private matter.

The weekly staff meetings were held in the dining room, the main social centre of the house. Residents were free to come to all or part of a meeting but could also spend time in other parts of the house if they chose. This demystified the meetings without requiring residents to attend them if they chose not to. Architecturally, the dining room was a very open room — there could be no sense of things happening behind closed doors.

There was also a daily house meeting for residents of the house and those staff and volunteers on shift. In the house meeting residents were able to discuss their needs and work out tensions between themselves and other residents or staff members. The form of this meeting was in constant transition — sometimes it was mainly a talk session, sometimes people gave one another relaxing massages or worked off excess energy by singing and dancing together.

Residents entered VEEC either by contacting the house directly, or by referral from another community agency. In the case of referrals, emphasis was laid on the fact that the prospective resident must be willing to come to VEEC — he or she couldn't be 'placed' there by a social worker or agency. The prospective resident was invited to the house, where he or she sat down with a staff member to discuss VEEC and possible residence there. If the person didn't want to stay at VEEC, or if the staff member felt that VEEC wasn't the proper place for that person, the contact was terminated. People who were not suitable for residence were those who had long-term, ongoing problems; who were mainly looking for a place to stay; who were violent; who had drug or alcohol problems; or who were unwilling to give up their use of psychiatric drugs. These limitations evolved through practice in the first few months of VEEC's existence and were always clearly explained to prospective residents.

During the early months several VEEC residents were very 'spaced-out', disorganised people whose lives had been in continual crisis. Although they enjoyed staying at VEEC and felt much better when they left, little change had been made in their overall way of dealing with the world. The VEEC staff decided that, with a five-bed house that was nearly always full to capacity, it was better to restrict residence to people who were in the midst of an immediate crisis. It was also felt that since there were facilities in the city for people with drug and alcohol problems and for people who wanted to use psychiatric drugs, it was better to provide services that were available nowhere else.

Shortly after admission each resident was encouraged to make a contract, in which he or she set forth the problems that had brought him or her to VEEC, as well as the desired life changes the resident wanted to make. It wasn't always possible to write the contract right away, and the policy was flexible. The idea behind the contract was that residents were expected to be actively working on making the kinds of life changes that would make it possible for them to leave VEEC with better perspectives on their future. Often, residents had practical problems, such as needing a place to live, and were helped with these practicalities by the staff. Residents were free to modify their contracts at any time.

A typical day at VEEC centred around meals, activities, and the daily house meeting. Meals were usually prepared by staff members or volunteers, although residents were often involved as well. The emphasis was on healthy, nutritious food, with lots of fresh fruit and vegetables. Activities were organised around people's interest. Outings to nearby parks for noncompetitive athletics were popular. Residents were free to come and go as they liked; some residents stuck close to the house and seldom left it, while others were involved in job hunting, apartment hunting, or other errands that took them out of the house, either with or without a staff member, as they chose. Occasionally, the problem arose of a resident who spent so much time outside the house that he or she seemed to be using it for little else than a crash pad - but when such problems arose, they were dealt with at a house meeting. Both residents and staff members were free to criticise one another and were encouraged to be open about their criticisms. Staff members emphatically discouraged being thought of as remote authority figures who had their own lives in perfect order. On the rare occasion when a resident would be asked to leave, it would be worked out among residents and staff members at a house meeting.

Another method of facilitating open communication was the house log book. Residents, staff members, and volunteers could all write in the log book about their interactions with one another and their reactions. Everyone expressed their emotions - anger and fear, but also pleasure and joy - in the pages of the log, as well as in direct, face-to-face contact with one another.

The physical setup of the house encouraged interaction, while allowing people to have private spaces to withdraw to when needed. On the main floor was a living room, dining room, kitchen, bathroom and a tiny office with a desk and a telephone. This was the 'public' part of the house, where people could sit and talk, eat, drink tea, listen to music (or make their own), read, or just generally hang out. Upstairs were three bedrooms and another bathroom. In the basement was a small meeting room, a utility area, and the screaming room, a tiny room whose floor was covered with mattresses, where residents (or staff) could go and let out tension in complete safety. (In a public service radio ad about VEEC, mention was made of the screaming room, and VEEC received several calls from people inquiring whether they could drop in just to use the room.)

Of course, not everyone who came to VEEC was helped by it, but most residents found VEEC supportive and helpful, and some experienced dramatic, life-changing events. The following account was written by 'Cinnamon', who stayed at VEEC for three weeks:

> During the month of March, 1974, I had what I would presume to be, a nervous collapse, which in turn, brought about a complete mental breakdown. I was barely able to call the Crisis Center, and they in turn referred me to the Vancouver Emotional Emergency Center. I called them and spoke at length to one of the workers. I was crying convulsively and could find no apparent reason for my condition. I was convinced by the worker that I needed someone to talk to personally and some time to relax away from my demanding job of being a single parent. I agreed to go to the Center, and so, due to the fact that I could barely walk because of emotional stress and tension, the Crisis Center Flying Squad was called in and I was picked up and driven to VEEC.
>
> Once I was there, I was served tea, and accepted the offer of a quiet place to sit and talk. After a couple of hours

of talking to two workers, I decided to become a resident for a short time, with the understanding that I could leave at any time and was there because I chose to be. The staff were of great help in assisting me in finding temporary care for my three-year-old son.

After a couple of days of sleeping, not eating and generally being very withdrawn, I began to take part in group sessions, which consisted of yoga, exercising, massages, and group discussions which were often held over a large pot of tea. At first I kept pretty quiet, not saying much. I felt angry and resentful towards almost everyone, including the other residents. There were one or two of the workers who could talk with me quite successfully, and soon they encouraged me to *deal with* my anger instead of shutting it up. The end result was that before long I was able to express my hurt and bitterness towards the people and events which had caused me to suffer for so long. Much of the feeling that I was able to put out was shouldered patiently by the people working with me and I remember very little of the actual occurrences during my time there, but rather I recall the depths of emotion I felt, the reasons I discovered, but more than this I learned how to feel genuine emotion and through this I discovered myself.

I believe that the basic reason for my ability to overcome my emotional breakdown was the fact that I was helped and encouraged by kind, understanding workers. I was not hindered by any tranquillising or elevating drugs, but rather encouraged to avoid their use.

The people that were most able to help me were also able to admit their own weaknesses and did not in any way appear superior to me in my weakened state. I was extremely vulnerable and needed constant attention, but I am sure that the genuine friendship and caring was what convinced me to trust those around me, which in turn enabled me to pull through my fears and doubts.

I am convinced that the kind of help offered by Vancouver Emotional Emergency Center is one of the things lacking in institutional treatment. As I at one time was a patient in the provincial mental hospital for three months, I believe my opinion to be a valid one. I would like to encourage those involved in the support and organisation of such places as VEEC to continue their efforts, for I believe in human involvement that is based on a more personal level than most institutions can offer. In closing, I offer my thanks and gratitude to those continuing their work at VEEC and I would like to say, may daffodils and sunshine be yours.[52]

Some of the log entries that Cinnamon wrote in the VEEC logbook during her stay reveal the dramatic events that she narrates so calmly in retrospect. During her first few days in the house, she became very withdrawn. She wrote:

I never complained when screaming was going on that ripped me apart, so please leave me alone or I'll scream so loud I'll destroy myself.[53]

Later, she recognised her fears and started to discuss them. After an emotionally charged, long rap with a staff member, she wrote:

Much is happening inside. I have discovered parts of me that I never even hoped existed. Good parts so far. I feel like I'm crawling out of a deep, dark hole, so deep I can perceive no bottom. Every now and then I'm forced back down by a fear so overwhelming there are no words to describe it. I fear most of all the insanity of continually falling and not being able to reach solid ground. I have love for so many people here and this frightens me, for it's so new and clean that I'm frightened I'll corrupt the realness of it, with my unreality. I'm slowly (13 days) beginning to accept the love offered and am beginning to give it back in small doses.[54]

Just before leaving VEEC, Cinnamon wrote:

I'm exhausted with existing. I want to live, to be aware of all my senses, all the needs that have been denied me, by others including myself.... I feel no loss at departing, but rather a continuation of what has already been ... I feel the freedom to love and respect my needs as well as to continually be aware, in a real sense, of others.[55]

VEEC closed in March 1976 because it was unable to find a new funding source. In its twenty-six months of existence it had served about 650 people.

While none of the alternatives that have been discussed in this chapter are patient controlled, all have made attempts to break down the hierarchical structure of traditional mental health facilities and to bring patients into the decision-making process. Residents, even when they do not take an active part in running things, at least are not mystified about where authority lies. Staff in these alternatives present themselves not as 'experts' but as human beings who, in common with residents, have feelings, experience problems, and try to make their lives as satisfying as possible.

There are also some critical differences. Soteria House was explicitly apolitical,[56] while the Elizabeth Stone House (based in feminism) and the Vancouver Emotional Emergency Center tried to make important connections between individual unhappiness and societal conditions. David Myers, who was a member of the VEEC staff during almost the entire existence of the house, is writing a critical examination of VEEC, focusing particularly on operating effectively as a collective and on the relationship between 'going crazy' and the political and social environment.[57] Making these political connections is essential in developing a true alternative, since it helps to locate the cause of people's distress in the very real pressures of their lives rather than believing that it arises out of some mysterious process.

In the future, as mental patients' liberation groups become stronger and more successful, they will become involved in setting up alternatives that will incorporate ex-patients' special perspectives on 'going crazy' and on 'coming sane'. Ex-patients, for example, probably would be able to relate better than the VEEC staff could to people in long-term crisis. Until then, nonprofessional alternatives are positive examples of the kinds of changes that need to be made so that those under-going the 'madness experience' can grow and change instead of being dehumanised and invalidated, as they are within the present mental health system.

NOTES FOR CHAPTER 5

1. David Mechanic, 'Some Factors in Identifying and Defining Mental Illness', in *Mental Illness and Social Processes,* ed. Thomas J Scheff (New York, Harper & Row, 1967), p 26.
2. Thomas S Szasz, *Law, Liberty and Psychiatry* (New York; Macmillan, 1963), p 34.
3. Thomas S Szasz, *The Manufacture of Madness* (New York; Harper & Row, 1970), p 27.
4. See, for example, Gregory Zilboorg, *A History of Medical Psychology* (New York; WW Norton & Company, 1941); Franz G Alexander and Sheldon T Selesnick, *The History of Psychiatry* (New York; Harper & Row, 1966), and Albert Deutsch, *The Mentally Ill in America, 2nd ed (New York: Columbia University Press, 1862).*
5. Miriam Siegler and Humphrey Osmond, *Models of Madness, Models of Medicine* (New York: Macmillan, 1974), p 186.
6. *Ibid*, p 41.

7. 'Interview with Thomas S. Szasz', *The New Physician*, June 1969, p 40. My disagreements with Szasz include the paternalistic attitude he frequently adopts towards people conventionally described as 'mentally ill', and his deep faith in American capitalism.

8. In interview with Lanny Beckman, in *Mental Patients' Association*, a film by Richard Patton, National Film Board of Canada, 1977.

9. Dianne Jennings Walker, 'Dianne: The Oppression of Psychotherapy', *Madness Network News 3*, no 6 (June 1976): p 1.

10. *Hurry Tomorrow*, a film by Richard Cohen and Kevin Rafferty, Tri-Continental Film Centre, New York, 1975.

11. Bette Maher, 'Personal Account', in *Voices from the Asylum*, ed Michael Glenn (New York: Harper Colophon Books, 1974), p 102.

12. Cynthia Cekala, 'If This Be Insanity', in *Voices from the Asylum*, ed Glenn, pp 80-81.

13. Ibid, p 83.

14. The Committee on Nomenclature and Statistics of the American Psychiatric Association, *Diagnostic and Statistical Manual of Mental Disorders*, 2d ed. (Washington, DC: American Psychiatric Association, 1974), p 44.

15. This point is made by Lanny Beckman, 'Millions of Homosexuals Cured ... Instantly!' *In a Nutshell: Mental Patients' Association Newsletter 3,* no. 2 (March 1974): p 4.

16. Anthony Brandt, *Reality Police* (New York: William Morrow & Company, 1975), p 133.

17. Kenneth Donaldson, *Insanity Inside Out* (New York: Crown Publishers, 1976), p 119.

18. Deutsch, *The Mentally Ill in America*, pp 77-79.

19. Ibid, p 79.

20. Ibid

21. Ibid, p 81

22. Ibid

23. Ibid, p 82.

24. Ibid, p 81.

25. Szasz, *Manufacture of Madness*, p 151.

26. Michael Foucault, *Madness and Civilisation* (New York: Pantheon Books, 1965), p 39.

27. Ibid, p 268.

28. Ibid, p 166.
29. *History of Medical Psychology*, p 415.
30. JW King and GW Brown, *Institutionalism and Schizophrenia* (Cambridge, Cambridge University Press, 1970), p 177.
31. Maxwell Jones, *The Therapeutic Community* (New York: Basic Books, 1953), p 53.
32. Ibid, p 30.
33. Ibid, pp 27-28.
34. For an example of a therapeutic community that physically prevented patients from leaving, see Philip M Margolis, *Patient Power* (Springfield, Ill, Charles C Thomas, 1973) to which Jones wrote an enthusiastic foreword.
35. Mary Barnes and Joe Berke, *Mary Barnes: Two Accounts of a Journey Through Madness* (New York: Ballantine Books, 1973), pp 88-89.
36. Berke observed a dramatic example of this, too. Ibid, pp 89-92.
37. David Cooper, *Psychiatry and Anti-Psychiatry* (New York: Ballantine Books, 1971), p 117.
38. Ibid, p 121.
39. This account is taken from James S Gordon, 'Who Is Mad? Who Is Sane? RD Laing: In Search of a New Psychiatry', in *Going Crazy: The Radical Therapy of R.D. Laing and Others,* ed Hendrik M. Ruitenbeek (New York: Bantam Books, 1972), p 87.
40. RD Laing, 'Metanoia: Some Experiences at Kingsley Hall, London', in *Going Crazy*, ed Ruitenbeek, p 12.
41. Ibid (italics in the original).
42. Barnes and Berke, *Mary Barnes*, p 3.
43. Ibid, p 271.
44. Personal interview with David Parker, December 8, 1976.
45. Soteria House brochure, quoted in Loren R Mosher, 'A Research Design for Evaluating a Psychosocial Treatment of Schizophrenia', *Hospital and Community Psychiatry 23*, no 8, (August 1972): p 232.
46. Alma Menn, 'Growing at Soteria', in *In Search of a Therapy*, ed Dennis T Jaffe (New York: Harper Colophon Books, 1975), p 86.
48. 'The Elizabeth Stone House: A Boston Womens' Residential Mental Health Alternative', provided by the Stone House, nd
49. Ibid.
50. Ibid.

51. 'VEEC Drug Statement', *In a Nutshell: Mental Patients' Association Newsletter 3,* no. 3 (June 1974): p 10.
52. 'Vancouver Emotional Emergency Center Report and Evaluation', August 1, 1974, pp 22-24.
53. Ibid, p 22.
54. Ibid.
55. Ibid.
56. Mosher, Reifman, and Menn, 'Characteristics of Nonprofessionals', p 393.
57. Personal interview with David Myers, December 20, 1976.

Chapter Six

Inside the Mental Patients' Association

People do not have to be in a life-crisis situation to need help and support. Most people need help at some point in their lives. Seeking help with one's problems, however, can be regarded as a stigmatising act, an admission of weakness. This will remain the case despite mental health propaganda to the contrary, until seeking help is seen as a normal aspect of human behaviour and people give and get help and support freely from one another. The present system, in which the givers of help derive status and financial rewards, while those who seek help are seen as needy or sick, perpetuates the rigid separation between the helper and the helped. Detachment and impartiality, which mental health professionals believe are the proper therapeutic attitudes, become, in practice, either cold formality or the shallow pretense of friendliness. Alternative services replace medical and bureaucratic distance with real friendliness — not the bland, impartial 'friendliness' of a person behind a desk but the open give-and-take of a relationship between equals. Having problems is seen as a normal component of living in a sometimes difficult and threatening world and not as part of an illness existing only in some unfortunate people.

Former mental patients need many special kinds of help, not because they are sick but because in addition to experiencing personal crises, they have been through the often debilitating experience of psychiatric institutionalisation. Ex-patients may need special help with places to live, with dealing with bureaucracies, and with finding jobs. Most services offered to ex-patients continue to place them in the category of needy, incompetent individuals who couldn't possibly help themselves or one another without outside intervention. When problems are called mental illness, they become entirely the province of professionals. Mental patients are taught to think of their difficulties as 'symptoms', which require professional expertise to treat. Even practical problems, such as finding a job or a place to live, tend to be handled by social workers within the overall psychiatric framework. And within this framework, every difficulty the patient or ex-patient experiences may be viewed as an indication of mental illness. Patients are also taught to distrust one another, since help is seen as coming only from professionals.

Patient-run alternatives break down these barriers. When ex-patients work together, without professional supervision or control, no one is seen as inferior. Humiliating features of professionally run services (closed files and meetings, for example) are eliminated. Patients are able to turn to one another and to find that a relationship of equals provides help in a warm and supportive way that is entirely new. A model for a good alternative service for ex-patients must include the following elements:

1. The service must provide help with needs as defined by the clients.

2. Participation in the service must be completely voluntary.

3. Clients must be able to choose to participate in some aspects of the service without being required to participate in others.

4. Help is provided by the clients of the service to one another and may also be provided by others selected by the clients. The ability to give help is seen as a human attribute and not as something acquired by education or professional degree.

5. Overall direction of the service, including responsibility for

financial and policy decisions, is in the hands of service recipients.

6. Clients of the service must determine whether participation is limited to ex-patients or is to be open to all. If an open policy is decided upon, special care must be taken that the nonpatients do not act oppressively toward the ex-patients. In other words, such a service must be particularly sensitive to issues of mentalism (as previously defined).

7. The responsibility of the service is to the client, and not to relatives, treatment institutions, or the government. Information about the client must not be transmitted to any other party without the consent of the client, and such information must be available to the client.

In the detailed examination that follows of the operations of the Mental Patients' Association (MPA) in Vancouver, particular attention is paid to how closely this model is followed. While MPA does not follow the model in every respect, it has been selected for this detailed study because it is the largest and most successful organisation that approaches the model.

The founding of MPA was described in Chapter 3. Today, six years after it was founded, MPA operates a drop-in centre and five co-operative residences. The drop-in centre is open seven days a week from 8.00am to midnight, and provides social and recreational activities. Members are free to come at any time for coffee, to use the arts and crafts room or the photography darkroom, to sit, talk to others, sleep, watch TV or listen to the radio, to use the phone, or for any other reason. Drop-in centre co-ordinators, elected by the membership and placed on salary for six-month terms, are always available to members, to teach a skill or just to talk.

At the weekly drop-in centre meeting, co-ordinators and members resolve questions or problems in connection with the running of the drop-in centre. All questions are decided by majority vote, co-ordinators and members together. The meeting determines the allocation of the centre's budget, plans activities, and resolves any disputes among the membership.

MPA also runs five co-operative residences, which altogether have a capacity of forty-nine. Each house is responsible for the running of its own affairs, including the election of two co-ordinators, who are placed on salary by MPA for six-month terms. The co-ordinators (who do not live in the house, although they may be residents of another MPA house), are available as resource people to the residents of the house, to help them with whatever particular needs or problems they may have.

The entire organisation is run by the membership. Day-to-day administrative matters are handled by the office and research co-ordinators, also elected by the membership for six-month terms. During the weekly business meeting co-ordinators and members make decisions about overall MPA policy. Every third week there is a general meeting, which is the main decision-making body of MPA. During 1976, the general meeting voted the board of directors out of existence and legally became the governing body of the organisation, 'to conform to the practice of a society which is based on power reversal and self-help'.[1]

The organisation defines a member of MPA as anyone who has come to the drop-in centre more than once or who lives in an MPA residence. (Many residents don't come to the drop-in centre.) There is no requirement that a member be a former mental patient, although most are. Co-ordinators are members of the organisation who have been selected by the membership for additional responsibilities.

Funding for MPA has been obtained from a number of Canadian government sources, local, provincial, and federal, over the years. While it is difficult to make direct comparisons between Canadian and US government programmes, most of the funding could be broadly compared to US antipoverty grants. (MPA's funding will be discussed in detail in Chapter 7.)

MPA serves several hundred members through its various facilities and activities. There are no membership dues, no applications, no formalities. It is truly an open door. An informative and entertaining newsletter, *In a Nutshell,* is written, illustrated, and produced by MPA's membership.

The drop-in centre is located in a storefront building in a residential section of Vancouver. The present centre, which was acquired by MPA in 1974, was renovated by the membership. Three former stores were combined to provide a large living room, an office, a kitchen, a crafts room, a darkroom, a workshop, a TV room, quarters for the caretaker, two small bathrooms, and a storage area. The living room is a large open area with attractive built-in furniture providing seating for about twenty people. Fish swim in an aquarium, provided by a hobbyist member. An upright piano against the wall provides the opportunity for frequent impromptu concerts. A ping-pong table gets heavy use.

The best way to understand MPA is to spend a typical day at the drop-in centre. It is 8.00am and the caretaker has just unlocked the door. The caretaker is an MPA member (elected, of course, by the membership) who sleeps overnight at the drop-in centre. The co-ordinator on the 8.00am to 1.00pm shift has arrived, as have several early-morning regulars. Someone sets up the large percolator and soon the fragrant aroma of coffee begins to drift from the kitchen to the living room. The morning regulars are mostly quiet sorts who sip coffee, read the paper, or nap on the couches. The day starts slowly.

By midmorning, the office, which adjoins the living room, is busy. The phone has begun to ring regularly. Extension phones are located all over the drop-in centre — members make and receive calls on the same telephone lines that are used to conduct the official business of the organisation. While this may not lead to efficiency, efficiency is not the most highly prized value at MPA. Members walk freely in and out of the office, chatting with the office co-ordinators. Everyone is one a first-name basis. Small groups of people are conversing in areas throughout the centre — topics range from the weather to intimate personal problems, and everything in-between. The ping-pong table is in use. A member brings some food from the grocery store across the street and cooks himself breakfast. Some members live in furnished rooms without cooking facilities. 'Clean Up After Yourself', warns a sign above the sink, mostly observed.

Shortly after eleven o'clock, the weekly drop-in centre meeting is called to order. The five drop-in co-ordinators, the workshop co-ordinator, the transportation co-ordinator, the caretaker, and perhaps eight members are present. The meeting takes place in the living room, and not all members present choose to participate in the meeting. A list is passed around so that the co-ordinators can sign up for their shifts. The first item of discussion is planning the activities for the forthcoming week. The transportation co-ordinator lists the times he is available to drive the MPA van, which is used for grocery shopping for the residences as well as for drop-in centre activities. Everyone suggests activities, and those eliciting the most enthusiasm are scheduled. There will be a trip to a local movie theatre, a bowling night, and an afternoon at a public swimming pool. One of the drop-in centre co-ordinators has been delegated to get free tickets for as many local events as he can, and he reports that he has obtained fifteen tickets for a hockey match. A spirited discussion begins about the fairest way to distribute these much-desired tickets. It is finally decided that five tickets will be available by lot to the residences, ten by lot to the drop-in members, and that no one on salary can get a ticket unless there are any left over. There is a lot of groaning from the co-ordinators who are hockey fans.

Discussion then turns to problems created by Richard, a member who has been violating one of the drop-in centre rules; specifically, he has been refusing to leave at the midnight closing time. Richard has been asked to be present at the meeting in order to try to resolve the problem. The caretaker explains the rule to Richard again and details several incidents when he has had great difficulty persuading Richard to leave. Several other complaints against Richard also come up. Richard tries to explain his difficulties, but finally agrees that they are irrelevant to the question at hand. He agrees to co-operate with closing time in the future. Several people indicate to him that they would like to get to know him better — perhaps he will come to them the next time he is upset.

Noon — the time of the weekly business meeting — is approaching, and the drop-in centre meeting is brought to a close. By this time about twenty-five people are gathered in the living room. Since it is a larger group, the business meeting operates slightly more formally. A chairperson is selected — first volunteers are asked for, and if none are forthcoming, individuals are asked if they want to chair. An effort is made to find someone who has not chaired a meeting for a while. A secretary is selected by the same method. An agenda is prepared — some items are carried over from previous meetings, others have been placed there by people who have specific questions to raise. Several additional items are added to the agenda as the meeting starts. Last week's minutes are read. A member, Larry, asks that the meeting consider the subject of lifting a ban that has been in force against him for the past six months. It is decided to consider this item first.

Larry had been banned from the drop-in centre for six months (bans are instituted by a vote of the membership) for breaking one of the large plate-glass windows. Many people present remember the incident and have strong feelings about it. The chairperson makes sure each person who wants to speak is recognised. A number of people ask Larry to pay for the window he broke, and a payment schedule is worked out with him. Larry explains that he had been using illegal drugs at the time of the incident and is now determined to stay clean. A motion is made that Larry be allowed back to the drop-in centre on the conditions that he pay for the window and refrain from using illegal drugs. Larry indicates that the motion is acceptable to him, and it is then put to a vote and passed.

The usual first agenda item, 'the roundabout', then begins, during which each person present is able to speak on his or her activities during the past week. Since MPA is a large organisation, this gives everyone a chance to be kept up to date on everything that is happening. A number of interesting things are mentioned. One of the office co-ordinators has received a request for several speakers to do a presentation about MPA to a college class, and volunteers are found. Gerry, who has been handling MPA's books and financial affairs since the organisation began, mentions a problem he has had recently in placing fire insurance coverage for the residences. The insurance agent has asked him whether the houses were for sick people. Gerry tells the meeting, 'I tried to give him a short course in what MPA was all about, and I think it helped'. He is expecting to hear shortly about the insurance.

The meeting continues until about 2.30pm, covering a diversity of items — vacancies in the MPA residences, requests for more volunteers to work on the *Nutshell,* plans for a series of Saturday night dances. The major item of the day's meeting is a discussion of the budget for the forthcoming fiscal year. A large chart is displayed showing how much money the organisation has been getting from the various funding sources and how the money is spent. The focus of the discussion is what areas should be expanded if additional funding is secured. Several alternative proposed budgets have been prepared by the office co-ordinators, and the meeting votes on which one to adopt. The final decision will be made at the next general membership meeting.

The drop-in centre empties out for a while after the meeting ends. The co-ordinator on the afternoon shift sits around talking with some of the people who remain, and gradually the room begins to fill again. Friendly groups chat in different parts of the room. Another pot of coffee is made. The phone rings continually. Constant cries of 'Is Joanne here?' 'Has anyone seen Fred?' 'When will Anne be back?' Again, no distinction is made between personal calls and 'official' ones. Occasionally, a person unfamiliar with MPA calls and asks to speak to 'the director' — it can take a while to explain that there is none and to find out who can best help the caller.

By mid-evening, the drop-in centre is fairly noisy. Many people are old friends who obviously enjoy being together. Although there is a constant influx of new members, some have been coming to MPA for years. Occasionally, as with any large groups of people, there are disagreements, and voices are raised. MPA is a free and easy place, but violations of the four rules, the four basic MPA principles, are immediately dealt with. The rules, posted prominently on the wall, read:

1. No alcohol
2. No nonprescription drugs
3. No violence
4. No disturbing the peaceful enjoyment of others.

At the drop-in centre, violations are dealt with immediately by an emergency meeting of those present. The parties to the dispute, and witnesses, all address the group, which then decides how the situation is to be handled. Examples of those situations (which occur infrequently) are:

A loud argument erupts between Bob, a quiet man who has been reading the newspaper, and Ed, who has been insistently trying to start a conversation. 'Just mind your own business', snaps Bob, which provokes a new round of badgering from Ed, who finally rips the newspaper from Bob's hands. Bob snatches the newspaper back, and in a moment the two men are grappling with each other. Several people help to separate them. 'What's going on?' asks Fred. 'Did anyone see what happened?' A number of people begin talking at once. Fred announces that a meeting of those present is necessary to resolve the issue. Bob, Ed, and a number of other people describe what happened, and with a lot of interrupting and disputing, the full story is pieced together. Suggestions are solicited from the group as to how to deal with Bob and Ed. Most people agree that Bob had been harassed, but they are divided on whether he was justified in fighting with Ed. A number of people say that they have been bothered by Ed in the past, and someone suggests banning him. Steve points out that this is the first time Ed has actually been violent, and perhaps banning is too drastic. Lucy remarks that Ed has frequently violated the rule about the peaceful enjoyment of others. After much discussion, the group decides to warn Ed that he will be banned the next time he physically assaults anyone *or* harasses anyone. The group decides that Bob should not have escalated the violence, but that he had been provoked. This leads to a discussion of a member's responsibility to get the group to deal with potentially violent incidents — Bob could have initiated a meeting to deal with Ed's verbal harassment before the situation turned into a fight.

'Leave me alone', screams Debbie, 'just stop bothering me'. 'What's wrong, Debbie?' asks Mike. 'Is Andrew hassling you?' 'This is about the tenth time I've told him to keep his hands off me.' Mike walks up to Andrew and tells him that bothering Debbie is against the rules. 'We're going to have a meeting and discuss it', Mike tells Andrew, who mumbles that he wasn't doing anything wrong. The people in the living room listen to Debbie, who says angrily, 'I'm sick and tired of guys who grab at women. I told Andrew to leave me alone, but he trapped me in the corner'. Mike explains to Andrew that disturbing another member is a violation of the rule. Andrew agrees that he will leave Debbie alone in the future. 'Not just me', Debbie tells him. 'You can't bother *any* woman around here — you can't just grab women.' As the impromptu meeting breaks up, Mike talks quietly to Andrew about how to talk to women. Several men join the discussion. 'And don't call them chicks', Mike warns. Several people talk quietly with Debbie and comfort her.

Jim, whose ban for fighting is still in effect, walks into the drop-in centre and loudly argues with Mark, a member who points out to him that he should leave. Mark begins to call loudly for a meeting, and people begin to sit down in a circle in the living room. Alice, the co-ordinator on shift, asks Mark what has happened. 'He's not supposed to be here,' says Mark. 'He was banned last month for throwing a book at me.' 'That's true', says Alice, turning to Jim. 'If you want to ask that your ban be lifted, you can come to the next drop-in centre or business meeting, but until then you're not allowed in the drop-in centre.' 'I really want to come back', says Jim, 'I'm sorry I threw the book and sorry I got kicked out. I'll come to the next meeting. I hope people will let me come back'.

Rule breaking is not a frequent event at MPA. It has been covered in detail because it illustrates clearly the unique qualities of the organisation. The membership truly runs MPA. Even in the drastic step of banning a member, the excluded person sees that it is not an arbitrary decision made by someone he or she barely knows but is a direct consequence of his or her own actions, decided upon by the group. There is no back-up authority, no one person to whom members can turn and say, '*You* make the decision'. Membership control would be a sham (as it is in the typical ex-patients' social club, for example) if this kind of back-up authority figure existed.

To return to our typical day ... it is now late evening, and the day's activities are coming to an end. A small group is gathered quietly in the TV room. A few people are reading or napping in the living room. Several people are emptying ashtrays, washing the coffeemaker, and sweeping up. The evening co-ordinator and the caretaker start reminding people that midnight is approaching. One by one, people say goodnight and depart. The caretaker locks the door and turns off the lights.

The drop-in centre is one major component of the Mental Patients' Association: the residences are the other. The residence programme grew out of needs that became obvious in the early months of the drop-in centre's existence. Some members asked to be allowed to sleep in the drop-in centre — they literally had no other place to go. Others lived in isolated furnished rooms so depressing that they simply could not bear to go back to them after spending stimulating hours at MPA. The needs of members who wanted MPA as a place to live were in conflict with those who wanted it as a social centre. It became obvious that the two functions would have to exist in physically separate locations.

The first residence was started in a rented house after MPA had been in existence for about six months. The basic operating principles are radically different from halfway houses or boarding homes, the two main types of living arrangements available to recently discharged patients. Decision-making is in the hands of the residents. This includes not only trivial day-to-day decisions — what should be served for dinner, for example — but also major ones. Prospective new residents are accepted into the house by the vote of current residents. In order to provide practical and emotional support for residents, the position of residence co-ordinator was created, and two residence co-ordinators were elected by the residents of the first house, and put on salary by MPA. The co-ordinators were not the 'directors' of the house; they were there to help out with problems as defined by the residents. Over the years the residence programme has grown so that there are now five residences, each conducting its own affairs, yet each a component part of MPA.

The MPA residences are located in residential neighbourhoods in Vancouver and are indistinguishable from the houses around them. MPA believes that a residence is a group of people living together as a family and thus should be able to locate in single-family areas. After years of effort, MPA has been successful in getting the Vancouver City Council to agree to a special zoning designation of 'Community Residential Facility' for its houses, as well as for any similar group-living arrangements. Community Residential Facilities are legally able to locate in any neighbourhood. Previously, the city had tried to classify the houses as boarding houses, which have to make elaborate and expensive physical alterations and are limited to certain zones. It was MPA's successful argument that since their residents live together in a family manner, they should be considered families for zoning purposes. Similar zoning regulations are being introduced in a number of cities, making it easier to establish similar family-style residences there.[2] The zoning question will be discussed further in Chapter 7.

Again, the best way to understand the MPA residence programme is to look at a typical day in a residence. There is no official wake-up time. As each resident gets up, he or she prepares breakfast and washes the dishes. A schedule pinned to the wall shows the day each resident is scheduled to cook dinner; another schedule sets out the various housekeeping responsibilities. This week Steve is to clean the living room, Eleanor is to do the bathroom, and so forth. The jobs rotate each week. A bulletin board shows a schedule of MPA activities. House members are free to come and go. A few have jobs, many are on welfare, some of whom are registered for a part-time work programme (often performed at MPA) that gives them an additional fifty dollars a month. While some residents prefer to spend most of the day at home, others spend time at the drop-in centre, visiting friends, going to school, or participating in training sessions. How residents spend their time is up to them.

The two house co-ordinators stop by frequently. Their function is to serve the needs of the residents. This can take the form of refereeing interpersonal disputes, helping a resident to deal with welfare or other bureaucracies, and being available for informal discussion and advice. The co-ordinators influence the running of the house, but decision-making power lies in the collective hands of the residents, expressed at the weekly house meeting. Often a resident new to the house and freshly out of a mental hospital will try to cast the co-ordinator in the role of director, and it may take a long time to convince him or her that there is no director.

Some residents are under psychiatric outpatient care. Whether or not to get psychiatric treatment is the decision of each resident. Occasionally, a resident may be legally required by the terms of his or her discharge to go for outpatient treatment, but even in these situations it is the responsibility of the resident to arrange it. Of course, the co-ordinators are available if a resident wants a companion or advocate to accompany the resident to a doctor's or clinic appointment. Residents who are taking psychiatric medication are responsible for taking and safeguarding their own pills.

By midmorning all the residents are awake. Diane, one of the two co-ordinators, has arrived and is having a cup of coffee with some of the residents in the kitchen. There is spirited, informal discussion of several pressing issues, particularly several residents' dissatisfaction with Eric, a newcomer to the house. 'Let's talk about it at the house meeting tonight,' Diane suggests.

Diane, together with several of the residents, straightens up the living room and lays out ashtrays. This week the house is playing host to the weekly residence council meeting, which rotates among all the MPA residences. The council consists of all ten residence co-ordinators plus residents of the houses.

Several of the residents plan to attend the meeting, while others choose to avoid it. The meeting is attended by several residents of other houses and most of the co-ordinators. There are several important agenda items for today's meeting, particularly the upcoming MPA general election. Each house must elect two co-ordinators for the next six months. (Residence co-ordinators, like co-ordinators who work at the drop-in centre, are placed on salary by MPA.) The discussion centres on how to run the elections. Most of the co-ordinators want to continue to work for their houses, and the likelihood is excellent that all will be re-elected to their positions. Some houses have requested that they not have to interview additional candidates.

In the past the policy has been that anyone who was interested in running for a residence co-ordinator position visited each of the houses and got to know the residents. The discussion turns to how democratic it is to limit the residents' choices. 'The people in my house don't want their privacy violated by lots of strangers wandering in', says Nick. 'They say they're satisfied with Jane and me and want to re-elect us.' 'But suppose someone came around who they thought was really terrific?' asks Lisa. 'They shouldn't make up their minds in advance.' 'Remember', Don points out, 'our terms run for only six months. Even if we want our jobs again, there's no guarantee that the house will vote for us, and there shouldn't be. Sure, I want to get re-elected, but I also want the house to get the best possible people for the job. I want them to see everyone who's available'. 'But what if the residents decide, like the people in our house have, that we're satisfied?' says Francine. 'We like Nick and Jane, we think they're doing a good job, and we don't want a bunch of other people to come, thinking that maybe they might have the job, when we know we're going to vote Nick and Jane back in. It's not fair to let people think they have a chance of being elected when they don't. It's just a waste of everyone's time.'

The discussion continues, the many sides of the question being more and more deeply explored. No final conclusion is arrived at; the co-ordinators decide to go back to their houses and raise the whole question for thorough discussion.

Debbie raises the next topic. 'The people at our house have been complaining about activities. Sometimes a lot of people want to go on an activity, and then it gets cancelled. And people who want to go swimming say that it hasn't been scheduled for ages.' 'There isn't enough co-ordination between the drop-in centre and the residences about activities', agrees Don. 'I've been planning to go to the drop-in centre meeting and talk to them about involving the residences more in activities. I'll definitely go next week.' 'That's a good idea', says Debbie. Don says he will report back next week about the results of the meeting.

A report is made by each house as to the number of vacancies. A list of vacancies is kept in each residence and in the drop-in centre so that prospective residents can be referred to houses that have room. Prospective residents then visit the house (or houses), get to know the residents and the set-up of the house, and then return to the weekly house meeting, where the house members vote on whether to accept the prospect as a resident. The discussion turns to one house that has had vacancies for several weeks but has not voted in any new residents. 'The people in our house are getting fussy', says Lisa. 'They are pleased at how well the house has been running recently and don't want anyone who will rock the boat.' 'That's very nice', says Debbie, 'but they need to fill up the house. There's simply not enough money to pay all the bills if you're not getting all the income. You've got to remind people to think back to when they needed a place. Suppose people hadn't been willing to vote them into the house? Where would they be now'? 'I'll try', promises Lisa, 'I'll go over the budget figures with them and try to show them we need more residents. And I'll remind them that once they were applicants too, and people agreed to take a chance on them.'

When the meeting breaks up, the house is quiet. Only a few residents are at home, and they sit drinking coffee and chatting quietly in the living room. Les, the other house co-ordinator, has stayed after the meeting and is down in the basement with several of the residents, clearing out a largely unused storage room. Joe, who is helping in the basement, asks Les if he knows where Joe can find a job. Les offers to accompany him to the employment office, and they make an appointment for the next morning.

In the late afternoon Joe goes into the kitchen and checks the cooking schedule. Eric, the new resident, is supposed to cook dinner, but he is upstairs in his room. Joe goes up and knocks on Eric's door. He talks to Eric, who says he is very doubtful of his cooking ability and afraid the other residents will criticise his hamburgers. 'They used to criticise mine', Joe tells him. 'The first time I made dinner here, I made hamburgers. I wasn't sure how long to cook them, and by the time I decided they were done, there wasn't much left to them. But I've gotten better at it now. Do you want me to help you out today, considering it's your first time?' Relieved, Eric agrees, and he and Joe head for the kitchen.

While Eric and Joe prepare dinner, Les and Diane chat with residents and Ellen, a prospective resident, in the living room. The weekly house meeting is scheduled for immediately after dinner; the co-ordinators stay for dinner on this day, and Ellen has been invited. Nearly everyone is home by suppertime — missing a house meeting is frowned upon. Joe and Eric call people into the dining room and set out a meal of hamburgers, salad, and potatoes. Everyone compliments Eric on his cooking. After dinner the dishes are cleared away, and the house meeting begins.

Diane looks at Lynn, who had been complaining about Eric that morning, saying that he didn't seem to be fitting into the house. 'This morning', says Lynn, 'a lot of us were worried about you, Eric. You have hardly ever said a word to anyone since you moved in. But I feel better about you now. You were more relaxed and friendly tonight'. Eric smiles. 'I really wasn't sure about this place till today. I expected somebody to criticise me every time I turned around — I was just bracing myself. I was scared to cook dinner and scared to ask for help. But Joe was just so great. He showed me how, and it wasn't hard at all. And it was nice when everyone said it tasted good'.

The upcoming election is discussed. Les summarises the discussion of the residence council and asks for comments. He has previously told the residents that he does not plan to run for re-election. 'Then we have one position open', says Carol. 'No, we have two', replies Joe. 'Diane is running, but she has to run just like everyone else. We interview candidates, including Diane, and then we elect two co-ordinators. I think you'll get elected', he remarks to Diane. 'I hope so,' says Diane, 'but I think you are right. You should consider everyone who applies, and pick the best people. Of course, I hope you vote for me'.

Cleaning and housekeeping chores for the week are rotated, and everyone is reminded of his or her new assignment. The next week's cooking schedule is drawn up, and each person indicates when and what he or she will cook. Shopping, one of the rotating chores, is done once a week in conjunction with several other MPA residences, using the MPA van and going to the most inexpensive stores. On the basis of the week's planned menu, a shopping list is drawn up.

Ellen has sat quietly through the meeting. 'What about it?' she asks now. 'Can I move in?' 'What do *you* think of it?' she is asked. 'Do you think you'd like living here?' 'I think so', she replies. 'I was in a halfway house before, and I didn't like the way they treated me there. Then I went back in the hospital, and when I was ready to leave, I didn't know where I could go. Then, someone told me about MPA. I like the way you have these meetings and discuss everything. I hope you'll vote for me. The hospital says I'm ready to leave as soon as I find a place to live.' 'You'll be my roommate if you move in', says Carol. 'I enjoyed talking to you during dinner. I think we'll get along well together.' Ellen is asked to leave the room for the vote. No one raises any objections to Ellen, and the vote is unanimous. Carol goes to tell Ellen the good news, and they come back into the room in animated discussion.

Diane and Les say goodnight. 'Don't forget tomorrow', Joe reminds Les. 'I want to talk to those employment people, but I don't want to go alone.' 'Of course', says Les. 'I'll be here at nine. Be ready.'

After the co-ordinators leave, a few residents sit in the living room watching TV. Joe and Eric clean up the kitchen. Carol and Ellen make plans to go shopping together after Ellen moves in the next day. 'I hate to go back to the hospital, even for one more night', says Ellen. 'I know', says Carol, 'but after tomorrow you'll be living here. Isn't it great?' Ellen leaves to catch a bus back to the hospital.

As the evening wears on, the residents go off to bed one by one. By midnight, only a few night owls are still watching the television set, turned down low so it will not disturb those who are sleeping.

A study of the residence programme, which was tabulated by a long-time MPA resident, clearly shows the effectiveness of the MPA houses. Over a ten-month period, 118 people lived in the five houses. Only 10 per cent returned to the hospital; 42 per cent went on to other living arrangements in the community; the rest continued to live at MPA. In the opinion of the co-ordinators and other residents, 66 per cent of the residents improved during their stay in the house. The average length of stay in an MPA residence is seven months.[3]

Now that MPA has been described, I will examine it in conjunction with the model for a good alternative service that I proposed earlier.

1. *The service must provide help with needs as defined by the*

clients. MPA clearly fits this description. MPA was organised by ex-patients who recognised that their needs were not being met by the existing mental health system. I believe that only in a service founded by clients can this criterion be met. When the service is formulated without input from clients, needs will be predefined, and clients will have to fit that structure in order to use or benefit from the service. At MPA, new needs are continually presented, and the organisation has grown in response to these needs. Experiments have been tried — some successful, others not. At one point there was a rural residence, but, in the words of one member, 'at the farm...there was no support from the community for a self-help group. The distance from MPA prevented the development of the kind of support co-ordinators and residents needed. We gave up the idea that fresh air and the country life had some magic curative effect'.[4] The group has been free to change in response to needs because there was no master plan to fulfill. Flaws can be recognised and dealt with because there is no bureaucracy to defend an unsuccessful plan. Ideas fail or succeed based only on whether or not they work.

MPA's nonbureaucratic, nonhierarchical structure is an essential element in fulfilling the model. Participatory democracy works to ensure that needs are articulated and plans are made to deal with them. Of course, the model does not always work exactly as it is supposed to. From time to time, people with strong and compelling personalities have managed to attain a degree of personal power. There are times when indifference among the membership has been a serious problem. But it is impressive that MPA tries to deal with these problems. The structure of the organisation encourages open discussion. Agendas of all meetings are open to any item any member wants dealt with. All meetings (of which MPA has many) are open for any member of the organisation to attend. Even when a committee is formed to deal with a particular subject or problem, nonmembers of the committee can sit in on meetings. This structure helps the organisation to rebound from situations where membership control has temporarily lapsed.

2. *Participation in the service must be completely voluntary.* MPA meets this standard completely. Usually, the initial contact with the drop-in centre is made by the prospective member. In the residences it is sometimes a hospital social worker who makes the first enquiry, but the prospective resident makes all the arrangements. No one can 'place' a person at MPA. I believe that complete voluntariness is one of the keys to MPA's success. People who have been in mental hospitals are accustomed to plans being made for them in which they have little say, and their attitude towards their 'placements' (whether in hospitals, outpatient clinics, halfway houses, or the like) reflects this lack of control over their lives. MPA, on the contrary, is really whatever the members make it. If they don't like it, they can either stop coming or work to change it. Voluntariness and membership control are directly linked. People who are involved in a compulsory activity know that they do not control it, no matter what they may be told.

An incident that occurred several years ago illustrates what happened when participation in MPA was made compulsory for a member. Marilyn, a member of MPA, ended up in jail on a minor charge. An arrangement was made with Marilyn, MPA, the court, and a probation officer that the charges against her would be dropped and she would be placed on probation on the condition that she live in an MPA residence. Understandably, Marilyn did not feel that the residence was her home, the way the other residents did. She had spent much of her life in institutions — jails, orphanages, and mental hospitals — and she looked on the house as her latest prison. MPA principles that were true for the other residents didn't apply to her. Marilyn did not control her own life. Even though MPA tried not to be 'in charge' of her — for example, Marilyn participated in writing the reports MPA was required to submit to her probation officer — Marilyn resented the situation and decided to leave. In a later assessment, MPA decided that the experiment had been a failure. MPA principles cannot work when the organisation has control of a member's life.

3. *Clients must be able to choose to participate in some aspects of the service without being required to participate in others.* No one at MPA has a 'programme'. Each member chooses for him or herself what aspect of the organisation to participate in. Some members partake only of the 'service' aspects without getting involved in decision making. Many residents never go to the drop-in centre. Some members wouldn't dream of missing a business or general meeting, others attend infrequently. A few people are seldom seen except at the free Wednesday night dinners and Saturday morning breakfasts. *MPA does not keep records on members.* No one keeps track of a member's utilisation of activities and services. Members are seen as responsible people who do not have to be compelled to do things 'for their own good'. A member who complains of having nothing to do might be advised to go to an activity of particular interest. Someone might suggest to a member who was lonely and wanted friends that he or she might spend more time at the drop-in centre. But these are suggestions, not requirements. An organisation is not truly voluntary if members *must go* to meetings in order to go swimming (or vice versa)[7].

Requiring people to do things 'for their own good' means there must be an authority figure, a person who decides what other people do. When a person is required to do something and then told that it is what he or she 'really' wants, the power of the authority figure is mystified. This is what commonly happens to people in mental institutions and other kinds of institutions that control people's lives. Often, what the person is told he or she 'really' wants is something clearly undesirable. Instead, 'MPA insists that people who have been in mental hospitals can make the necessary changes to manage their own lives, take responsibility for their own welfare, and be involved in healing themselves while living in the community'[5]. The principles of MPA are an attempt to reverse the process of mystification. Members make the decisions openly together.

During my visit to MPA, some members complained about a small clique who made many of the decisions themselves. The existence of such a clique is antithetical to MPA principles, and this is an issue the organisation will have to grapple with.

4. *Help is provided by the clients to one another and may also be provided by others selected by the clients. The ability to give help is seen as a human attribute and not as something acquired by education or professional degree.* MPA was started as a self-help organisation, one in which people turned to one another and everyone was equal. An important and significant difference between MPA and many other 'self-help' organisations is that MPA did not develop under professional sponsorship, nor did it employ or consult outside 'experts'. The people who founded MPA were largely sceptical about the abilities of mental health professionals. Decisions about whether or not to consult professionals were felt to be purely personal ones. MPA *as an organisation* takes neither a pro-psychiatry or an anti-psychiatry position. Some members see mental health professionals as useful and helpful, others do not.

I attribute the lack of a position on psychiatry to a short-circuiting of the consciousness-raising process that led to the formation of the organisation. Because MPA got involved in service delivery so early in its existence, major attention had to be paid to practical matters rather than theoretical (or personal) ones. Meetings necessarily became focused around immediate issues. Because service delivery costs money, enormous amounts of energy went into fund raising. Members could easily agree on the importance of fund raising, running the drop-in centre, and setting up the residences. Coming to a group position about psychiatry was time-consuming, served no immediate practical purpose, and was potentially divisive. Opinions about psychiatry vary widely within MPA. Some members trust psychiatrists and hospitals, others turn to them reluctantly in situations of extreme distress, and others want nothing to do with them. Some members feel a strong commitment to self-help principles, while others think professional expertise is usually necessary. When a member becomes extremely distressed, there is a tendency to encourage that person to seek professional help, *even if such help has proved unhelpful to that person in the past.* Ideally, a client-run alternative service would pay more attention than has been done in MPA to the development of self-help, by holding ongoing consciousness-raising meetings, for example.

5. *Overall direction of the service, including responsibility for financial and policy decisions, is in the hands of service recipients.* MPA has avoided splitting off certain kinds of decision-making to a small group within the organisation. This is one of its greatest strengths. Membership control is meaningless if policy decisions come from above. It is impressive to observe participatory democracy in action. The twice-yearly general elections provide the most dramatic example. There are more than twenty co-ordinators to be elected or, in the case of residence co-ordinators, ratified by the general meeting. There is no nominating committee — people place themselves on the ballot. The living room is crowded with fifty or sixty members, many sitting on the floor or crowded in the doorway. There are usually about fifteen applicants for the six drop-in co-ordinator positions. Each candidate has five minutes to speak and five minutes to answer questions. Then ballots are marked and collected.

Office, research, and transportation co-ordinators are elected next. As the ballots are tabulated, the winners are announced. Then, the houses'. choices are announced and are subject to ratification. No one is guaranteed a job. A few people have been with MPA for years, but only because the membership continues to re-elect them. The process lasts well into the night, an exhausting but exhilarating process.

Another example of MPA's democratic process was the 1976 funding crisis. MPA, which had previously received federal government funding, was in the process of switching over to local and provincial funding. The residence programme was to come under a new programme that would impose regulations about length of stay and would remove the residents' financial independence. The residents of the houses voted to reject the funding and to seek another, less restrictive funding source. When no other source could be found, the residents, faced with the possibility of losing their homes completely, voted to accept the funding on an interim basis. (This situation will be described more fully in Chapter 7). Anything short of this is not true membership control.

6. *Clients of the service must determine whether participation is limited to ex-patients or is to be open to all. If an open policy is decided upon, special care must be taken that the nonpatients do not act oppressively toward the ex-patients. In other words, such a service must be particularly sensitive to issues of mentalism.* MPA has, since its beginning, been open to anyone who wants to join. This position has significant strengths and weaknesses. A positive effect of open membership is that MPA does not define the needs of ex-patients and nonpatients differently. Everyone is seen as benefiting from participation. However, some members feel that MPA has not been sufficiently sensitive to mentalism, which needs to be dealt with as an ongoing problem. Although the open membership policy was not set up with this result in mind, what has evolved is that most

of the nonpatients in MPA are co-ordinators — people put on salary by the organisation. One of the unintentional results is that nonpatients are seen as more competent, less needy people, since their role in MPA is largely giving help to others rather than getting it for themselves. Ideally, open membership should lead to the recognition that *all* people, not just those who have been labelled mentally ill, benefit from caring and emotional support, but, in order to reach this ideal, I believe there must be an ongoing consciousness-raising process. This has not happened at MPA.

7. *The responsibility of the service is to the client, and not to relatives, treatment institutions, or the government. Information about the client must not be transmitted to any other party without the consent of the client, and such information must be available to the client.* MPA's policy of keeping no individual records is significant. The keeping of records by an alternative service creates problems both of confidentiality (for outside parties) and of access (of members to their own records) that are probably insurmountable. Record-keeping implies that some people need to keep track of other people: and a two-class system is created. In MPA, when utilisation reports are necessary for government agencies (for funding purposes), surveys of the membership are made. This is another example of the importance of down-valuing efficiency. While it might be easier to write a report if attendance records were kept for each member, it would destroy the character of the organisation.

Clearly, while MPA does not fit the proposed model completely, it provides a good example of a functioning, successful alternative service for former mental patients. It stands in strong contrast to the professionally oriented 'alternative' services examined in Chapter 4. The differences are fundamental. In MPA, the membership is the organisation. The people who perceived the problems were the same people who set up the structure and used the services. Membership control is essential to making a service that truly meets the needs of the people it was designed to service. In addition, membership control helps people to think of themselves as strong and competent rather than weak and needy.

Most of the problems facing former patients are purely practical ones — where to live, how to get a job, or how to obtain welfare. People come out of hospitals with little faith in their own ability to deal with life. When they turn to an institution or organisation for help, this perception of themselves is further reinforced. People who come to an alternative, on the other hand, receive help with far more than the immediate problem. Ex-patients see a whole new way of dealing with problems. Instead of remote experts, they see people like themselves helping one another to find solutions. They learn that they, too, have the capacity to help others.

I believe that alternative services limited to ex-patients will be able to accomplish this even better than has been the case in MPA. The presence of nonpatients makes it difficult for people to be fully open about the difficulties they may be experiencing, out of a fear of being thought mentally ill by people who have never been through their experiences. Most people have had experiences that could be labelled 'crazy', but the prejudice against ex-mental patients makes it hard to see that people are more like one another than they are different. This is another example of the pervasiveness of mentalism. The presence of nonpatients also makes it difficult for ex-patients to talk frankly about their bad experiences in mental hospitals without being thought 'paranoid'.

I believe that an ongoing consciousness-raising process is essential for building self-confidence and counteracting the effects of mentalism. Like racism and sexism, mentalism infects its victims with the belief in their own inferiority, which must be consciously rooted out. By working together in self-help organisations, ex-patients can gain experience in helping themselves and one another. But the belief in one's own inferiority can continue unless active efforts are made to combat it.

Consciousness-raising helps ex-patients to demystify their hospital experiences and see what has been helpful or harmful. In a consciousness-raising group, ex-patients can compare their experiences with one another and discover that they can be truly helpful to each other, often far more successful than the professionals have been.

Many services for ex-patients are permeated with mentalism. The hidden message is that ex-patients are unequal. This MPA member expressed it well:

> I dislike the housing in a boarding home compared to an MPA home. It is too undemocratic in a boarding home. But in an MPA home the residents run the house. I feel that you are placed in a boarding home, and that's that. But in an MPA residence you are voted in by residents of the house whether you stay or not. I like the MPA system.

> You have restricted entertainment in a boarding home. It is simply that they want to supervise your outings. You must be in by 11pm. No yesses, no's, or maybes. You just be there. But in MPA you are put in a situation that you must socialise. It is that that I think is good. And there is no curfew.

> I dislike the food system in a boarding home. You are herded like cattle for meals. Meals are always the same time every day. It gets very boring. If you don't sign the sheet for being out for meals you simply don't get any. In MPA you are not restricted for meals at all. You don't sign a blasted sheet for meals. You eat when you want to eat, and that's that.

The supervisor must know when visitors are coming. Visitors can stay for only a short time because the supervisor wants you to talk to other clients in the boarding home. But in an MPA residence you can have visitors whenever you want as long as they don't bother other people in the house. There is no time span. I feel this is a good system because it's like a real home.

In an MPA home you have complete control of your money. You even get a chance to open a bank account. But in a boarding home someone dishes out some of your $25 comfort allowance money every day, and I think this is terrible.[6]

Living under these kind of restrictions and regulations shows ex-patients that they are not trusted or thought of as responsible people. Even though they may be told that being discharged from the hospital means they are 'well' again, they are treated as disabled. The message is clear: 'Ex-mental patients are inferior'.

Alternative services combat mentalism by refusing to divide people into 'sick' and 'well'. All people are seen as having a need for emotional support; being needy is not considered a sign of mental illness, nor does it disqualify the presently needy person from helping others. When the service is run entirely by ex-patients, it illustrates dramatically that ex-patients can be successful without supervision or control.

A frequent objection that is raised to the self-help model is that some people are seen as 'too sick to help themselves.' This is the same rationale that is used for involuntary commitment. 'Too sick' is used to mean 'unwilling to do what someone else has decided is best'. Mentally ill people are frequently seen as refusing needed services as a consequence of their mental illness. Of course, people who have absorbed this concept of mental illness will be sceptical about client-run services. MPA, however, 'believes that giving the decision-making power to the members is basic to a mentally healthy organisation. If people are not in control of the major decisions concerning their lives there can be no development of self-worth — only mind-control and adaptation'[7].

Every alternative service must decide what relationship it will maintain with traditional mental health services. A group must choose whether it will attempt to handle all situations itself or whether there is a point when the group will turn to psychiatry. The way this question is answered will determine much about the nature of the service. The best way to go about making this decision is through the consciousness-raising process, where each member of the group has an ongoing chance to express his or her feelings about being an ex-patient and what that means in terms of being a competent and worthwhile person. Feelings of inferiority have many sources; for many ex-patients, the feelings frequently stem from the constant put-downs they encounter from other people and in the mass media. In a consciousness-raising group, members have a place to discuss their reactions to these encounters with mentalism. Feelings of strength and self-worth can grow with this kind of support. Problems that the group might have at one time found itself unable to handle become less frequent as the sense of capability develops. It becomes less and less necessary to turn to the mental health 'experts', as fewer and fewer group members are seen as people who are 'too sick' for self-help.

When group members have the opportunity to discuss and compare their hospital experiences, they are able to look more clearly at how psychiatry works. Many of the experiences people have had become comprehensible when they are not hidden by psychiatric language. I have seen people in consciousness-raising groups make the exciting discovery that they can draw meaning from what had been dismissed as 'hallucinations' or 'delusions'. As their own psychiatric symptoms become comprehensible, the 'crazy' behaviour of others becomes less frightening. Mental health professionals are usually remote and distant to people whom they think of as 'crazy' (or whichever psychiatric term they may use); but people who can recognise elements of their own behaviour in that of the 'crazy' person can offer closeness and support. Since a person in crisis may be very frightened by his or her behaviour, it can be extremely reassuring to be told by other members of the group that they, too, have undergone similar experiences. This is exactly the kind of support that is almost impossible to find in traditional mental health services.

Is the alternative going to be a component part of the mental health system, or will it exist outside and in opposition to it? Each group must develop its own answer to this question through its own group process. This stance will depend on the attitudes and experiences of the membership.

One of the problems within MPA is that the organisation has never taken a group position on these very basic questions. Some members have enormous faith in psychiatry (often despite many bad experiences with it) and see the group as existing on one end of a continuum of services. Others believe that the organisation should place itself in sharp contrast to the mental health system, which they think of as inherently dehumanising and unhelpful. Others take positions somewhere in between: still others have not considered the question at all. This lack of perspective makes it more difficult to deal with a member experiencing a crisis than it might otherwise be. No one is quite sure just what to do.

It must be kept in mind that MPA was set up to deal not with crisis situations but with the ongoing, day-to-day problems of the membership. One unfortunate result is that when a member does experience a crisis, often MPA can be of only limited help. However, there is a question as to whether crises and ongoing life problems can be dealt with together. People in crisis usually require a lot of personal attention and can be disruptive of ongoing programmes. On the other hand, rejecting a person experiencing a crisis can increase the amount of distress and alienation that person is experiencing.

Ideally, an alternative service will maintain ongoing self-evaluation that will help the group deal with these problems as they arise. Flexibility is far easier to maintain with this kind of group structure than it is in a bureaucratic organisation, with its predefined categories and procedures. In fact, a willingness to change in response to needs is one of the distinctive features of alternative groups.

Ex-patients are not all the same, nor do they all have similar problems and difficulties. For some people, mental hospitalisation is a one-time incident, while others go back again and again. Also, the difficulties someone faces when coming out of an institution after being there for many years are different from those resulting from a brief hospitalisation. Frequently, traditional 'aftercare' services divide people on the basis of length of hospitalisation. There are lower expectations that long-term patients will be able to succeed 'on the outside' without intensive services. This can be a self-fulfilling prophecy. MPA has shown that there is another way of dealing with long-term patients.

The membership of MPA encompasses people with one hospitalisation and many, people who may have been in institutions for several weeks or many years. Rather than segregating long-term patients into special groups with lowered expectations, MPA provides a place where all members can define for themselves what their involvement will be. A person intimidated by meetings, for example, can choose not to attend them. Even when a meeting is dominating the living room at the drop-in centre, there are many places in the centre to which a member can retreat. Eventually, a person might observe that MPA meetings are not that frightening, since he or she is likely to see parts of a number of the meetings that take place at the drop-in centre. Members can choose, without penalty, not to participate in the decision-making process. The organisation does not require the participation of every member in every decision. There is a place for people who want only services. But no one is ever arbitrarily defined as 'too sick' or 'too institutionalised' to be a participant.

Of course, practical difficulties do arise. A member making his or her first attempt to speak up at a meeting, one who is unskilled at forcefully presenting a point of view, may be overlooked or not listened to seriously. Meetings tend to be dominated by experienced members (of course, this is true of all kinds of groups and is not a problem unique to ex-mental patients). Groups committed to membership control must exercise ongoing efforts to ensure that leadership does not centralise in a small clique. What happens in practice at MPA is that most members participate in meetings from time to time, but only a minority take an active part in the day-to-day running of the organisation. There is a commitment to being open to new voices, a commitment that occasionally lapses. There is a place for the people that conventional agencies would define as 'too sick' for a self-help group.

MPA recently began making an effort to reach another kind of long-term patient — those still in the hospital. In late 1976 MPA established a branch of the drop-in centre at Riverview Hospital, near Vancouver, which is the only public mental hospital in the province of British Columbia. Many of the patients making use of the drop-in centre are people who have been in the hospital for years and have become quite institutionalised. The MPA drop-in centre is the only place in the institution where patients can go and not be under the surveillance and control of hospital staff. The five project staff members are elected by the membership of MPA and placed on salary; four of them are former Riverview patients. The MPA Riverview Extension Program is set up

> to develop relationships with patients classified as 'chronic', patients in locked wards and those with grounds privileges and day passes, in order to aid in the process of reintegration into the community. Project staff will be available to accompany patients off grounds as requested. We will provide liaison between patients and appropriate local community service personnel. We will help patients about to be discharged from hospital to obtain suitable living accommodation within the community and attempt to provide transportation for this purpose when necessary.

> We will provide a drop-in centre at the hospital for patients to socialise, develop new relationships, secure assistance in legal matters, and obtain advocacy in hospital-related affairs.

> We will encourage patient use of services currently available both at Riverview and in the community. Also, we will provide necessary services not presently existent such as an adequately developed housing registry, familiarising patients with the Lower Mainland transit system, and attempting to provide or secure necessary and suitable short-term accommodation to enable patients to make use of overnight or weekend passes. In addition, an attempt will be made to supply any other services within our means that are deemed necessary but not available during the life of the project.[8]

The MPA Riverview drop-in centre quickly became a popular gathering place for patients. Coffee was always available, and the patients recognised that the centre provided a free space where there was no pressure and where they could be comfortable. In the first few weeks of its existence, the drop-in centre found five patients who were ready for discharge and assisted them in finding accommodations in boarding homes.

The project is not run completely along MPA principles, although there are plans to convert to participatory democracy as soon as possible. Working with patients who are still in the hospital is quite different from being with ex-patients. One project staff member, himself a Riverview ex-patient, told of realising just how institutionalised people could become when he found that many of the patients addressed him as 'sir'.[9] Undoing patients' reliance on authority figures is difficult with institutionalised patients, who must, in fact, defer to authority figures all day long. For the present, patients are excluded from the daily project staff meeting. An exciting innovation introduced by the MPA Riverview Extension Program is a weekly meeting among Riverview staff, project staff, and patients. In the meeting I observed, patients had a chance to question the clinical director of the hospital in a democratic setting that was not available anywhere else in the institution.

The MPA Riverview Extension Program raises a number of questions about the relationship between a self-help group and an authoritarian mental hospital. The programme wants to establish a patients' council, in which current and former patients would meet regularly with hospital staff to discuss patients' rights issues. Members of the programme's staff believe that incidents of patient abuse and other rights violations are high. The hospital has made it difficult for MPA to visit the long-stay wards, where many abuses are believed to occur. During one meeting between the programme's staff and Riverview administrators, a hospital official asserted that hospitals are not democratic places.[10] The interests of the hospital would obviously not be served by an independent patients' council, and it is doubtful that a council will be set up on the model proposed by MPA. Since the interests of the hospital and MPA are so different, it is questionable that negotiations could produce any meaningful compromise, and the possibility of co-option is great. It would be advantageous to the hospital for the MPA programme to become comfortable with the concessions they have been granted and decide not to push for more at the risk of losing the drop-in centre. At present, the programme's staff is determined to resist co-option.

In Boston, the Mental Patients' Liberation Front has taken a very different approach to organising patients' rights groups. MPLF began visiting Boston State Hospital in May 1974, giving patients copies of the patients' rights handbook the group had written, which led to discussions between the patients and MPLF members (who were all former patients). MPLF arranged with the director of volunteers to run a weekly current events group for patients, which informally developed into a patients' rights meeting, since this was the main subject everyone wanted to discuss. After several months the hospital administration attempted to bar MPLF from meeting with the patients. Several patients drew up a petition, which was signed by over 80 per cent of all the patients on the wards that had been involved in the group. Faced with this overwhelming show of support, the hospital administration was forced to back down, and the group has met regularly ever since.

MPLF's approach was to establish contact with the patients first. The existence of the patients' rights group was not a concession that was won from the hospital; it was already an ongoing group when the administration became aware of its existence. With this base of support among the patients, MPLF was in a good position to resist the hospital's efforts to abolish the group. It is to be hoped that the MPA Riverview Extension Program will gain similar patient support.

There are other, smaller patient-run alternative services for ex-patients. Project Release's community centre in New York City has already been described in Chapter 4. There are some significant differences between Project Release and MPA. Project Release has rejected the concept of providing 'services'. Instead, they define their work as setting up a true community, where people are not designated as staff or as clients. They believe that relationships between equals are the best way to operate self-help programmes and that designating some members as staff works against this process.

In Kitchener, Ontario, another Project Release (not formally connected with the New York group) operates a six-day-a-week drop-in centre staffed by ex-patients. The group, which started in 1976, is now trying to expand to provide crisis and residential services as well. In Cleveland, Project Renaissance was started jointly in 1975 by members of the Patients' Rights Organisation and the Legal Aid Society and operates five days a week. Committed to a nonhierarchical structure. Project Renaissance employs a social worker as its salaried co-ordinator whose role is to facilitate the evolving co-operative structure. All other jobs are filled by ex-patient volunteers. Originally, activities were mostly of the arts and crafts variety, but the group has expanded to provide madness consciousness-raising, history of crazy people, assertiveness training, and yoga. Plans are under way for Project Renaissance to set up businesses that will provide employment for members and financial support for the organisation.[11] In Boston, the Mental Patients' Liberation Front operates a drop-in centre that is open one evening a week. Staffed by ex-patients, the centre provides a place for former patients to meet with one another and to obtain information about housing, welfare, and other needs.

Patient-run alternative services provide an atmosphere that is entirely different from professionally provided or sponsored services. Replacing paternalism with co-operation and hierarchical structures with democratic ones, these alternatives provide places where ex-patients can grow strong as they help themselves and one another.

NOTES FOR CHAPTER 6

1. 'MPA Constitution' *In a Nutshell: Mental Patients' Association Newsletter* 4, no 3 (July 1976): p 10
2. Fran Phillips, 'Housing Designation,' *In a Nutshell* 4, no 4 (October 1976): p 10

3. 'Residence Program — A History of Residents at the Mental Patients' Association', November 1976, provided by MPA.
4. 'Residents No Longer MPA Orphans'. *In a Nutshell* 2, no 8 (December 1973): p 2.
5. Mental Patients' Association, 'Application for Project Grant', 1976, p 2.
6. 'Funding Problems', *In a Nutshell* 4, no 3 (July 1976): p 2.
7. MPA, 'Application for Project Grant', p 2.
8. Funding application, quoted in Dave Beamish, 'MPA Riverview Extension Program', *In a Nutshell* 4, no 4 (October 1976): p 5.
9. Personal interview with Dave Beamish, December 17, 1976.
10. Meeting at Riverview Hospital, December 17, 1976.
11. Personal communication from Kathy Palumbo, Project Renaissance co-ordinator, April 14, 1977.

Chapter Seven

Money — and Other Practical Problems

After deciding on the philosophical basis of the alternative they wish to create, no easy task in itself, the founding group must next turn its attention to a number of practical matters. First among these is money. The group must study the costs of their proposal, draw up a budget, and find a source of funding. Another important practical decision is the location of the proposed facility. The group may find itself studying local building and zoning codes, visiting real estate agents, and possibly facing local opposition when they do find a suitable and reasonably priced building.

Other practical problems involve philosophical considerations as well. Internal organisation is one such problem. There will be strong tendencies to move away from group decision-making as the group becomes larger and more involved in service delivery. The commitment to collective decision-making requires constant evaluation to make sure a gradual slide toward bureaucracy does not set in.

Still another problem that the group may face has been discussed earlier — the belief (both by outsiders and by ex-patients themselves) that mental patients are incapable of managing their own affairs. The consciousness-raising process should be incorporated into the internal organisation of the group so that members can combat their own mentalism. And the group should practice good public relations (perhaps under a less unpleasant name) by speaking to community groups and college classes and by appearing on local radio and television programmes.

By showing the community that ex-mental patients are successfully operating their own alternatives, the group will help to combat mentalism in the community.

No matter what kind of alternative service a group decides to set up, it will face the problem of finding the money to run it. Funding sources for innovative programmes are difficult to find. It is perhaps lack of money more than any other single factor that has led to so few alternative facilities advancing beyond the planning stage.

As soon as a group advances past the stage of meeting in one another's living rooms, it will need some source of money to provide a place to meet, telephone service, postage, and similar expenses. Initially, this money can come directly from the members, but fund raising will have to expand beyond this source as the group moves from planning to action. Decisions about money are interconnected with those concerning programme and policy. The entire group should be involved in making these decisions.

Some projects require very little money. In New York, Project Release has a housing programme they call 'all-the-way houses'. Members of Release have set up three communal apartments, and more are in the planning stage. Members have simply come together with one another and found suitable apartments, sharing the rent and other expenses. Release has served as a place for people to meet and find one another. Communal housing for ex-patients, without any formal therapeutic function or staff, can be financed out of the residents' earnings or welfare cheques; no outside funding is necessary.

In Vancouver, the Mental Patients' Association also provides communal housing for its members, but since each MPA residence (described in Chapter 6) has two paid co-ordinators (nonprofessional, live-out staff), funding is necessary. It is important to note that MPA's costs are considerably lower than those of typical, professionally oriented halfway houses.

A crisis house will require a higher budget than a residence, since more intensive supportive services are necessary for people in crisis situations. Again, it must be pointed out that the costs of these intensive services are far lower than those provided through the mental health system. The Vancouver Emotional Emergency Center, for example, had, in 1975, a per diem cost of $65, while three area hospitals cost $116.50, $89.50. and $101.40 respectively.[1]

The cost advantage that alternative services have over traditional ones is one of their most salable features in the search for funding. The group should investigate the costs of services locally — the nearest mental hospital, community mental health centre, general hospital psychiatric ward, halfway house, psychiatric boarding home, or other facility — and compare it to its own projected cost. A number of factors contribute to the lower cost of alternatives. These services are usually located in existing houses or apartments in relatively inexpensive areas, and often in quite run-down ones. Furniture and equipment are donated or bought cheaply secondhand. Members of the group do the maintenance, cleaning, and repairs themselves. The biggest saving, of course, is in salaries. Alternatives employ no high-priced professionals, and if salaries are paid, they are usually minimal. Project Release's community centre in New York is run totally on the volunteer labour of the members, although this might be a utopian solution. At the Mental Patients' Association, which pays its co-ordinators, a policy of equal salaries reinforces the collective structure. When MPA began, co-ordinator salaries were pegged to the welfare rate, although practicalities soon overrode idealism, and salaries have been raised a number of times. This was done, of course, by a vote of the entire membership. MPA co-ordinator salaries are currently about six hundred dollars per month. The kinds of people who are attracted to working in alternative facilities are usually willing to work for modest salaries.

Conventional services are almost invariably organised as

hierarchies, with several layers of prestige and power. Hierarchies tend to isolate decision-making in the higher levels, while day-to-day service delivery is in the hands of lower-paid workers. Clients, of course, are left out of decision making entirely. Hierarchies are inherently more expensive than collective, democratically run structures, which do not require a supervisory staff. We have already seen that hierarchical mental health facilities are alienating and dehumanising; the alternative is not only better but cheaper as well.

Applying for funding, whether through government or private sources, is usually an elaborate process. If a member of the group has had experience with writing grant proposals in the past, this experience will prove valuable. Otherwise, the group may want to seek out a friend or acquaintance with such experience who will be willing to serve as a consultant, or the group may want to consult with other local community organisations in order to find someone with grant-writing experience. Two useful books to consult are *The Art of Winning Government Grants* by Howard Hillman and Kathryn Natale and *The Art of Winning Foundation Grants* by Howard Hillman and Karin Abarbanel.[2] While the major portion of the grant proposal should be written by the people directly involved in planning the project, it is helpful to have an experienced person to give advice and suggestions.

Possible sources of funding are the government, foundations, and local community service organisations. Government sources may include federal, state, county, and city agencies, since all are involved in various aspects of mental health. Groups should also look into locally operated charitable foundations, which usually limit the projects they fund to the immediate area. These foundations may be obscure, but since they operate in a limited geographical area, they are valuable to know about. Other possible funding sources in the local community include the Community Chest, civic groups, and churches. No matter what funding source(s) are selected, groups proposing to start innovative alternative mental health services face a number of obstacles. Their project will probably be dramatically different from those the funding source is familiar with. Concepts such as self-help, collective structure, and participatory democracy may be viewed as radical and impractical. The participation of ex-patients may evoke scepticism, as may the lack of professional direction. These are real obstacles that should not be minimised.

Ongoing discussions should be held within the group about the progress of a funding application. Often, the funding agency may ask for changes in the proposal. It is important that the group evaluate changes so that they do not find their proposal distorted beyond recognition. Before the funding process is undertaken, it is a good idea to make sure that the group agrees about which principles should not be compromised. It is useless to gain funding if the project is stripped of its alternative nature in the process.

In 1975 I was a member of a group attempting to start an emotional emergency centre in Bellingham, Washington. Our project was modelled largely on the Vancouver Emotional Emergency Center, and we received invaluable help from VEEC staff members in writing and presenting our proposal. Our first step had to be gaining the approval of the county Mental Health Advisory Board, and we prepared a brief proposal and a tentative budget for presentation. Since the board had a quite conventional approach to mental health services, they viewed as weaknesses the very things we saw as our strengths — our lack of professionals, our opposition to psychiatric drugs, and our collective decision-making process. The Bellingham Emotional Emergency Center never made it past the planning stage. I relate this story only to show the real difficulties inherent in finding funding for such projects.

One reason that two successful alternative services, the Mental Patients' Association and the Vancouver Emotional Emergency

Center, were set up in Vancouver is the liberal funding policies of the Canadian government. Both VEEC and MPA got their early funding from the Local Initiatives Project, a federal programme designed specifically to fund community-based, innovative social service projects. It is easier to gain approval for an alternative service if the deciding body is concerned with social services rather than specifically with mental health.

The history of the Mental Patients' Association illustrates the way in which various funding sources influence the kinds of services provided. The initial funds for MPA came in the form of a one-thousand dollar grant from the graduating class of the University of British Columbia, which provided for the rental of a house to serve as the drop-in centre and office. Next, a six-month grant from the Local Initiatives Project enabled MPA to elect co-ordinators and pay salaries. Long-term funding was found through the Local Employment Assistance Project, a branch of the federal government concerned with getting unemployed and unemployable people back into the job market. After receiving this funding for three years, MPA was told to turn to local sources and now receives provincial and municipal funding. It was necessary to split up the various aspects of MPA's programme among various government departments, which has caused some practical difficulties, such as more complicated bookkeeping and reporting procedures.

One near-casualty of the change in funding sources was the MPA residence programme. Out of its federal grant, MPA had paid the salaries of the ten residence co-ordinators. All other expenses of the houses were covered by the monthly fees paid by residents: rent or mortgage, utilities, general upkeep, and food. Most residents were eligible for welfare and paid their room and board costs out of their welfare cheques. Those residents who were employed paid the same amount per month as the welfare recipients. Employed residents served as valuable role models for residents who were not yet ready to face the job market. When MPA approached the provincial government with a request to continue the funding on this basis, they were turned down. Instead the government proposed to fund the MPA residences in the same manner as it funded private, proprietary, psychiatric boarding homes. The operator of the house (in this case, MPA) would be paid a per diem amount for each person actually in residence. Residents would not receive full welfare cheques, but instead would receive a twenty-five dollar monthly 'comfort allowance'. Employed residents would either have to pay an exorbitant monthly fee or leave.

The decision as to whether or not to accept the new funding was made by the residents. A vote was held in all the houses, and the residents voted to reject the per diem funding and continue the search for a funding source that would allow MPA residents to maintain control of their own money and their own lives. Residents expressed dissatisfaction with a system that would reduce them to receiving twenty-five dollar a month 'comfort allowances' as too much like being in a hospital or other institution. Several months later, when no other funding source was located, the residents reluctantly voted to accept the new funding rather than shut the houses down.

When I visited MPA in December 1976, membership dissatisfaction with this funding was growing. Residents complained about no longer feeling that the MPA house was their home, since they were now hemmed in by bureaucratic restrictions they had never faced before. The name of each person in residence had to be reported weekly to the Vancouver Resource Board. Residents were faced with arbitrary regulations on how long they could remain in the house, where previously this had been the individual resident's own choice. Linda, who has been an MPA resident for three years, complained:

> The new residence funding is terrible. I'd prefer to get my own money to spend the way I want. Now you always have to be afraid that you'll be kicked out because of some regulation. We've always said that MPA residences are

like our own homes, but in your own house, you can stay as long as you want. Now it's like a baby-sitting service. We have to report to the VRB all the time. If you want to go away for a few weeks or if you have to go back in the hospital, you can lose your bed. Before, you knew you had a place to come back to. I was in hospital for seven weeks in '74, but I knew I had a place to go when I got out, and that made it a lot easier.

Our principles have been damaged by the funding. The residents don't have the say in things that they used to. We have to keep lots of records that we didn't have to keep before. We used to just be able to budget the way a family does, but now it's more of a business-type thing.

What can you do with a twenty-five dollar a month 'comfort allowance'? If you smoke, there's twenty-five dollars right there. We have no flexibility at all. Before, everyone paid rent, and that helps you feel it's your home. This way, it's just like being in a boarding home. If they manage to turn us into regular boarding homes, we'll fold up the houses rather than do that.[3]

In a currently pending application for a federal demonstration project health and welfare grant, MPA detailed the reasons why per diem funding is unsatisfactory:

Since the inception of MPA's residence programme, the emphasis has been on personal and fiscal self-sufficiency, by establishing five individual communal families each member of which contributed a share of the operating costs of the homes.... Under outright funding of co-ordinators' salaries and a small subsidy for operating expenses of the programme, we were able to maintain a mix of people with various sorts of income. Some received handicapped pensions, some had independent incomes, some worked, some had welfare assistance. From this mix our residents have had living examples before them of other alternatives. In August, 1976, rather than close our homes, we were forced to accept per diem funding for our residence programme. Per diem funding is directed toward the individual, not the organisation and its programmes. The rules and regulations of this cost-shared funding dictate against our money management programme; dictate against our members making any financial decisions; dictate against our mix of people, in short, turn MPA homes into very expensive boarding homes.

The regulations also dictate that the length of stay in the programme shall be six months. Our experience has taught us that clients must stay in the programme for as long as they feel the need, be this one month or three years. To set a time limit within which vastly differing individuals must acquire basic living skills, acceptable social behaviour, a comfortable feeling about themselves and the confidence to live independently in the community is completely unrealistic. Fragile people can regress very quickly when they are removed prematurely from a support system. Because of the restrictions of per diem funding we will no longer be able to demonstrate that self-help and power reversal are effective methods of returning people from dependence to independent living in the community.[4]

This account of MPA's funding history shows some of the disadvantages of government funding: rigid programmes and bureaucratic red tape. A truly innovative service was not comprehensible to the bureaucracy in any but the most conventional terms. The government lumped MPA's resident-run communal homes together with proprietary psychiatric boarding homes and insisted on identical funding policies for both. For example, when residents learned they were eligible for clothing allowances, they called the Vancouver Resource Board to apply. The VRB requested house co-ordinators to draw up and submit lists of residents who were eligible, as if residents were incapable of managing this for themselves. MPA is continuing its search for less restrictive funding.

Project Release in New York provides an example of private funding. For more than a year, Project Release had an office in a Universalist church on the Upper West Side of Manhattan. When they decided to seek larger quarters so that they could open their community centre, the church helped put them in contact with a foundation connected to a Unitarian church on Long Island. The foundation was interested in Project Release's innovative programme and gave them a ten-thousand-dollar grant, enough to run the community centre for a year. The main expense is rent; money is also used for office expenses. No one at Project Release receives a salary.

Another possible funding source is the local Community Chest or United Fund. These groups provide funding largely to established organisations and may or may not be open to proposals from innovative alternative services, depending on the composition of their boards. Alternative groups should explore the willingness of such groups in their own community to fund nontraditional services.

Still another approach to fund raising is to set up a business or service that will generate income, as well as employment, for group members. Both Project Release in New York and Project Renaissance in Cleveland are exploring this method of raising money. Project Release is attempting to start a printing co-operative, while Project Renaissance is considering several ventures, including a low-cost moving service aimed toward the poor and the elderly. The aim is for these services to become self-supporting and also provide employment for group members.

How much should an alternative service cost? Alternatives that do not pay salaries can be amazingly inexpensive. Both the

Elizabeth Stone House in Boston and Project Release in New York operate on annual budgets of about ten thousand dollars. These groups help people to stay out of traditional mental health facilities, which are not only ineffective but usually expensive as well (in tax dollars if not in direct costs). Project Release, which has focused on the whole question of recidivism, points out that traditional aftercare services, which cost the state of New York $39,018,200 in fiscal 1975, encourage emotional dependency, produce low self-esteem, and further damage ex-patients' self-image, while self-help promotes self-reliance, self-direction, and individual creativity.[5]

If a project does decide to pay salaries, costs will go up considerably. There are strong arguments both for and against salaries. When all jobs are performed by volunteers, the equality of all members is stressed. It is undeniably true that salaried people (whether they are called co-ordinators, staff, or whatever) are placed in a different role from other members. It is possible for them to become a controlling group. On the other hand, salaries emphasise that helping to run the alternative is important, serious work. Salaried people are free from the scramble of holding down a job while devoting large amounts of time to the service.

If a group decides it wants to pay salaries, it must also put into effect procedures that will prevent the salaried people from becoming the 'establishment'. MPA's practice of holding semiannual elections for salaried positions was begun for precisely this reason. Another important MPA principle is equalised salaries — all co-ordinators make the same amount, with an adjustment based on the number of dependents. MPA's annual budget is in excess of $200,000 a year, most of which goes toward salaries.

It is not accidental that most alternative facilities operate with some kind of collective structure. Breaking down role distinctions is impossible within the usual hierarchical structure of most mental health facilities. By making decisions collectively, alternatives provide clear examples of the benefits of working without hierarchies. Collective decision making can be time-consuming and tedious, but the benefits are enormous. Groups that operate collectively allow all members to take part in the decision-making process. Decisions can be easily changed or modified if they do not work out well in practice, since people are not separated into 'workers' and remote 'policy makers'. Ideally, collective decision-making should involve all people included in the service, whether as workers or clients (to the extent that these distinctions are maintained at all). Groups that exclude clients from the decision-making process are not true alternatives.

Outside requirements (when applying for funding or becoming incorporated, for example) often require that certain individuals be designated as officers. This can be done within the collective structure by making clear within the group that these are ceremonial positions only. Similarly, a requirement that there be a board of directors can be handled by giving overall decision-making power to the group, and only advisory powers to the board of directors. (MPA, as pointed out earlier, voted to abolish even their weak board of directors and make the general meeting the legal governing body of the organisation.)

Working collectively can be difficult, especially at first. But with a genuine commitment to the collective process and to the open discussion of disagreements, collectively run groups can achieve a flexibility and openness impossible with any other kind of internal organisation.

Fund raising does not end once a grant has been secured. The group must look ahead to the end of the grant period. Alternative sources of funding should be investigated long before termination, so that the group does not find itself facing a funding crisis. On the other hand, the group should also be constantly monitoring its own usefulness and not become another automatically self-perpetuating institution.

Funding problems are not the only obstacles to starting viable alternative organisations. Another major difficulty is finding a suitable location for a residence, drop-in centre, or crisis house. Groups will find that they are unwanted in many neighbourhoods. Often, zoning restrictions will make their existence all but impossible. Landlords may be fearful of renting to them as well.

The group should carefully consider exactly what kind of facilities they need. Many kinds of physical structures may be suitable. Drop-in centres, for example, have been located in houses (MPA), storefronts (MPA and Mental Patients' Liberation Project), industrial space (Project Release, Kitchener), or apartments (Project Release, New York). A crisis house or a residence needs a homelike atmosphere and is best located in a single-family house or a spacious apartment. This is where problems of zoning and neighbourhood preference are most likely to arise.

Single-family zoning has been under legal challenge in many cities by people who choose to live communally, by students, and by people who cannot afford rents in particular areas without sharing. Some courts have upheld the rights of communities to limit occupancy to related people, while other courts have said that people living together as families must be regarded as families for zoning purposes. The Community Residential Facility designation achieved by MPA in Vancouver, which permits MPA residences in single-family zones, should be introduced into zoning codes in other cities. A group attempting to establish an alternative facility may find itself enmeshed in local politics, attending zoning board and city council hearings and fighting for less restrictive local zoning laws, before it can even open its doors or else to keep a newly opened service from being closed down.

There are ethical as well as legal issues involved here. Should a community have the right to exclude former mental patients from living there? I believe that a community should no more have this right than it should the right to exclude racial minorities, which is now illegal. The change to allowing people of all races to live where they choose was not accomplished by minority groups passively waiting until the majority decided to allow them to live in their community. Instead, minority groups fought discrimination on many fronts — by buying houses in previously all-white areas, by taking individuals (or even entire communities) to court, by demanding that their rights be respected. Former mental patients, who are similarly discriminated against in regard to housing, should emulate these tactics. In Vancouver, for example, the Mental Patients' Association believes that since its 'members represent a cross-section of people from all areas of society', citizens have a 'responsibility to facilitate the return of people to similar neighbourhoods from which they have come'[6]. MPA's policy has been to assume the right to move into any neighbourhood and to face whatever community opposition may surface. In one case, MPA was forced to give up a rented house when neighbourhood children taunted residents, but most MPA residences have existed peacefully in their chosen neighbourhoods.

Another method of dealing with neighbourhood opposition (one that has been specifically rejected by MPA) is to seek the approval of neighbours before moving in. This implies that ex-patients do not have a right to live where they choose but can live only where other people decide it is permitted. Like racial minorities, ex-patients who wait for neighbourhood permission before moving in are co-operating in their own oppression. The issue is not whether the neighbours want blacks or ex-patients living next door, but whether they have the right to exclude them.

There are strong arguments to be made for the proposition that people living together in a family manner should be considered families for zoning purposes. The legitimate need of a city to establish different residential criteria for families and for hotels, boarding houses, and the like is to regulate public health and safety. Places where people live as strangers to one another need special structural requirements, such as fire stairs, restaurant-type kitchens, lighted exit signs, and so on, because people who are strangers do not assume group responsibility. When people live together in a family manner, on the other hand, these requirements are burdensome and unnecessary restrictions. A group of unrelated people who live together as a family should be no more subject to these restrictions than should a family of the same size. Since these zoning requirements are in dispute in many areas, groups planning to start alternative facilities should thoroughly research local zoning regulations and work to change those that are unreasonable. (A number of states, including California, Colorado, Minnesota, Montana, and Virginia have recently adopted laws permitting group homes in areas zoned for single family use.)

In Boston, the Elizabeth Stone House was visited early in its existence by the city building inspector. 'They told us it was a residential neighbourhood', said a staff member. 'We told them that's what we're doing here — residing.' When the group heard a rumour that the neighbours were unhappy about having them there, staff members visited families on the block. Not only did the rumour prove untrue, but local residents offered to submit a statement to the city that the Elizabeth Stone House was a good neighbour.[7] This approach is much more likely to produce good results than trying to prepare a neighbourhood for the arrival of a facility. Mentalism — the unreasonable fear of mental patients — is likely to influence people who are approached to give permission for the location of a residential alternative service in their community. Asking permission implicitly suggests that there is some reason why the prospective facility is undesirable. Ordinary neighbours are not expected to win community approval before they move in.

Of course, the alternative facility has the obligation to be a responsible neighbour. Neighbourhood standards of cleanliness should be observed. The house should not be unduly noisy. If large numbers of people come and go (as in a drop-in centre), they should avoid loitering in the area, which might be distressing to local residents. By being a good neighbour, the alternative facility can ease community fears about strange, crazy mental patients in their midst.

In New York, the Upper West Side community, which has often united in opposition to traditional halfway houses and aftercare facilities, has been quite supportive of Project Release. They believe that the reason is that the community, sees Project Release members acting as responsible adults, while clients of traditional mental health facilities are maintained in long-term dependency relationships. And, they point out, 'We do live here and feel we are members of the community and make no separation between our needs and everyone else's'[8].

One additional practical problem that must be faced by the group is its relationship with mental health professionals. Again, this is a philosophical as well as a practical matter. A patient-controlled alternative is not merely another part of the mental health system. On the other hand, it will probably want to maintain some communication with traditional psychiatric services. It will want present mental patients to know of its existence. It will want to locate sympathetic professionals who may refer some of their patients to the alternative. It will want to maintain contact with any of its members who may have to return temporarily to mental institutions.

Mental health professionals are often really puzzled by alternative facilities. They are so used to thinking of patients as people who need taking care of that they may find it hard to deal with the fact that ex-patients are the administrators as well as the clients of the alternative. But faced with actual, functioning alternatives, mental health professionals will be forced to deal with the fact that ex-patients are doing what they are supposed to be incapable of doing. This can be a consciousness-raising experience for the professionals.

Another problem that may arise is that some professionals may try to dump their most difficult, undesirable patients on the alternative, using it as a place of last resort. Patient-controlled alternatives should include as members all people who want to participate, not just the rejects of the psychiatric system. As we have seen with MPA, groups must develop ways of dealing with troublesome people as part of their programme.

In one sense, this designation of some matters as purely practical is artificial. Questions of funding, of internal structure, of relations with the community are philosophical questions as well as practical ones. A group that is running (or attempting to start) an alternative facility is challenging some of the basic ideas with which society views the 'mentally ill'. This is a profoundly political act.

NOTES FOR CHAPTER 7

1. Vancouver Emotional Emergency Centre, 'Funding Application', January 1976, p 2.
2. Howard Hillman and Kathryn Natale, *The Art of Winning Government Grants* (New York: Vanguard Press, 1977); and Howard Hillman and Karin Abarbanel, *The Art of Winning Foundation Grants* (New York: Vanguard Press, 1975).
3. Personal interview with Linda, December 21, 1976.
4. Mental Patients' Association, 'Application for Project Grant', 1976, pp 5-6.
5. Project Release, 'Proposal for One Year Grant to Operate A Community Centre', 1976, pp 3-4.
6. Fran Phillips, 'Housing Designation', *In a Nutshell: Mental Patients' Association Newsletter* 4, no 4 (October 1976): p 10.
7. Karn Lindsey, 'Creating A Communal — and Feminist — Therapy'. *Boston Phoenix,* March 4, 1976.
8. Howie T Harp, 'Project Release and the Community', *Silent No Longer! The Newsletter of Project Release* 1, no 4 (n d): p 10.

Chapter Eight

Coercion or Co-operation?

The alternative system that has been described is a completely voluntary one. It is set up to serve people's needs as they define them, not to enforce arbitrary standards of correct behaviour. Alternative institutions are different from mental hospitals — different in underlying philosophy, not just in appearance. They exist out of their clients' needs and are responsive to changes in those needs. Because people cannot be coerced into participating in alternative programmes and because coercion is so basically a part of the traditional mental health system, the most common objection to alternative facilities is that they don't reach the bulk of people who need psychiatric services, people who supposedly are so 'mentally ill' that they don't know that they need help. Involuntary commitment, supposedly, exists so that these people can be cared for. Without involuntary treatment, so the argument runs, the world will be full of 'crazies' wandering the streets, frightening people, and committing crimes.

In different periods of history, the 'mad' have been banished, whipped, or kept locked in cellars or attics. In seventeenth-century Europe, they began to be confined in large institutions, not for purposes of treatment but to remove them from society.[1]

It is only in the past two hundred years that the incarceration of the mentally ill has been held to be treatment. Institutions, which had existed for purposes of confinement, were transformed into hospitals offering treatment — less by changes within the institutions than by changing the names of things. Inmates became patients, directors became medical superintendents, and the various methods of enforcing discipline (cold baths, solitary confinement, and straitjackets among them) became medical treatments.[2] Since the mentally ill were almost universally loathed and feared, no one objected to their incarceration and brutalisation (except, one suspects, the 'mad' themselves, and no one listened to them).

These attitudes toward mental illness are not merely part of the past. They exist today, side by side with the contemporary mental health ideology that declares that mental illness is an illness like any other. Despite this, suspected mental illness is simply not viewed in the same category as suspected pneumonia or heart disease. Even those ex-patients who have been pronounced cured of mental illness by psychiatrists are viewed with suspicion, as Thomas Eagleton discovered when he tried to run for vice-president. Mental illness is not strictly a medical concept; the judgement that an individual is 'crazy' is usually made by lay people and then confirmed by medical opinion. The public fear of mental patients includes ex-patients as well.

Mental health professionals are not immune to this prejudice. They, too, tend to view the mentally ill as strange beings, unable to communicate directly, always needing care, and never to be trusted. One study of 'schizophrenics' states that 'the chronic schizophrenic is intriguing because he negates many criteria which have been used to distinguish men from other animals.... The chronic schizophrenic ... violates so many functional definitions of man (that) there is heuristic value in studying him with an approach, like that which would be used to study any alien creature'.[3]

In addition to viewing their patients as strange, psychiatrists also frequently don't listen to them. Psychiatrists are prone to interpret clear verbal messages of patients as having hidden meanings, especially when the patient is saying something the psychiatrist doesn't want to hear. Psychiatrist Philip Margolis has presented the case of a patient in his 'therapeutic community' — her statements are juxtaposed with Margolis's comments (which appear in brackets):

> I broke the door. I was venting my anger. Just sitting here on pins and needles. They were waiting to decide how to dispose of me (the use of the word 'dispose' is significant: (the patient) had succeeded in getting everyone angry with her). They are planning long-term hospitalisation (true). Last night I demanded my release. Nobody took me seriously (true). I was very serious. There is nothing legal holding me here — nothing but brute strength and locked doors (in essence, this was also true). I don't like it here (not true).[4]

Margolis, who wants to believe that the ward he runs is humane, ignores the patient's clear expressions of anger at her treatment, instead labelling her behaviour 'acting out'.[5] Although it is clear from Margolis's account that this patient was being held in violation of her legal rights, it is justified because it is what she 'really' wants and needs.

The enormous distance between patients and staff members in mental institutions makes meaningful human contact difficult or impossible. There is no real equality. Patients are under the control of staff members, whose job includes reporting on the conversations and activities of patients. Patients who complain of feeling spied on are often labelled paranoid. Patients are required to be open about their thoughts and feelings, but personal questions asked of staff members are seldom directly answered, and all sorts of pathological motives may be imputed to even asking them. Psychologist David Rosenhan, during his stay in a mental hospital as a 'pseudopatient', observed a patient who was beaten by an attendant after telling the attendant, 'I like you'.[6] Patients are frequently addressed by their first names but are required to use last names and titles when addressing staff members.[7]

The long history of the coercive mental health system, with its emphasis on control, makes it difficult to imagine that a truly open system can work. But there is a vicious cycle of reasoning at work here. Patients, viewed as dangerous and untrustworthy, are kept under strict control, which further increases the suspicion in which they are held. People begin to believe that only through control can the mentally ill be kept from 'running amok', and the image is perpetuated. Even though patients are seldom violent, this is attributed only to the effectiveness of control. A noncoercive model becomes impossible to imagine.

Intertwined with the belief in strangeness is the belief that mental patients are dangerous. The National Association for Mental Health USA), which usually pushes the line that mental illness is no different from any other disease and is not a stigma, publishes a booklet for police officers, instructing them on how to take mental patients into custody. People are not usually hauled in by the police because they have heart disease, diabetes, or cancer — mental illness is clearly *not* an illness like any other. The NAMH book instructs police officers in how to apply armlock holds or 'restraints such as leather cuffs and anklets that are used in mental hospitals' when apprehending people who are 'violently disturbed'.[8] The possibility that it is the fact of being forcibly restrained that causes the expressions of rage is not even considered. This is just another example of how behaviour that is considered normal (such as fighting back when attacked) becomes abnormal once someone is considered mentally ill. The 'patient' is expected to acquiesce to treatment others would fight, and the patient's struggle is considered a 'symptom'.

The myth of dangerousness is continually perpetuated. Television crime shows would go out of business without the 'psychopathic killer', whose murderous frenzies are attributed to mental illness.[9] Thriller movies frequently use the same subject. Although few mental patients commit crimes, those who do are widely publicised. Ex-patients who live law-abiding lives generally go unnoticed. As psychologist Thomas Scheff has pointed out, 'An item like the following is almost inconceivable: 'Mrs Ralph Jones, an ex-mental patient, was elected president of the Fairview Home and Garden Society at their meeting last Thursday'.[10] The media do not report a person's ex-patient status in order to be objective; an 'ex-mental patient' is a code word for a violent, dangerous, unpredictable individual.

Not only are the mentally ill not especially dangerous, but many studies have shown that psychiatrists are unable to predict dangerousness — and it is the psychiatric prediction of dangerousness that results in involuntary commitment. Psychiatrists for some reason have seldom even researched the question of whether or not they are accurate predictors of dangerousness. Lawyer Alan M Dershowitz found fewer than a dozen such studies after conducting a thorough survey of the literature.[11] Those studies that were made showed that psychiatrists regularly overpredicted dangerousness. The Dershowitz study found 'that for every correct psychiatric prediction of violence, there are numerous erroneous predictions. That is, among every group of inmates presently confined on the basis of psychiatric predictions of violence, there are only a few who would, and many more who would not, actually engage in such conduct if released'.[12]

Thomas Scheff has pointed out that 'physicians learn early in their training that it is far more culpable to dismiss a sick patient than to retain a well one. This rule is so pervasive and fundamental that it goes unstated in textbooks on diagnosis'.[13] While this may work to the patient's benefit in most areas of medcine, in psychiatry 'the assumption that medical diagnosis can cause no irreversible harm to the patient's status is dubious'.[14]

Involuntary commitment has become a substitute form of preventive detention. It is illegal in the United States to lock someone up in a jail or prison because of the expectation that the person will commit a crime if allowed to remain at liberty. This principle is one of the foundations of the American legal system. But once the prospective criminal is presumed to be mentally ill, a different set of standards applies. A psychiatric allegation of potential dangerousness *can* result in confinement (called 'treatment') in a mental hospital. Patients, under these circumstances, quite rightly view their confinement as punishment, not treatment.

The increasing involvement of psychiatry in the criminal justice system is, I believe, a dangerous trend in the United States today.[15] Some psychiatrists have even argued that crime is a product of mental illness, and that criminals require psychiatric treatment.[16] Psychiatrists have gained enormous power within the prison system, and prisons have come increasingly to resemble mental hospitals. Psychoactive drugs and behaviour modification programmes are the most common forms of prison psychiatric 'treatment'. The increasing psychiatric involvement in the criminal justice system has not led to the decrease in crime rates that optimistic penal psychiatrists used to predict.

Perhaps the prison most like a mental hospital is the Patuxent Institution for Defective Delinquents in Jessup, Maryland. Patuxent's 'patients' are convicted criminals who have been labelled 'defective delinquents'. Any convicted Maryland prisoner can be sent (at the request of the court or the state prison) to Patuxent for examination; those prisoners adjudged by the Patuxent staff to have compulsive criminal tendencies are transferred to Patuxent, and their criminal sentences are transformed to indefinite terms. Patuxent's 'patients', no matter the length of their criminal sentences, remain incarcerated until adjudged cured. Prisoners found to be 'criminally insane' do not go to Patuxent but to state hospitals. Patuxent's 'patients' are prisoners considered sane enough to fall outside the criminally insane category but not sane enough to escape the compulsory attention of psychiatrists.

Once committed to Patuxent, patients face a rigidly structured environment that punishes any form of non-confirmity. Only by attending mandatory group therapy, obeying the rules of the institution, and showing the correct attitude can a 'patient' earn such 'privileges' as a later bedtime or access to recreational facilities.

Not surprisingly, most psychiatrists approve of such a system. Dr Karl Menninger, for example, suggests that citizens of Maryland should be 'as proud of their remarkable Patuxent as they are of their Johns Hopkins' and expresses surprise that lawsuits have been brought against Patuxent.[17] Menninger's opinions are representative of psychiatric thinking — he has received the Isaac Ray Award for contributions to the fields of law and psychiatry.

Nonpsychiatrists who have studied Patuxent come away with a somewhat different impression. Journalist Phil Stanford interviewed a Patuxent 'patient' who had been sentenced to four years for auto theft at age seventeen, yet was still in Patuxent with no hope of release after serving fourteen years. His refusal to co-operate with the treatment staff, because he thought their practices were oppressive, was viewed by the staff as pathological.[18]

In her book *Kind and Usual Punishment,* Jessica Mitford interviewed a volunteer teacher who had worked at Patuxent for nine years. Although he originally approved of Patuxent, he discovered that 'defective delinquents' were so loosely defined that nearly any prisoner could qualify. He also found that the supposedly humane indeterminate sentence severely demoralised the prisoners, who saw in it, quite rightly, 'the naked, absolute power of the state'.[19]

Mitford also tells the dramatic story of a Patuxent 'patient' who spent six years appealing his conviction, refused compulsory treatment, and was kept on the lowest 'tier' for six years. Patients at this level are kept locked in their cells virtually twenty-four hours a day, are allowed only one shower a week, and are denied mail and visitors. Most Patuxent 'patients' remain on the lowest tier for thirty to sixty days, but staff kept this 'patient' on the lowest tier because of his refusal to accept 'treatment'. When his case came before the Supreme Court, the horrified justices ordered his immediate release, finding that compulsory psychiatric interviews violated his Fifth Amendment right to remain silent.[20]

Psychiatrist Thomas Szasz has stated, 'Patuxent is worse than the way they use mental institutions in Russia, except that when they haul someone off over there everyone here gets upset',[21] The concern of Americans with Soviet political dissidents does not extend to the social and cultural dissidents in American mental institutions.

To the psychiatrists who designed Patuxent and similar programmes, compulsion is benign, since the purpose is to 'help' the inmate. But coercion often precludes the possibility of any real help being offered, since, as Szasz has pointed out over and over again, combining the roles of helper and jailer means that only the jailer's definition of help is acceptable. In a legal brief defending Patuxent's practices, the state claimed that it had the 'right to compel co-operation' by 'an indeterminate stay in the diagnostic area (the lowest tier) of Patuxent until co-operation is obtained'.[22] Such practices violate the commonsense meanings of both 'help' and 'co-operation'.

How effective is Patuxent's programme? In 1972, after eighteen years of operation, Patuxent had held a total of 985 committed prisoners (in addition to those held for examination before transfer back to regular prisons); of those, only 115 have been pronounced cured and released. Thirty-eight per cent of all Patuxent's 'patients' are kept beyond the term of their original sentence.[23] A further breakdown of statistics shows that in 1972 only 38 per cent of Patuxent 'patients' were serving time for the crimes of murder, second-degree murder, assault with intent to murder, and forcible rape (or attempted rape). Fifty-one per cent were guilty of robbery, robbery with a deadly weapon, breaking and entering, housebreaking, car theft, and similar crimes, including two 'rogues and vagabonds', two forgers, and two bad-cheque passers. Eleven per cent were serving time for sex crimes, including 'perverted practices' (twenty-nine cases), indecent exposure, and 'attempted perversion'.

Psychiatrists frequently express the desire to treat the 'potentially dangerous' before they commit crimes, thus averting violent incidents. Psychiatrist Renatus Hartogs, for example, wrote a book that claimed that early psychiatric treatment could have prevented the assassination of President Kennedy by Lee Harvey Oswald and Oswald subsequent murder by Jack Ruby.[24] (Hartogs, unlike many people who have studied the assassination, is convinced of Oswald's guilt.) Hartogs was chief psychiatrist at Youth House in New York City when he saw Lee Oswald, who had been sent to the facility because of truancy. On the basis of a single psychiatric interview, Hartogs diagnosed the thirteen-year old Oswald as having a 'personality pattern disturbance with schizoid features and passive-aggressive tendencies' and recommended psychiatric treatment on either an outpatient or a residential basis.[25] Both Oswald and his mother resisted psychiatric interference in their lives, and they eventually left the city. Hartogs clearly believes that had Lee Oswald gone into treatment, the assassination of President Kennedy might never have happened. Hartogs attributes Oswald's murder by Jack Ruby to Ruby's failure to receive psychiatric treatment as an adolescent, as well.

Because of his truancy, Oswald was required to report regularly to a probation officer. After the assassination, the probation officer expressed the same belief about the 'tragedy' of Oswald's not getting early psychiatric treatment.[26] There is absolutely no evidence to support such faith in the efficacy of institutionalisation and 'treatment'. There is, in fact, some indication that children placed in residential facilities go on to become more antisocial. Recidivism in juvenile facilities approaches 80 per cent.[27] Yet both Oswald's probation officer and his psychiatrist recommended possible residential treatment. The probation officer paints a somewhat idyllic picture of what life in such a facility is like: 'They have cottages for youngsters in trouble, with supervision by cottage 'mothers' and most of all, psychiatric treatment and follow-up therapy'.[28] In actuality, facilities that go under the name of training schools and the like are grim places with heavy emphasis on custody and frequent instances of brutality. Educator Kenneth Wooden, who visited juvenile detention facilities around the country, found a pattern of staff violence and neglect in nearly every strate.[29] Many institutions are miniature jails, with high fences topped with barbed wire, barred windows, and solitary confinement cells. Corporal punishment is frequent and severe, while education is infrequent or, in some cases, nonexistent. Is this the system that would have 'saved' Lee Harvey Oswald?

A better example of the results of the juvenile justice system is Charles Manson, who, unlike Oswald, did not escape incarceration at the age of thirteen. His 'crime' was that his mother didn't want him.[30] From then on, he was seldom out of institutions, and his brief periods of freedom usually ended with the commission of a crime and sentencing to still another institution. (Manson had not been a lawbreaker before he was institutionalised.) Wooden finds that 'Manson was the product of too many impersonal institutions, too many endless days in solitary confinement, too many sexual assaults by older boys and far too many beatings by guardians and institutional personnel.'[31] While psychiatrists might argue that state training schools are not treatment facilities and that with more money and more treatment, conditions would improve, we have already seen that psychiatric 'treatment' often includes dehumanisation and solitary confinement and that brutality in mental hospitals is all too common. The historical confusion of confinement with treatment has had, and continues to have, tragic consequences. Putting people in detention facilities called mental hospitals is considered humane. Improving mental hospitals then becomes a matter of providing more treatment. It doesn't matter if the patients call it torture.

In 1960, Morton Birnbaum, a lawyer and a medical doctor, published a paper that argued that mental patients have a Constitutional right to treatment. According to Birnbaum, 'If a person is involuntarily institutionalised in a mental institution because he is sufficiently mentally ill to require institutionalisation for care and treatment, he needs, and is entitled to, adequate medical treatment'.[32] Birnbaum clearly believed that there were effective and safe forms of psychiatric treatment, and that, given additional appropriations, state hospitals would be transformed from custodial institutions to active treatment centres. Both these assumptions are questionable, at best. While Birnbaum argued that a patient who was denied treatment should be released, he made no provision for patients to object to the form of treatment. Birnbaum, with humane motives, refers to mental patients as sick people who need psychiatric treatment, but at the same time he never questions the coercive circumstances under which most people become mental patients. If mental patients have, as Birnbaum claims, a Constitutional right to treatment, why can't they exercise that right in the same way as medical patients — by seeing their doctors when they find their condition distressing? The right to treatment is not a device to protect mental patients from coercion. On the contrary, so long as the patient is being subjected to active treatment, even if under protest, the right to treatment expressly defends the state's right to hold him or her.

The right to treatment has formed the basis for several important lawsuits concerning the rights of mental patients. In Alabama, patients at the state hospital and state school for the retarded sued the state, arguing that the totally inadequate conditions at the institutions violated their Constitutional right to treatment. On April 13, 1972, the federal district court ruled that patients did have a right to treatment and that the state was violating the patients' rights by providing only custodial care. In order to guarantee that patients' rights would be respected, the court set minimum staffing standards, provided that each institution establish a human rights committee, required that each resident have an individualised treatment plan, and set up a number of other requirements. The decision was upheld by the Court of Appeals on November 8, 1974.[33]

Bruce Ennis, a lawyer for the Mental Health Law Project who argued the patients' case, has stated his reservations about the concept of a right to treatment. He refused to take a number of earlier right to treatment cases because he saw the right to treatment as 'a legitimising stamp on involuntary commitment, another basis for depriving people of their liberty'.[34] In the Alabama case, his use of the right to treatment was a tactic:

> I became involved in the Alabama 'right to treatment' case because we had some advance information that the judge in that case would not only say there is something in the abstract called the 'right to treatment', but that he would set standards so high that the state of Alabama literally would not be able to meet them. For example, he required that there be at least one PhD psychologist for every sixty 'mentally retarded' children in institutions. There simply were not enough psychologists in the state of Alabama to staff the institutions at that ratio with the then current resident populations. Using that ratio meant that instead of hiring more psychologists Alabama was going to have to discharge many of the residents in its institutions.[35]

The right to treatment, according to Ennis's interpretation, was to be used not to provide more psychiatric treatment to often unwilling patients but to force the states to free thousands of patients.

Another important right to treatment case was brought by Kenneth Donaldson, an involuntary patient who was held in a Florida state hospital for fifteen years. Donaldson began fighting his commitment as soon as he was institutionalised, but his numerous writs of habeas corpus were ignored by the court. When he saw a newspaper article about the right to treatment theory, he wrote to Dr Birnbaum who became his legal advisor. Later, Bruce Ennis also joined Donaldson's legal team. Donaldson did not want treatment, he wanted freedom, but he saw the right to treatment as a device to force the hospital to release him, since it provided no treatment and only the most minimal custodial care. Donaldson's case eventually went to the United States Supreme Court, which ruled, on June 26, 1975, that 'a State cannot constitutionally confine without (treatment) a nondangerous individual who is capable of surviving safely in freedom by himself or with the help of willing and responsible family members or friends'.[36] The Supreme Court did not specifically rule on whether or not there was a Constitutional right to treatment. Donaldson, in any case, was fighting for the 'right to treatment or release'.[37]

The Mental Health Law Project has also been involved in promoting another new right for mental patients. The right to the least restrictive alternative was advanced in a case brought in 1973 against the District of Columbia and the Department of Health, Education and Welfare, which administers Saint Elizabeth's, the District's 'state' hospital. Although a study by the National Institute of Mental Health (a branch of HEW) in 1970 had found that more than half of the hospital's patients could be discharged to community facilities, there were no such places for them to go, and the patients remained in the hospital. The lawsuit, brought in the names of several individual patients, argued that they had the legal right to treatment in the community and that holding patients in the overly confining atmosphere of the hospital violated their right to treatment. On December 23, 1975, the federal district court ruled in favour of the patients and directed that community facilities be set up.[38]

Ex-patient groups have argued that rather than a 'right' to treatment, which many patients neither need nor want, mental patients should have the right to refuse treatment. A major lawsuit testing this right was filed by seven patients at Boston State Hospital, many of whom had been members of a patients' rights group that was conducted weekly in the hospital with the aid of the Mental Patients' Liberation Front. The suit, *Rogers v Macht,*is scheduled for trial in federal district court in Boston in the summer of 1977. Since both sides have stated that they will appeal an adverse decision, it will probably be several years before there is a final judicial determination as to whether patients do indeed have a right to refuse treatment. If the position of the patients is upheld and the right to refuse treatment is recognised, mental hospitals will no longer be permitted to force patients to take medication or to put patients in seclusion except in tightly defined emergency situations.

The right to refuse treatment suit highlights the distinctions between coercion and treatment, distinctions that are now blurred. The right to refuse treatment will allow mental patients to play the same role in deciding their treatment that medical patients now play. Medical patients consult doctors when they believe that they are ill, are advised of diagnosis and possible treatment, and choose which treatment they will receive (or choose to receive no treatment or to consult another doctor). When mental patients are allowed to choose whether to accept treatment and what treatment to accept, stupefying patients with drugs or locking them in solitary confinement will no longer be allowed to pass for treatment. If psychiatry has truly valid treatments to offer, treatments that benefit the patient (from the patient's point of view), then people in distress will be truly served by mental hospitals. Psychiatry has never had to face this test.

Meanwhile, people who want real help with their problems are badly served by a system of coercion masquerading as treatment. People who go voluntarily to mental hospitals, expecting care and concern, are in for a rude awakening. I know — I was one of them. Once inside the institution, all patients, voluntary and involuntary, people seeking help with their problems and people wanting only freedom, are treated exactly the same way. Patients who expect to find counselling and advice get tranquillisers instead. Patients who don't co-operate are often considered troublemakers, even if their 'nonco-operation' is an attempt to find the help that mental health ideology teaches is readily available in mental hospitals.

It is this group of mental patients — those who are troubled and looking for ways to get their lives in order — who can be better served by alternative facilities than by the traditional mental health system. People who are motivated to make changes in their lives do not need the mindless routine of the typical mental hospital, with its premium on following orders and not making waves. They do not need locked doors (or open doors they are forbidden to walk through). The shock of finding themselves in a prisonlike atmosphere when they were expecting warm, supportive human contact often increases the problems they brought with them to the hospital. And the stigma they face upon discharge provides an added handicap.

In alternative facilities, to which these people will come willingly since they are troubled and are seeking help, there is no deadening institutional routine, no naked exercise of power. If they do not find the help that is provided satisfactory, clients can make demands that things be changed (demands that must be taken seriously in a true alternative), or they can leave and find another source of help. Facilities that clients find unsatisfactory must change or go out of business, since (unlike mental institutions) their clients are always free to leave.

And what of the other group of mental hospital inmates, those who are there against their will, who do not view themselves as needing help? What would happen to them in a truly voluntary, noncoercive mental health system? Obviously, they would not come to alternative facilities, since they don't think they have problems and aren't looking for any help. My answer is simple, although it will not satisfy those who believe that psychiatric diagnoses justify involuntary detention for purposes of 'treatment'. People who are believed by others to be 'mentally ill', who do not themselves want treatment, should be free to live their lives as they choose, unless they commit crimes (which statistics show is unlikely). As the Supreme Court ruled in the Donaldson case, 'the mere presence of mental illness does not disqualify a person from preferring his home to the comforts of an institution'.[39] Since those 'comforts' usually include barren surroundings and total powerlessness, perhaps the choice not to enter a mental institution should be seen, in itself, as evidence of 'sanity'.

The public fear of the 'mentally ill' is not sufficient reason to justify involuntary commitment. The public dislikes mental patients, mentally retarded people, the physically disabled, the deformed or disfigured — and often such people are incarcerated in institutions euphemistically called hospitals, schools, and homes. Attorney Bruce Ennis, who has fought many legal cases for those in mental institutions, recognises that these unpopular groups cannot depend on the public's goodwill:

> I think that most people don't like 'mental patients'. They don't like anyone whom they cannot categorise neatly into an acceptable niche that is comfortable for them. I think if it were put to a popular referendum, the people in this country would favour massive custodial warehouses where people are swept off the streets and kept for the rest of their lives and drugged, tranquillised, shocked, whatever is necessary to keep them off the streets. I literally believe that is the way people feel about it.[40]

The public's aversion to people who are different is not sufficient reason to justify locking them up. When the differences are psychiatric judgements of pathology, a category is created that could, and does, include nearly anyone. The state does, of course, have the right to intervene in people's lives and perhaps to incarcerate them if they violate the rights of others. People who talk to themselves, dress oddly, don't eat right, or display other psychiatric 'symptoms' are not criminals. Being odd or unusual is simply not in the same category as being assaultive. People who attack others should be locked up, and sufficient laws exist to accomplish this without recourse to psychiatric justifications. (The many flaws of the criminal justice system lie outside the scope of this book.) People who are subjected to involuntary commitment are almost always people who would go free if the state had to prove that they had committed criminal acts, or even that they were truly — rather than potentially — dangerous.

Millions of people are incarcerated in mental institutions who have violated no law, but who have committed the 'crime' of being offensive to others and have therefore been diagnosed as mentally ill. The American public is not ashamed of this. Perhaps some day it will be.

NOTES FOR CHAPTER 8

1. For an account of the history of the confinement of the mad in Europe see Michel Foucault, *Madness and Civilisation* (New York: Pantheon Books, 1975). For a similar account of it in the United States, see David J Rothman, *The Discovery of the Asylum* (Boston: Little, Brown & Co, 1971).
2. Foucault, *Madness and Civilisation,* pp 266-267.
3. Schooler and D Parkle, 'The Overt Behaviour of Chronic Schizophrenics and its Relationship to Their Internal States and Personal History', quoted in *Methods of Madness* by Benjamin M Braginsky, Dorothea D Braginsky, and Kenneth Ring (New York: Holt, Rinehart and Winston, 1969), p 32.
4. Philip M Margolis, *Patient Power* (Springfield, Ill: Charles C Thomas, 1973), p 49.

5. Ibid, p 50.
6. DL Rosenhan, 'On Being Sane in Insane Places', Science 179 (January 19, 1973): p 256.
7. For an example, see Robert Perrucci, *Circle of Madness* (Englewood Cliffs, N.J.: Prentice-Hall, 1974), p 60.
8. Robert A Matthews and Lloyd W Rowland, *How to Recognise and Handle Abnormal People* (Arlington, Va: National Association for Mental Health, 1975 edition), pp 13-14.
9. Otto Wahl, 'Six TV Myths About Mental Illness', *TV Guide,* March 13-19, 1976, pp 4-8.
10. Thomas J Scheff, *Being Mentally Ill* (Chicago: Aldine Publishing Company, 1966), p 72.
11. Alan M Dershowitz, 'The Psychiatrist's Power in Civil Commitment: A Knife That Cuts Both Ways', *Psychology Today* 2, no 9 (February 1969): pp 43-47.
12. Ibid, p 47.
13. Scheff, *Being Mentally Ill,* p 110.
14. Ibid, p 114.
15. Thomas S Szasz has written extensively on this point. See, for example, *Law, Liberty and Psychiatry* (New York: Macmillan, 1963) and *Psychiatric Justice* (New York: Macmillan, 1965).
16. See, for example, Karl Menninger, *The Crime of Punishment* (New York: Viking Press, 1968), or Seymour L Halleck, *Psychiatry and the Dilemmas of Crime* (New York: Harper & Row, 1967).
17. Menninger, *Crime of Punishment,* p 243.
18. Phil Stanford, 'A Model, Clockwork-Orange Prison', *New York Times Magazine,* September 17, 1972, p 80.
19. Jessica Mitford, *Kind and Usual Punishment* (New York: Alfred A Knopf, 1973), pp 110-111.
20. Ibid, pp 109-112.
21. Stanford, 'A Model Prison', p 71.
22. Quoted in Mitford, *Kind and Usual Punishment,* p 112.
23. Stanford, 'A Model Prison', pp 78-80.
24. Renatus Hartogs and Lucy Freeman, *The Two Assassins* (New York: Thomas Y Crowell Company, 1965).
25. Ibid, pp 229-231.
26. The newspaper interview with Oswald's probation officer is reprinted in *Lee Harvey Oswald and the American Dream* by Paul Sites (New York: Pageant Press, 1967), pp 72-76.

27. Kenneth Wooden, *Weeping in the Playtime of Others* (New York: McGraw-Hill Book Company, 1976), p 25.

28. Quoted in Sites, *Lee Harvey Oswald,* p 74.

29. Wooden's *Weeping in the Playtime of Others* is not an 'objective' study. It is a horrified (and horrifying) look at the way American society treats its unwanted children.

30. Ibid, p 48.

31. Ibid

32. Morton Birnbaum, 'The Right to Treatment', *American Bar Association Journal* 46, no 5 (May 1960): p 503.

33. Information about *Wyatt v Stickney* from 'The Docket: Test Case Litigation', *Mental Health Law Project Summary of Activities,* March, 1975, pp 2-3.

34. Leonard Roy Frank, 'Interview with Bruce Ennis', *Madness Network News* 2, no 2 (February 1974): p 10. Reprinted in *Madness Network News Reader,* ed Sherry Hirsch et al (San Francisco: Glide Publications, 1974) pp 162-167.

35. Ibid

36. Quoted in Kenneth Donaldson, *Insanity Inside Out* (New York: Crown Publishers, 1976), p 327.

37. Ibid, p 330.

38. Information about *Dixon v Weinberger* from Paul R. Friedman, 'Beyond Dixon: The Principle of the Least Restrictive Alternative', *Mental Health Law Project Summary of Activities* 2, no 1 (March 1976): pp 1-3.

39. Quoted in Donaldson, *Insanity Inside Out,* p 328.

40. Frank, 'Interview with Bruce Ennis', p 10.

Chapter Nine

People, not Patients

My experiences in mental institutions were not unique. I was lucky — I wasn't committed for very long (although at the time it felt like eternity), and, unlike most troubled people, I finally was able to find a truly caring and helpful alternative. While millions of Americans have experienced the desolation and horror of mental institutions (and many have had far worse experiences than mine), only a handful have been fortunate enough to find the real help offered by true alternatives. Unless drastic changes are made in the way this society deals with those in emotional pain, people will continue to find indifference and neglect (as well as outright brutality) far more often than care and concern.

We need to look at our conceptions of mental 'health' and mental 'illness' and to challenge the psychiatric myths that pervade our culture. When troubled people are defined as 'mentally ill', they suffer the additional pain of psychiatric 'treatment' and the stigma of becoming mental patients. But the patients are not the only ones who suffer. Because psychiatric ideology mystifies people's difficulties into an 'illness' that only experts are thought capable of treating, we are all rendered a little less human. By turning our friends, our relatives, and ourselves over to psychiatry, we abandon and isolate people when they most need love and nurturance. The continual redefining of various kinds of problems as psychiatric in nature, requiring expert intervention, continually limits the extent to which people reach out to one another and increases the isolation in which we twentieth-century Americans more and more find ourselves. Rather than caring for one another, we turn to remote authority figures and experts, reinforcing the notion that one needs professional degrees and credentials in order to avoid doing irreparable harm to troubled people. And when the system fails to work, when our mental institutions turn out people more troubled, more frightened than they were before, we call for more experts, for newer treatments, unable (or unwilling) to acknowledge that the mental health system is a monster that damages, degrades, and often desroys those people it claims to help.

This is a problem not just for patients and ex-patients but for everyone, because anyone can become a mental patient. As we have seen, people who don't fit smoothly into their assigned social roles, people who are troubled or unhappy (or 'excessively' happy) can easily find themselves psychiatrically labelled and the subjects (or perhaps one should say, the objects) of compulsory treatment. Or troubled people may voluntarily enter mental hospitals, often to discover too late that no real help is offered and that they may not be allowed to leave.

There is much that must be done in order to build a system of viable alternatives. It is not a job that can be turned over to the 'experts', who have already failed. It is a task that must be done by all of us, ordinary citizens, working together. Those of us who are ex-patients have a vital role to play, since we know firsthand the inner workings of the present system and how it differs from the face it presents to the world. By experiencing consciousness-raising together, we can learn to see clearly the ways in which the psychiatric system has damaged us and the kinds of services that will provide true alternatives to paternalism and oppression. By working together to build alternatives that truly serve our needs, former patients can help ourselves and one another to grow strong.

As I have tried to show, setting up an alternative facility involves many different kinds of activities. The group must define needs and actions. This is best done side by side with consciousness-raising, without the presence of nonpatients. Ex-patients must deal with their own mentalism before they can challenge the mentalism of others.

But everyone, ex-patient or not, can begin to challenge mentalist attitudes wherever they may be found. What do we mean when we call a person 'sick' because we don't like his or her behaviour? We don't *really* mean that the person is suffering from an illness; it's an easy way to discredit or dismiss that person's ideas or actions, a way not to listen to what he or she is saying. It's a way of turning the 'problem' over to the experts — the psychiatrists — even though we know that we wouldn't want that to happen to us. We use words that sound clean and sterile, 'mental illness' and 'mental hospital', when we know we mean 'crazy' and 'snake pit' and 'booby hatch'. We draw away from anyone we know who is a mental patient, and we draw away from the unknown and mysterious areas within ourselves. Mentalism cripples us all.

We must begin to turn toward the people we now isolate — the troubled (and troubling) relatives and friends we both love and fear. It will not be easy. The mental hospital system has developed precisely because this is a job we would rather leave to others. We must encourage and support the kinds of alternatives that will allow troubled and unhappy people to change and grow, even though it means we will no longer be able to sweep the problems out of sight. We must support the establishment of neighbourhood crisis centres, drop-in centres, community residences, and group homes — in our own neighbourhoods, not merely somewhere else, safe and far away. And we must welcome back into our communities even those people so damaged by years of psychiatric incarceration that they may always remain a bit different, a little odd. Only by bringing an end to the mental hospital system can we prevent a new generation of these chronic patients, people who have been lost behind the walls that have hidden psychiatry's mistakes for too long. Only by building a network of real, community-based alternatives will we be able to prevent today's troubled people from being similarly damaged and crippled.

As we struggle to create real alternatives, we must also guard against what has been termed, by Thomas Szasz and others, psychiatric imperialism — the spread of psychiatric power and control throughout society. We must distinguish true alternatives from mini-mental institutions and work to ensure that community facilities are controlled by their communities and by their clients, not by a centralised psychiatric bureaucracy. 'Community' facilities, too, can have locked doors and rigid, hierarchical structures; they, too, can dehumanise and control. We must demand only services that are responsive to their communities and their clients, alternatives that differ from one another to meet local and individual needs. Otherwise, we will not have solved the problem; we will have changed only the terminology, and we will continue to dehumanise troubled people.

Community has become an important word in psychiatry. 'Community' mental health centres have been established around the country, and many professionals now call themselves 'community' psychiatrists. But the typical community mental health centre is no more a part of the community in which it is built than is the typical state hospital. Most community mental health centres are run by psychiatrists, or other mental health professionals, chosen by a state bureaucracy, who follow policies established by that bureaucracy. Professionals tend to categorise community residents only as patients or potential patients, or at best as 'paraprofessionals', who perform in the lowest-paid, lowest-status jobs. No real community is created, just the same old hierarchies. If this is to become the 'alternative' to mental hospitals, nothing essential will have changed.

Community mental health centres are not replacing the state hospital system; they are a growing, parallel bureaucracy. Community mental health centres *need* state hospitals as weapons with which to threaten their 'difficult' patients. And the state hospital bureaucracies, which have held power within each state for well over a hundred years, are not simply folding their tents and stealing away into the night. In many states, new state hospitals are being built (and filled). And in nearly every state the scandals of patient mistreatment and abuse continue, quietly for the most part, but occasionally breaking out into the open, sparking investigations that usually die down quickly and without inspiring any real changes.

For real change is impossible in a system that continues to transform people into mental patients, whether the system is 'community based' or not. Only by providing alternatives in which people help one another will we break the cycle in which we strip troubled people of their humanity and then turn from them in fear. Only by reaching out to one another, by replacing professional 'expertise' with human concern and psychiatric labelling with the recognition of our shared humanity, will we create the opportunity for all of us to change and develop.

We cannot eliminate 'problems'. But we can do away with a system that stigmatises those who have problems and makes us all fear to recognise the problems within ourselves. The psychiatric system damages us all, because it teaches us (falsely) that those kinds of difficulties it claims to treat are illnesses and that the people who suffer from them are essentially different from other, 'normal' people. Only by developing true alternatives can we prove that we can care for one another far better than psychiatry has 'cared' for its patients who have suffered under its control for too long.

Appendix

List of UK groups run by patients and ex-patients

The groups listed below are made up of users and ex-users of mental health services. The addresses and contacts were correct at the date of publication but are liable to change. If you are unable to contact one of the groups listed or if there isn't a group listed for your area, indeed if you are interested in forming a group, MIND's consumer network worker will do her best to help.

MIND Consumer Network Worker, 22 Harley Street, London W1N 2ED. Tel 01-637 0741.

NATIONAL

Survivors Speak Out, c/o Peter Campbell, 33 Lichfield Road, London, NW2 2RG

Schizophrenia Survivors Group,
c/o Chesterfield & District Branch of the National Schizophrenia Fellowship, Unit 19/20, Central Avenue, Boythorpe, Chesterfield

British Network for Alternatives to Psychiatry,
158 Rivermead Court, Hurlingham, London SW6

LONDON

Barnet Action for Mental Health Group, c/o Dee Kraaij, (Community Worker) 16 High Road, East Finchley, London, N2 9PJ

Camden Mental Health Consortium, c/o Emma Baatz, 8 Burgess Hill, London NW2 2WA

Ealing Mental Health Action Group, c/o John Ainsworth, 52A Burlington Gardens, Acton, London, W3

City and Hackney Federation of Users of the Mental Health Services, c/o CHC, 210 Kingsland Road, London E2 8EB

Hackney Union of Mental Patients, c/o Stoke Newington Community Association, Leswin Road, London N16

About Turn Co-operative, 16 Dalston Lane, Hackney, London, E8

Hackney Mental Health Action Group, c/o CHC, 210 Kingsland Road, London, E2 8EB

Islington Mental Health Forum, The Old Darkroom, The Laundry, Sparsholt Road, Islington, London N19

Sagacity in Community Care, General Secretary, 3A Steele Road, Chiswick, London W4

Westminster Mental Health Action Group, c/o Westminster MIND, 526 Harrow Road, London W9

BAKEWELL

NETWORK, c/o Medway Centre, Bath Street, Bakewell, Derbyshire

BOLSOVER

Buckle Club, c/o The Vicarage, High Street, Bolsover, North Derbyshire

BRIGHTON

INSIGHT, c/o Richard Pennell, Brighton Mental Health Group, 17-19 Dichling Rise, Brighton, BN1 4QL

BRISTOL

Bristol Crisis Service for Women, c/o Missing Link, 248 Stapelton Rd, Easton, Bristol.

Bristol Survivors Network, c/o MIND, 43 Ducie Road, Bartin Hill, Bristol

Womankind, 43 Ducie Road, Bartin Hill, Bristol.

CHESTERFIELD

Contact, Chesterfield Community Centre, Tontine Road, Chesterfield, S40 1QU

North East Derbyshire and Chesterfield Association of Self Help Groups, The Secretary, c/o Chesterfield Community Centre, Tontine Road, Chesterfield

CLAY CROSS

Therapeutic and Social Club, c/o 1-3 Woodside Place, Holmegate, Clay Cross, Chesterfield

CRESWELL

Creswell Open Door, c/o Creswell Community House, Duke Street, Creswell, Worksop

DERBYSHIRE

West Derbyshire Federation of Mental Health Support Groups, The Secretary, c/o 113 Dale Road, Matlock, Derbyshire

DRONFIELD

CHAT, c/o Contact Club, Snapehill Lane, Dronfield, Sheffield

GLASGOW

LINK, 2 Queen's Crescent, Glasgow, G4 9BH

HULL

PEGS (Patients/Ex-patients Group Support),
c/o 73 Grammar School Road, Hull, HU5 4NY

MATLOCK

SPECTRUM, c/o 113 Dale Road, Matlock, Derbyshire

MILTON KEYNES

Milton Keynes Mental Health Advocacy Group,
c/o John Drozd, Cripps Lodge Resource Centre,
Broardlands, Netherfield, Milton Keynes, MK6 4JJ

NOTTINGHAM

Nottingham Patients' Council Support Group, 114
Mansfield Road, Nottingham, NG1 3HL

SOUTHAMPTON

The Cafe Club, 28 The Avenue, Southampton, SO1 2SW

WESTON-SUPER-MARE

Weston Survivors, c/o Friend, 39 A-B Oxford Street,
Weston-Super-Mare, Somerset BS23 1TN

WINCHESTER

Winchester Mental Health Action Group, c/o Glen
Cawes, 22 Devon Close, Chandlers Ford, Eastleigh,
Hampshire